Tell Me Why

How were the mountains made?

Can a hummingbird stand still in mid-air?

When did the world's most popular sports originate?

Tell Me Why

By Arkady Leokum

Answers to Questions about:

THE WORLD AROUND US

HOW IT BEGAN

THE HUMAN BODY

HOW OTHER CREATURES LIVE

Hamlyn

London · New York · Sydney · Toronto

Introduction

In this book will be found answers to over three hundred questions that intelligent young people ask.

To cater for many interests, these questions have been drawn from as wide a field as possible; they cover the world in which we live, its origins, its relationship to other planets, its past and its future; they deal with the complex society that countless generations, labouring over the centuries, have fashioned for themselves and their heirs, a society that has been transformed by technical progress to which a multitude of inventors, famous and anonymous, have made their contribution. Other questions touch on the wonders of the workings of the human body and the mysteries of the animal kingdom.

The purpose of this book is not merely to impart information but to stimulate enquiring minds to undertake further search for knowledge.

Today many share the conviction that knowledge should be the heritage of all; it is appropriate therefore, that this book would have been planned for an international, worldwide audience.

Published by
THE HAMLYN PUBLISHING GROUP
Astronaut House, Feltham, Middlesex, England
First published 1966
Second edition, fourteenth impression 1983
© Copyright 1966 by Arkady Leokum
All rights reserved under International and Pan-American Copyright Conventions
Published pursuant to agreement with Grosset and Dunlap Inc., New York, N.Y., U.S.A.
All rights reserved. No part of this publication may be
reproduced, stored in a retrieval system, or transmitted
in any form or by any means, electronic, mechanical, photocopying,
recording or otherwise, without the permission of The Hamlyn
Publishing Group Limited.
ISBN 0 600 38661 9
Printed in Czechoslovakia
51091/15

Contents

Chapter II
How It Began

Chapter III

The Human Body

Chapter IV

How Other Creatures Live

Chapter 1

THE WORLD AROUND US

HOW BIG IS THE UNIVERSE?

It is impossible for the human mind to conceive a true picture of the size of the universe. We not only don't know how big it is, but it is hard for us even to imagine how big it might be.

If we start from the earth and move out, we'll see why this is so. The earth is part of the solar system, but a very tiny part of it. The solar system consists of the sun, the planets that revolve around it, the asteroids, which are tiny planets, and the meteors.

Now, this whole solar system of ours is only a tiny part of another, much bigger system called "a galaxy." A galaxy is made up of many millions of stars, many of which may be much larger than our sun, and they may have solar systems of their own.

So the stars we see in our galaxy, which we call "the Milky Way," are all suns. They are all so far away that distances are measured in light years instead of in miles. Light travels about 6,000,000,000,000 miles in a year. The bright star nearest to the earth is Alpha Centauri. Do you know how far away it is? 25,000,000,000,000 miles!

But we're still talking only about our own galaxy. This is believed to be about 100,000 light years in width. This means 100,000 times 6,000,000,000,000 miles! And our galaxy is only a tiny part of a still larger system.

There are probably millions of galaxies out beyond the Milky Way.

And perhaps all these galaxies put together are still only a part of some larger system!

So you see why it is impossible for us to have an idea of the size of the universe. Incidentally, it is believed by scientists that the universe is expanding. This means that every few billion years two galaxies will find themselves twice as far apart as they were before!

WHY IS THE SOLAR SYSTEM THE WAY IT IS?

As far as we know, there is no reason why the solar system is arranged exactly as it is. It might have been arranged differently, just as there are other solar systems in the universe arranged differently. This has to do with the way it originated. But man has discovered certain laws of nature that seem to keep the solar system in its present pattern.

Earth, like the other planets, follows its path, or orbit, around the sun. The period of time that the earth takes to go around the sun is called a year. The other planets have orbits larger or smaller than the earth's.

How this solar system came to be and how the planets came to have the size, location, and orbits they have, astronomers cannot fully explain. But they have two main types of theories. One type of theory suggests that the formation of the planets was a part of the gradual change of the sun from a whirling mass of hot gas to its present size and brilliance. The planets formed as small whirling masses in the giant gas and dust cloud as it turned.

Another group of theories is based on the idea that at some time there was a near-collision between the sun and another star passing nearby. Large pieces of the sun were pulled away and began to revolve around the sun at different distances. These are now planets.

No matter which theory is right, the solar system came to be as it now is more or less by chance. Why does it stay this way? Kepler's Laws of Planetary Motion state that all planets travel about the sun in an elliptical (oval) path; that a planet moves faster in its orbit as it nears the sun; and that there is a relation between its distance from the sun and the time it takes to make an orbit. Newton's Law of Gravitation, of which Kepler's three laws were an indispensable part, explained how two objects attract each other. So the solar system remains as it is because certain laws of nature maintain the relationship of the sun and the planets.

WHAT KEEPS THE SUN SHINING?

It may be hard for you to believe, but when you look at the stars that shine at night and the sun that shines by day, you are looking at the same kinds of objects!

The sun is really a star. In fact, it's the nearest star to the earth. Life as we know it depends on the sun. Without the sun's heat, life could not have started on earth. Without sunlight, there would be no green plants, no animals, no human beings.

The sun is 93,000,000 miles from the earth. The volume, or bulk, of the sun is about 1,300,000 times that of the earth! Yet an interesting thing about the sun is that it is not a solid body like the earth.

Here is how we know this: The temperature on the surface of the sun is about 6,000 degrees centigrade. This is hot enough to change any metal or rock into a gas, so the sun must be a globe of gas!

Years ago, scientists believed that the reason the sun shone, or gave off light and heat, was that it was burning. But the sun has been hot for hundreds of millions of years, and nothing could remain burning for that long.

Today scientists believe that the heat of the sun is the result of a process similar to what takes place in an atom bomb. The sun changes matter into energy.

This is different from burning. Burning changes matter from one form to another. But when matter is changed into energy, very little matter is needed to produce a great deal of energy. Twenty eight grams of matter could produce enough energy to melt more than a million tonnes of rock!

So if science is right, the sun keeps shining because it is constantly changing matter into energy. And just one per cent of the sun's mass would provide enough energy to keep it hot for 150 thousand million years!

WHY DO SUNSETS LOOK RED?

A beautiful red sunset, the colors warm and glowing, is one of the loveliest sights we can imagine. And sometimes, when we look at it we might say, "See how red the sun is!"

But, of course, we know that the sun itself hasn't become red or changed in any way. It merely looks that way to us at that particular time of day. In fact, at that very moment people are looking at that same sun

thousands of miles to the west and it doesn't look red to them at all.

What produces the colors of a sunset is the distance that the sunlight must travel through our atmosphere. The lower it is, the more of our earth's atmosphere does that light travel through.

But first, let's remind ourselves that sunlight is a mixture of light of all colors. Normally, this mixture of light appears as white to our eyes. But the atmosphere has molecules of air, dust, water vapor, and other impurities present in it. As the light passes through them, different colors are scattered by these particles. Now, it so happens our atmosphere scatters out violet, blue, and green light more than it does the reds and yellows. So when the sun is low, this scattering leaves more reds and yellows for us to see and we have a reddish sunset.

By the way, this scattering of light also explains why the sky looks blue. Violet and blue light have short waves and are scattered about 10 times more than red light waves by our atmosphere. This means that the red rays go straight through our atmosphere, while the blue waves don't come through directly but are scattered by the air, water, and dust particles. It is this scattered light that we see as the blue sky when we look up.

WHAT IS THE EARTH MADE OF?

Man is now preparing to explore the moon and other planets—and he still doesn't know exactly what his own earth is made of!

A sort of rough answer to this question would be: The earth is a big ball, or sphere, made mostly of rock. Inside the earth the rock is melted, but the outside cover is hard rock. Less than one-third of the earth's surface is land and more than two-thirds are water.

Now let's consider this in a little more detail. The outside of the earth is a crust of rock about 10 to 30 miles thick. This crust is sometimes called "the lithosphere." The high parts of this crust are the continents, and the low parts of it hold the waters of the oceans and the great inland seas and lakes. All the water on the surface, including the oceans, lakes, rivers, and all the smaller streams, is called "the hydrosphere."

Men have been able to examine only the outermost part of the crust of rock that forms the outside of the earth, which is why it's so hard to know what the earth is like on the inside. In drilling wells and digging mines, it has been found that the deeper the hole is made, the higher the temperature becomes. At two miles below the surface of the earth, the temperature is high enough to boil water.

But scientists have also been able to find out about the inside of the earth from studies of earthquakes. They believe that the temperature does not increase as rapidly deep down as it does in the crust. So they think that at the core or center of the earth the temperature may not be more than 5,500 degrees centigrade. Of course, that's very hot—since a temperature of 1,200 degrees would melt rocks!

The crust of the earth has two layers. The upper layer, which makes the continents, is of granite. Under the layer of granite is a thick layer of very hard rock called "basalt." Scientists believe that at the center of the earth is a huge ball of molten iron, with a diameter of about 4,000 miles. Between the central ball and the rocky crust is a shell about 2,000 miles thick called "the mantle." The mantle is probably made of a kind of rock called "olivine."

WHY ARE ECLIPSES SO RARE?

When the moon in its journey around the earth passes directly between the earth and the sun, it casts its shadow on the surface of the earth, and an eclipse of the sun takes place.

An eclipse of the sun occurs only when the moon is new, for then the moon is on that side of the earth facing toward the sun. Then why isn't there an eclipse of the sun every time there's a new moon? The reason is that the path of the moon around the earth does not lie directly in line with the orbit of the earth about the sun. In its 29-day trip around the earth, the moon passes sometimes above and sometimes below the path of the earth.

An eclipse of the sun can be total, annular, or partial. If the moon hides the sun completely, the eclipse is total. But the moon is not always the same distance from the earth. Often, it is too far from the earth to hide the sun

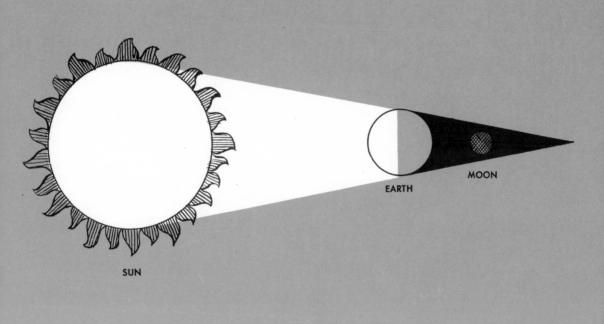

SUN

EARTH

MOON

completely. Then, when an eclipse takes place, the moon is seen as a dark disk which covers the whole sun except a narrow ring around its edge. This thin circle of light is called "the annulus," meaning "ring." This is an annular eclipse. An eclipse is partial whenever only part of the disk of the moon comes between the sun and the earth.

An eclipse of the moon occurs only when the moon is full, for then it is at the opposite side of the earth from the sun. When the moon comes directly behind the earth, as seen from the sun, it passes gradually into the great shadow-cone cast by the earth and disappears from view. A total eclipse of the moon then occurs. A partial eclipse takes place when the moon enters only partly into the shadow.

In some years, no eclipses of the moon occur. In other years, there are from one to three. Every year, there must be at least two solar eclipses, and there may be as many as five. At any one place on the earth's surface, a total solar eclipse will be visible only once in about 360 years.

The Constellation Aquila

WHAT IS A CONSTELLATION?

Have you ever looked at the stars and traced out squares, letters, and other familiar figures? In nearly all parts of the world, people of long ago did this and gave names to the group of stars they observed. Such a group is called "a constellation," from the Latin terms meaning "star" *(stella)* and "together."

The names of the constellations in use today have come down to us from the times of the Romans and from the even more ancient Greeks. What the Greeks knew about the stars came partly from the Babylonians.

The Babylonians named some of their star figures after animals and others after kings, queens, and heroes of their myths. Later, the Greeks changed many of these Babylonian names to the names of their own heroes such as Hercules, Orion, and Perseus. The Romans made further changes. The same ancient names are still used, but it is not always easy to make out in the sky the figures that suggested them. For example, Aquila is the eagle, Canis Major and Canis Minor are big and little dogs, and Libra is the scales, but the constellations don't look much like these figures to us.

About the year A.D. 150, the famous astronomer Ptolemy listed 48 constellations that were known to him. This list did not cover the entire sky; there were many blank spots. So, in later times, astronomers added constellations to Ptolemy's list. Some of these later constellations are named for scientific instruments, such as the Sextant, the Compasses, and the Microscope. Today, astronomers recognize 88 constellations in the sky.

A constellation is really an area in the sky. This means that every star lies in one constellation or another, just as any city in the United States is in some one state. The boundaries of the constellations used to be very irregular. Many of them had curved lines. But in 1928, astronomers decided to straighten them out so that the outline of any constellation includes only straight lines.

WHAT IS THE MILKY WAY?

There is probably nothing more mysterious and wonderful-looking in the sky than the Milky Way, stretching like a band of jewels from one end of the sky to the other. In ancient times, when people gazed at this spectacle, they were filled with the wonder and beauty of it just as you are. But since they didn't really know what it was, they made up all sorts of strange and .beautiful explanations of the Milky Way.

For example, in early Christian times, people thought it was a pathway for the angels, so they could go up to heaven on it. Or they imagined it was an opening in the heavens, so that we here on earth could have a glimpse of the glory that existed beyond.

Knowing the facts about the Milky Way, as we do today, doesn't remove any of the wonder of it. The facts are just as amazing as any "made-up" idea!

Our galaxy is shaped roughly like a watch, round and flat. If you could get above it and look down on it, it would look like an immense watch. But we are inside the galaxy, and when we look up we are looking towards the edge from inside the "watch." So we see that edge curving around us. And since there are millions of stars in it, we see it as the Milky Way.

Did you know that there are at least 3,000,000,000 stars in the galaxy? And here is an idea of its size. It takes eight minutes for light from the sun to reach the earth. For light from the center of the galaxy to reach the sun, it takes about 27,000 years!

The galaxy rotates about its center like a wheel. From our position in it, it takes about 200,000,000 years just to make one revolution!

WHAT IS THE BRIGHTEST STAR?

Have you ever looked up at the sky and tried to find the brightest star?

You may imagine that the number of stars you can see is countless. But the most that can be seen without a telescope are about 6,000 stars, and one-quarter of them are too far south to be seen in North America.

Ever since the days of the Greek astronomers, 2,000 years ago, the stars have been divided into classes according to their magnitude or brightness. Until the invention of the telescope, only six magnitudes, or degrees of brightness, were recognized. Stars of the first magnitude are the brightest, and stars of the sixth magnitude the faintest. Stars fainter than the sixth magnitude cannot be seen without a telescope. Today, stars can be photographed with modern telescopes down to the 21st magnitude.

A star of any given magnitude is about two and a half times fainter than a star of the magnitude above it. There are 22 stars of the first magnitude, the brightest stars, and the brightest star of all is Sirius, which has a magnitude of −1.6. This makes Sirius over 1,000 times brighter than the faintest star that can be seen with the naked eye.

The lower we go down in magnitude, the more stars there are in that class. Thus, there are 22 stars of the 1st magnitude and about 1,000,000,000 stars of the 20th magnitude.

WHAT ARE FALLING STARS?

For thousands of years men have looked up at "falling stars" and wondered what they were and where they come from. At one time it was believed that they came from other worlds.

Today we know that they are not "stars" at all. We call them "meteors." They are small, solid bodies which travel through space, and which may also pass through the earth's atmosphere.

When meteors come within our atmosphere, we can see them because they leave a fiery train of light. This is caused by the heat made by the friction, or rubbing, of air upon their surfaces.

Strangely enough, most individual meteor particles are quite small, about the size of a pinhead. Occasional meteors weigh many tons. Most meteors are destroyed entirely by heat as they pass through the earth's atmosphere. Only the larger meteor fragments ever reach the earth. Scientists believe that thousands of meteors fall to earth each day and night, but since most of the earth's surface is covered by water, they usually fall into oceans and lakes.

Meteors may appear in the sky singly and travel in practically any direction. But meteors usually occur in swarms of thousands. As the earth travels in its path around the sun, it may come close to such swarms of of meteors, they become fiery hot upon contact with the upper layers of the atmosphere, and we see a "meteoric shower."

Where do meteors come from? Astronomers now believe that the periodic swarms of meteors are the broken fragments of comets. When comets break up, the millions of fragments continue to move through space as a meteor swarm or stream. The swarms move in regular orbits, or paths, through space. One such swarm crosses the earth's path every 33 years.

When a piece of meteor reaches the earth, it is called "a meteorite." It has fallen to the earth because gravity has pulled it down. Far back in Roman times, in 467 B.C., a meteorite fell to the earth and its fall was considered such an important event that it was recorded by Roman historians!

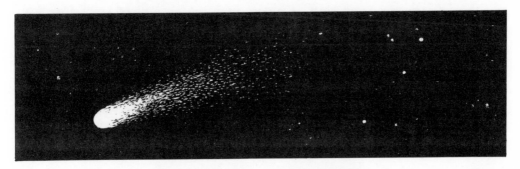

WHAT IS A COMET?

At one time, the appearance of a comet caused people to tremble with fear. They believed that comets were evil omens foretelling plagues, wars, and death.

Today, we have a pretty good idea of what comets are, though we still don't have all the answers about them. When a comet first appears, it is seen as a tiny point of light, though it may be thousands of miles in diameter.

This point of light is "the head," or nucleus, of the comet. Scientists think it is probably made of a great swarm of bits of solid matter, combined with gases. Where this matter originally came from is what is still a mystery.

As the comet approaches the sun, a tail usually appears behind it. The tail consists of very thin gases and fine particles of matter that are shot off from the comet's nucleus when it comes under the influence of the sun. Surrounding the nucleus of the comet is a third portion, known as "the coma." It is a glowing cloud of matter that sometimes reaches a diameter of 150,000 miles, or even more.

Comet tails are very different in shape and size. Some are short and stubby. Others are long and slender. They are usually at least 5,000,000 miles in length. Sometimes they are almost 100,000,000 miles long! Some comets have no tails at all.

As the tail grows, the comet gains in speed because it is nearing the sun, moving toward it head first. Then a curious thing happens. When the comet goes away from the sun, it goes tail first with the head following. This is because the pressure of light from the sun drives off the very small particles from the comet's head to form its tail, always in a direction away from the sun.

As a result, when the comet goes away from the sun, its tail must go first. During its journey away from the sun, the comet gradually slows down and then disappears from sight. Comets may remain out of sight for many years, but most of them reappear eventually. Comets make trip after trip around the sun, but they may require a long time to make a single revolution. Halley's Comet, for example, takes about 75 years to make its trip around the sun.

At present, astronomers have listed almost 1,000 comets, but there must be several hundred thousand comets in our solar system which remain unseen!

WHY DO ASTRONOMERS
THINK THERE MAY BE LIFE ON MARS?

As you know, scientists are now conducting all kinds of experiments to see if life can be found anywhere else in the universe. Naturally, it is easier to explore our own solar system for signs of life than it is to probe outer space. And one of the places where some scientists believe a form of life might be found is the planet Mars.

Why did they pick Mars? Well, Mars is considered to be a sort of twin of our own planet earth. It is the next planet beyond the earth in distance from the sun. Mars is about half the diameter of the earth and it rotates around the sun in just under two years. But Mars has a day that is almost equal in length to our day here on earth.

In observing Mars, astronomers have noticed certain things that indicate a form of life may be possible there. First of all, Mars has seasons like the earth. In fact, as the seasons change on Mars, there seem to be changes on its surface. The dark areas get stronger in the spring and summer, and the color changes from bluish-green to yellow. Could this be vegetation?

Astronomers also believe that there is at least a small amount of water vapor in the atmosphere of Mars, and this would be helpful in supporting life. Then, too, in 1887 an Italian astronomer, Giovanni Schiaparelli, reported seeing markings on the surface of Mars that resembled canals. "Could these have been built by Martians in order to carry water from the polar regions to the desert areas?" scientists wondered.

In 1976 two American Viking space probes landed on the surface of Mars. The instruments in the space probes searched the surrounding soil for signs of life and radioed their results back to earth. These results showed that either there are germs in the soil or that the soil is very unusual and not like that on earth. If life does exist on Mars it would be a very simple form of life.

CUMULUS

ALTOCUMULUS

STRATUS

STRATOCUMULUS

WHY ARE THERE DIFFERENT KINDS OF CLOUDS?

Here is how clouds are formed: Warm air, laden with moisture, rises into the sky. When it gets to a certain height, the warm air cools. At the cooler temperatures it can no longer hold all its moisture in the form of water vapor. So the extra moisture changes into small drops of water, or bits of ice, and this forms clouds.

No two clouds are exactly alike, and they are always changing their shape. The reason we have different types of clouds is that cloud formation takes place at different heights and temperatures. And clouds will be composed of different particles, depending on their height and temperature.

The highest clouds are called "noctilucent" clouds. They may be up as high as 30 to 50 miles! The next highest are called "nacreous," or "mother-of-pearl" clouds. They're 12 to 18 miles high. They are very thin, beautifully colored clouds composed of dust or water drops, and they are seen only after sunset, at night, or before sunrise.

The next highest clouds, which are five or more miles above the earth, are called "cirrus" clouds, "cirrostratus" clouds, and "cirrocumulus" clouds. The cirrus are feathery and threadlike, the cirrostratus are thin, whitish sheets, and the cirrocumulus are small, round clouds which form "mackerel" patterns in the sky. All these clouds are made of tiny bits of ice.

Lower clouds are made of little drops of water. The highest of these, the altocumulus clouds, are about two to four miles above the earth, and are made of larger, rounded masses than the cirrocumulus clouds. At the same levels are the altostratus clouds, which often cover the whole sky with a greyish veil through which the sun and moon shine as spots of pale light.

Lower still, about a mile high, are the stratocumulus clouds, large and lumpy. At the same level are the rain clouds. the nimbostratus, thick, dark, and shapeless. Very low, less than 610 metres above the ground, are the stratus clouds, which are sheets of high fog. Two other kinds of clouds, the cumulus, and the cumulonimbus, are the big, fat, "cauliflower" clouds that bring thunder and storms.

WHAT IS A NEBULA?

If you have seen pictures of nebulae in books, great spirals and whirlpools and clouds—don't expect to find anything like that in the sky. Most of the nebulae are so faint that they cannot be seen without a telescope. The word "nebulae," by the way, is really the Latin word for "mists" because they looked like mists when first observed through small telescopes.

There are two chief classes of nebulae, the galactic and the extragalactic. The galactic nebulae are found in our own galaxy (the Milky Way) and are composed of dust and gas. Since "extra" means "outside," the extragalactic nebulae are nebulae outside our own galaxy. They are made up largely of stars.

The galactic nebulae number less than 2,000. This means that most of the nebulae known to man are outside our own galaxy. How many are there? For all we know, there may be millions of them out there in the vast space beyond the Milky Way.

The extragalactic nebulae are sometimes called "island universes" or "galaxies." This means that if someone were looking at our own galaxy from out there he might well see it as a nebula.

The extragalactic nebulae have various forms. Some are irregular or elliptical. The most numerous are the spirals. The spirals, like our own galaxy, are made up of a large number of stars, big gaseous clouds, and vast tracts of dust. These nebulae usually have a nucleus in the center and from this, arms extend in spiral fashion. The spiral nebula Andromeda is the nearest to earth and the largest and brightest nebula known. It gives out about 1,500,000,000 times as much light as our sun!

WHY IS THE OCEAN SALTY?

Every now and then, we come across a fact about our earth which mystifies us and for which no answer has yet been found. Such a fact is the existence of salt in the oceans. How did it get there?

The answer is we simply don't know how the salt got into the ocean! We do know, of course, that salt is water-soluble, and so passes into the oceans with rain water. The salt of the earth's surface is constantly being dissolved and is passing into the ocean.

But we don't know whether this can account for the huge quantity of salt that is found in oceans. If all the oceans were dried up, enough salt would be left to build a wall 180 miles high and a mile thick. Such a wall would reach once around the world at the Equator! Or put another way, the rock salt obtained if all the oceans dried up would have a bulk about 15 times as much as the entire continent of Europe!

The common salt which we all use is produced from sea water or the water of salt lakes, from salt springs, and from deposits of rock salt. The concentration of salt in sea water ranges from about three per cent to three-and-one-half per cent. Enclosed seas, such as the Mediterranean and the Red Sea, contain more salt in the water than open seas. The Dead Sea, which covers an area of about 340 square miles, contains about 10,523,000,000 tonnes of salt.

On the average, a litre of sea water contains approximately 30 grams of salt. The beds of rock salt that are formed in various parts of the world were all originally formed by the evaporation of sea water millions of years ago. Since it is necessary for about nine-tenths of the volume of sea water to evaporate for rock salt to be formed, it is believed that the thick rock-salt beds that are found were deposited in what used to be partly en-. closed seas. These evaporated faster than fresh water entered them, and the rock-salt deposits were thus formed.

Most commercial salt is obtained from rock salt. The usual method is to drill wells down to the salt beds. Pure water is pumped down through a pipe. The water dissolves the salt and it is forced through another pipe up to the surface.

WHICH IS THE DEEPEST OCEAN?

In many ways, the oceans still remain a great mystery to us. We don't even know how old the oceans are. It seems certain that in the first stages of the earth's growth no oceans existed.

Today, man is exploring the bottoms of the oceans to learn more about them. Covering the floor of the ocean to a depth of 3,660 metres is a soft, oozy mud. It is made up of the limy skeltons of tiny sea animals. The floor of the deep, dark regions of the sea, where the water is more than four miles deep, is covered by a fine, rusty-colored ooze called "red clay." It is made up of tiny parts of skeltons of animals, the coverings of tiny plants, and volcanic ash.

The way the depth of oceans is measured today is by sending down sound waves which are reflected back from the bottom. The depth is found by measuring the time it takes for the sound wave to make the round trip and dividing this time in half.

Based on these measurements, we have a pretty good idea of the average depth of various oceans, and also the deepest point in each one. The ocean which has the greatest average depth is the Pacific Ocean. This is 4,281 metres. Next in average depth is the Indian Ocean which has an average of 3,963. The Atlantic is third with an average depth of 3,926 metres. The Baltic Sea is at the other extreme, with an average depth of only 55 metres!

The single deepest spot so far known is in the Pacific near Guam, with a depth of 10,790 metres. The next deepest spot is in the Atlantic off Puerto Rico where it measures 9,219. Hudson Bay, which is larger than many seas, has its deepest point at only 183 metres!

WHAT CAUSES THE WAVES?

If you've ever spent some time near a body of water, then you noticed that on a calm day there are very few waves in the water, and on a windy or stormy day there are many waves.

This, of course, explains what causes waves in the water. It is the wind. A wave is a way in which some form of energy is moved from one place to another. Some sort of force or energy must start a wave, and the wind provides that energy in the water.

When you watch the waves move, one after the other, the water seems to move forward. But if there is a piece of floating wood in the water, it will not move forward as the waves seem to do. It will only bob up and down with the waves. It moves only when the wind or tide moves it.

Then what kind of motion is taking place in a wave? A water wave is mostly the up-and-down movement of water particles. The movement passes on toward the shore, but not the particles of water. For example, if you have a rope you can send a kind of wave along the rope. The up-and-down movement passes along the rope, but not the particles of the rope.

As the bottom of a water wave strikes the ground a short distance from the beach, it slows up because of friction. The top keeps going, and then topples over, and thus forms a "breaker."

The energy that formed the waves loses itself against the shoreline. All you have to do is stand among the waves along a beach and you'll soon find out that they have energy!

In a water wave, the water particles move in a circular path, up and forward, as they are pushed by the wind. Then they move down and back as gravity draws the heaped-up water back to a common level. These up-and-down movements carry the wave along.

The distance from crest to crest of a wave is the wave length, and the low point is called "the trough."

WHAT ARE TIDAL WAVES?

On August 27, 1883, the island of Krakatoa in the Dutch East Indies practically blew up in a tremendous volcanic explosion. As a result of this explosion, huge waves rose more than a hundred feet in the air. They wiped out hundreds of villages. And they rushed across the ocean at speeds up to

700 miles an hour and made themselves felt on the coasts of Australia and California, thousands of miles away!

In 1946, there was an earthquake on the ocean floor near the Aleutian Islands. A gigantic wave was set up and in less than five hours it traveled 2,000 miles and struck Hawaii. It lifted houses and bridges and threw them hundreds of metres. More than 170 people were drowned.

Both of these great waves are what we call "tidal waves." They are completely unlike the normal waves at sea or those along the shore, and have nothing to do with winds or tides.

Scientists have a special name for tidal waves. They call them by the Japanese name *tsunami*. A tidal wave, or *tsunami*, is caused by some disturbance on the bottom of the sea. Usually, this is an earthquake that takes place on the ocean floor.

An earthquake on the ocean bottom produces a shock wave that travels through the water, just as a loud sound travels through the air. In fact, this shock travels through the water with the speed of sound.

If a ship happens to be in the 'region, it will actually be rocked by the shock, and it feels just as if the ship had struck a rock!

When an earthquake takes place on the ocean bottom, the ocean floor shifts and slides. It is this motion and the shock of the disturbance that produce tidal waves. Sometimes a great depression is suddenly created in the water, sometimes a huge mound of water is suddenly built up. The tidal wave is formed and begins at once to move across the sea at great speed.

When a tidal wave approaches land, the first sign, oddly enough, is a swell or rise that is just like an ordinary wave. Then the sea level falls for a number of minutes, as if it were very low tide. A big area of the ocean floor near the coast may be exposed. Then the great tidal wave comes crashing in!

WHAT IS A WHIRLPOOL?

When most of us think of a whirlpool, we imagine a huge spinning body of water into which people and ships can be sucked and pulled down to their death. While whirlpools are often dangerous, the fact is that there is no suction or downward-draft in them in the open ocean.

Let's see what a whirlpool is. You've probably noticed smaller whirlpools in a brook. They take place where a bank juts out into the current and gives a circular twist to the water.

As the water spins around in the narrow space behind the bank, it tends to pile up on the outside of the circle and to hollow out into a funnel-shaped hole in the center. This is the result of the action of centrifugal force. That is the same force which holds the water in the bottom of a bucket when the bucket is swung around in circles.

What causes the larger whirlpools, those we all know as dangerous to ships and men? When the tide comes sweeping in and it meets the ebb current of the preceding tide head-on, the ocean currents start to move in rotary fashion. This happens quite often in the narrow passages between groups of islands and the shores of the mainland.

When the narrow passage through which the tides flow is very deep, the rotary turning of the water sometimes changes to a spiraling flow and then a downward-draft to a deep center does take place. But as mentioned before, it doesn't take place in the open ocean. A whirlpool in the open ocean is nothing more than an eddy on a large scale, which simply means a flow of water in rotary fashion.

Whirlpools occur in many parts of the world. The three most famous ones are the Maelstrom, the Charybdis, and the whirlpool downstream from the Niagara Falls. The Maelstrom is located off the Norwegian coast, and the Charybdis lies in the narrow channel between Italy and Sicily.

WHAT IS THE GULF STREAM?

The Gulf Stream is an ocean current, the most famous ocean current of all. It is like a river that flows through the sea instead of on land. But the Gulf Stream is so vast that it is larger than all the rivers in the world put together!

The Gulf Stream moves northward along the coast of Eastern United States, across the North Atlantic Ocean, and then to northwest Europe. The Gulf Stream has a clear indigo-blue color and it can be seen clearly where it contrasts with the green and gray waters that it flows through.

The water of the Gulf Stream comes from the movement of the surface waters near the Equator in the Atlantic. This movement or "drift" is westward. So the Gulf Stream starts by moving north of South America and into the Caribbean Sea. It actually becomes what we call the Gulf Stream when it starts moving northward along the east coast of the United States.

Since the Gulf Stream starts in the warm part of the world, it is a current of warm water. And the presence of this huge current of warm water makes amazing differences in the climate of many places!

Here are some curious examples of this: Winds passing over this current in northern Europe (where it is called "the North Atlantic Drift") carry warm air to parts of Norway, Sweden, Denmark, The Netherlands, and Belgium. Result—they get milder winter temperatures than other places just as far north! It also means that ports along the Norwegian coast are ice-free the year round.

Thanks to the Gulf Stream, London and Paris enjoy mild winter climates, though they lie just as far north as southern Labrador, for example, which has bitterly cold winters. The winds that pass over the Gulf Stream are made warm and moist. When these winds become chilled, as they do near Newfoundland, dense fog results. And so we have the famous dangerous fogs of the Grand Banks of Newfoundland.

The Gulf Stream doesn't have as great an effect on the winter climate of North America as on Europe, because the winter winds don't blow over it and then inland, as they do in Europe.

WHY DOES WATER FLOW OUT OF A SPRING?

All the water that flows out of every spring once fell as rain. The rain water soaks into the soil and enters into rocks through cracks. Of course, much of the rain water remains near the surface and evaporates into the air, or plants absorb it through their roots.

The rest of the rain water is drawn downward by gravity, and it goes as far down as the openings in the rocks will allow. Below the surface of the land, but at a different depth in each place, there is a zone where all the openings in the rocks are completely filled with water. This is called "the ground water zone." The upper surface of this water is called "the water table."

A spring occurs when water finds a natural opening in the ground that is below the water table. That's why most springs are in valleys or low places. The ground water escapes as spring water through the cracks in the rocks along the sides or bottoms of these low places. A spring doesn't defy gravity; it is always flowing down from some water level above it.

Some springs receive water from deep within the water zone. These usually flow all year and are called "permanent" springs. Other springs have their openings near the water table. They usually flow only in the rainy season when the water table is at its highest. These are called "intermittent" springs.

Since all spring water passes through rocks during its underground travels, all spring water carries some mineral matter, such as sulphur or lime. Springs that have water containing an unusual amount of mineral matter are called "mineral" springs.

In some places, especially in areas where there have been volcanoes, the water in springs has been in contact with hot, underground rocks. This type of spring is called a "thermal," or "hot" spring.

An artesian well is quite different from a spring. In an artesian well, the rain water sinks down into the ground until it reaches a layer of porous rock or sand that is buried between two layers of solid rock. Pressure is built up around this water, and when a hole is bored down to reach it, the water escapes with a gush. The well must be driven at a point lower than that at which the water enters the ground.

HOW WERE THE MOUNTAINS MADE?

Because mountains are so big and grand, man thinks of them as unchanging and everlasting. But geologists, the scientists who study mountains, can prove that mountains do change, and that they are not everlasting.

Certain changes in the earth's surface produced the mountains, and they are constantly being destroyed and changed. Boulders are broken from mountainsides by freezing water; soil and rock particles are carried away by rainwash and streams. In time, even the highest mountains are changed to rolling hills or plains.

Geologists divide mountains into four classifications, according to how they were formed. All mountains, however, are the result of violent changes in the earth's surface, most of which happened millions of years ago.

Folded mountains were made of rock layers, squeezed by great pressure into large folds. In many places in such mountains, you can see the rock layers curving up and down in arches and dips, caused by the squeezing and pressure on the earth's surface. The Appalachian Mountains and the Alps of Europe are examples of folded mountains.

In dome mountains, the rock layers were forced up to make great blister-like domes. In many cases, molten lava, coming with great pressure from below the earth's surface, lifted these rock layers. The Black Hills of South Dakota are examples of dome mountains.

Block mountains are the result of breaks, or faults, in the earth's crust. Huge parts of the earth's surface, entire "blocks" of rock, were raised up or tilted at one time. The Sierra Nevada Range of California is a block that is 400 miles long and 80 miles wide!

Volcanic mountains are built of lava, ash, and cinders poured out from within the earth. The usual volcano is cone-shaped with a large hole, or crater, at the top. Among the famous volcanic mountains are Mounts Ranier, Shasta, and Hood in the United States, Fujiyama in Japan, and Vesuvius in Italy.

Many mountain ranges have been formed by more than one of the ways described. In the Rockies are mountains made by folding, faulting, doming, and even erosion of lava!

WHY ARE THERE
SO MANY DIFFERENT KINDS OF ROCKS?

Is there any boy anywhere in the world who hasn't filled up his pockets at some time with all kinds of strange rocks? The different sizes and shapes, some rough and some smooth, the different colors, some almost like precious gems, just make us want to collect them!

What makes rocks look so fascinating is the fact that they are composed of one or more minerals. It is these minerals which often give different rocks their wonderful colors, or make them sparkle like gems.

All rocks aren't formed in the same way. One kind of rock, called "sedimentary rock," has been formed by sediment. This means that substances were laid down long ago by water, wind, ice, or by the work of plants and animals. Since they are laid down in layers which are called "strata," these rocks are called "stratified" rocks. The tiny particles of which such rocks are made are usually rounded, since the sharp edges and corners have been worn off while the particles were being rolled along stream beds, washed by the waves, or blown by winds. Sandstones and limestones are typical sedimentary rocks.

Other rocks were once molten matter deep in the earth. They have been poured out on the surface or forced into cracks in other rocks. Such rocks are called "igneous" rocks, and examples of this type are granite and basalt.

The third kind of rocks was once in some other form (igneous or sedimentary), but has been changed into its present form by heat or pressure. This type is called "metamorphic" rock, and marble and quartzite are examples of this type.

In some rocks, different metal-bearing minerals are found mixed with the other rock substances. If there is enough of the metal to make it worth while separating it, the rock containing it is called an "ore."

HOW ARE CAVES FORMED?

Caves have long been linked with the history of man in many interesting ways. We know that late in the Old Stone Age, caves were the winter dwelling place of people who had no other shelter.

But long after man stopped using caves as homes, ancient people

believed many strange things about caves. The Greeks believed caves were
the temples of their gods, Zeus, Pan, Dionysus, and Pluto. The Romans
thought that caves were the homes of nymphs and sibyls. The ancient
Persians and others associated caves with the worship of Mithras, chief of
the earth spirits.

Today, huge and beautiful caves all over the world are tourist attractions. Caves are deep hollow places in the rocky sides of hills or cliffs. Large
caves are called "caverns."

Caves are formed in many different ways. Many caves have been hollowed out by the constant beating of the sea waves against the rocks. Some
caves appear under the surface of the earth. These are usually the old courses
of underground streams which have worn away layers of soft rock such as
limestone. Others are formed by the volcanic shifting of surface rocks, or by
the eruption of hot lava.

The most common type of cave in the United States is that made by the
wearing away of thick layers of limestone. This is done by the action of
water containing carbon dioxide. In Indiana, Kentucky, and Tennessee,
where there are great beds of limestone with an average thickness of 53
metres, such caves are numerous.

Some caves have openings through their roofs, called "sink holes."
These formed where the surface water first gathered and seeped down. Some
caves have galleries in tiers or rows, one above another. Underground
streams wind through some caves, though in many cases after a cave has
been formed, the streams that once flowed through it may find a lower level
and leave the cave dry.

In many cases, each drop of water that drips from a cave roof contains
a bit of lime or other mineral matter. As part of the water evaporates, some
of this matter is left behind. It gradually forms a stalactite, shaped like an
icicle hanging from the roof. Water dripping from the stalactite to the floor
builds up a column called "a stalagmite."

WHAT ARE FOSSILS?

The study of fossils is so important in helping man learn about his own past and that of animals who lived millions of years ago that it has developed into a separate science called "paleontology."

Fossils are not, as some people think, the remains of bodies buried ages ago. Actually, there are three different kinds of fossils. The first is part of the actual body of the organism, which has been preserved from decay, and which appears just as it was originally. But fossils may also be just the cast or mold of the shape of the body, which remains after the body of the plant or animal has been removed. And fossils may merely be the footprints or trails that animals have left as they moved over the soft muds or clays.

When a fossil is found that consists of part of the organism itself, it is usually only the hard parts, such as shells or skeletons, that are preserved. The softer parts are destroyed by decay. Yet, in some cases, even such soft-bodied animals as jellyfish, which are 99 per cent water, have left perfect fossils of themselves in rocks! And certain fossils found encased in ice not only have the skeleton preserved but also the flesh and skin on the bones.

Fossils have nothing to do with size. For instance, the fossils of tiny ants which lived millions of years ago can be found perfectly preserved in amber. The chances for animals being preserved as fossils depend mostly on where they lived. The most numerous of all fossils are water animals because when they die their bodies are quickly covered over by mud and so kept from decaying. Land animals and plants are exposed to the destroying action of the air and weather.

It is chiefly through the study of fossils that we know about animal life as it existed millions and hundreds of millions of years ago. For example, fossils taken from certain rocks tell us that millions of years ago there was an Age of Reptiles, with monsters so huge that they were 24 metres long and weighed 36 tonnes. These were the dinosaurs. And our entire knowledge about the earliest bird, called "the archaeopteryx," is based on just two fossils of it that have been found!

HOW ARE ICEBERGS FORMED?

We may think of icebergs as exciting and interesting things to see, but they are a great danger to ocean vessels when they drift into shipping routes. One of the greatest disasters at sea took place when the *Titanic* struck an iceberg on the night of April 14, 1912, and 1,513 people lost their lives.

An iceberg is a piece of glacier that has broken off. This happens where the glaciers (which are like rivers of ice) push down valleys until they reach the sea. The end of the glacier breaks off there and forms a floating iceberg.

Some glaciers do not reach the open sea but end in deep, steep-sided valleys called "fiords." The icebergs float down to the ocean from these fiords. In the case of some glaciers, the ends are worn or melted back by the waves. This leaves a big "foot" of ice submerged below the surface of the water. Such ice feet break off from time to time and rise suddenly to the surface as icebergs.

Icebergs vary greatly in size. Small ones up to 5 or 10 metres across are often called "growlers" by seamen. But icebergs which measure over 100 metres are very common, and there have been some giant bergs seen that measured as much as 1,000 metres across.

The ice in icebergs is only eight-ninths as heavy as sea water, so that only one-ninth of the iceberg sticks out above sea level and eight-ninths is below where it can't be seen. So a berg which rises 45 metres above the sea may extend 300 metres below! The amount of ice in an iceberg is almost unbelievable. Did you know that many of them weigh as much as 180,000,000 tonnes?

Because icebergs extend so far below the surface of the ocean, they don't drift with the winds but instead follow the ocean currents. Eventually most icebergs are carried to lower warmer latitudes where they melt. Very few of them last long after they meet the warm Gulf Stream east of Newfoundland, Canada. But those that do become a menace to ships. That's why the United States Coast Guard maintains an iceberg patrol there to warn ships of the location of icebergs.

WHEN DID THE ICE AGE END?

Most people think of the Ice Age as something that happened so long ago that not a sign of it remains. But did you know that geologists say we are just now reaching the end of the Ice Age? And people who live in Greenland are actually still in the Ice Age as far as they're concerned.

About 25,000 years ago, any people who may have been living in central North America saw ice and snow the year round. There was a great wall of ice that stretched from coast to coast, and the ice extended northward without an end. This was the latest Ice Age, and all of Canada, much of the United States, and most of northwestern Europe were covered by a sheet of ice over 1,000 metres thick.

This didn't mean that it was always icy cold. The temperature was only about 5 degrees lower than it is now in Northern United States. What caused the Ice Age was that the summers were very cool. So there wasn't enough heat during the summer months to melt away the winter's ice and snow. It just continued to pile up until it covered all the northern area.

But the Ice Age really consisted of four periods. During each period the ice formed and advanced, then melted back toward the North Pole. It is believed this happened four times. The cold periods are called "glaciations," and the warm periods are called "interglacial" periods.

It is believed that in North America the first period of ice came about 2,000,000 years ago, the second about 1,250,000 years ago, the third about 500,000 years ago, and the last about 100,000 years ago.

The last Ice Age didn't melt at the same rate everywhere. For example, ice that reached what is now Wisconsin began to melt about 40,000 years ago. But ice that had covered New England melted about 28,000 years ago. And there was ice covering what is now Minnesota until about 15,000 years ago!

In Europe, Germany got from under the ice 17,000 years ago and Sweden remained covered with ice until about 13,000 years ago!

WHY DO WE STILL HAVE GLACIERS TODAY?

The great ice mass that began the Ice Age in North America has been called "a continental glacier; it may have been about 4,500 metres thick in its center. This great glacier probably formed and then melted away at least four times during the Ice Age.

The Ice Age or glacial period that took place in other parts of the world still has not had a chance to melt away! For instance, the big island of Greenland is still covered with a continental glacier, except for a narrow fringe around its edge. In the interior, this glacier often reaches heights of more than 3,000 metres. Antarctica is also covered by a vast continental glacier which is nearly 4,000 metres high in places!

So the reason we still have glaciers in certain parts of the world is that they have not had a chance to melt away since the Ice Age. But most of the glaciers that exist today have been formed in recent times. These glaciers are usually the valley type of glacier.

It starts in a broad, steep-walled valley shaped like a great amphitheatre. Snow is blown into this area or slides in from avalanches from the slopes above. This snow doesn't melt during the summer but gets deeper year by year. Eventually, the increasing pressure from above, together with some melting and refreezing, forces the air out of the lower part of the mass and changes it into solid ice. Further pressure from the weight of ice and snow above eventually squeezes this mass of ice until it begins to creep slowly down the valley. This moving tongue of ice is the valley glacier.

There are more than 1,200 such glaciers in the Alps of Europe! Glaciers are also found in the Pyrenees, Carpathian, and Caucasus Mountains of Europe, and in southern Asia. In southern Alaska, there are tens of thousands of such glaciers, some from 25 to 50 miles long!

WHY DO VOLCANOES
APPEAR ONLY IN CERTAIN PLACES?

There are no volcanoes near New York City or London or Paris—nor are there likely to be any in the future. Yet there are parts of the world where there are several volcanoes quite near each other.

Central America, bordering the Pacific Ocean, is one of the most active volcano areas of the world. In fact, more than two-thirds of the active volcanoes and a large number of those which have been extinct for only a short time are found around the borders of the Pacific Ocean!

The reason is simply this: The earth's crust in these areas must be "weak" or have weak spots in relation to the earth's crust in other parts of the world. For without a weak spot in the crust of the earth, a volcano couldn't come into being.

Here is how a volcano is born: As you know, the center of the earth is hot. The deeper you go under the surface of the earth, the higher the temperature. At a depth of about 20 miles, it is so hot (1,000 to 1,100 degrees centigrade) that most rocks found there simply melt.

When rock melts, it expands and needs more space. In certain areas of the world, new mountain ranges have recently been formed (new in terms of thousands of years). Under and near these new mountain ranges, the pressure is less than elsewhere. It is a kind of "weak spot" in the earth's solid crust.

So the molten rock, which is called "magma," expands into these parts and a local reservoir of the molten rock is formed. This material rises along the cracks formed by the uplift. When the pressure in the reservoir of molten rock becomes greater than the strength of the roof over it, it bursts forth as a volcano. The eruption lasts until the gas is gone.

The material that comes out of a volcano is mainly gaseous, but large quantities of molten rock (which we call "lava") and solid particles that look like cinders and ash are also thrown out. The eruption is really a gas explosion, but some of the lava becomes finely powdered and makes the eruption look like black smoke.

WHERE DO MOST EARTHQUAKES OCCUR?

If you could look at a map that showed the entire surface of the earth and where earthquakes occur most often, you'd see a wavy ribbon that twisted up and down as it twisted around the earth. Some parts are missed entirely; others seem to have a habit of having frequent earthquakes.

The single region of the earth that has the most frequent earthquakes is Japan. There is an earthquake there almost every day of the year! Of course, most of these are very minor quakes and do no damage at all. Another region which has frequent earthquakes is the Mediterranean area. By contrast, consider the New England States. There have been no destructive earthquakes there since the Ice Age, many thousands of years ago!

The explanation for this is that the crust of the earth is not the same everywhere. In certain regions, the crust has not quite settled down firmly, and there is a "fault." A fault is a break in the rocks of the earth's crust. Where the break exists, one rock mass rubs against another with great force and friction. The energy of this rubbing is changed to vibration in the rocks.

While this vibration may travel thousands of miles, the earthquake is strongest, as you might imagine, right along the line of the fault made by the shifting of the earth blocks. The sides of the fault may move up and down against each other, or the sides of the fault may shift lengthwise.

Most of the changes that take place on the surface of the earth after an earthquake are seen along this fault line. The part of the fault line where the vibration is felt most strongly is called "the epicenter" of the earthquake. And if this is near a city, the destruction may be very great. The loss of life is usually due to falling buildings and fires that may be started by broken gas mains under streets.

The earthquake regions of the earth and the areas of recent volcanic activity are roughly the same. This is because both of these are regions where the earth's crust is not at rest.

HOW DOES THE WEATHERMAN
KNOW WHAT TO SAY?

All the conditions of the atmosphere are "weather." Whether it's hot or cold, dry or wet, sunny or cloudy, windy or still, it's "weather." The weather is changeable from day to day, and the total effect during a year is called "the climate."

There are many complicated reasons for changes in the weather, but the most important influence is the sun. The sun's heat evaporates water and warms the air, so that rising currents of warm air carry water vapor into the sky. There the air cools and the vapor condenses into rain. These things happen gently or violently. When they take place violently, we have storms.

In Great Britain there are approximately 200 weather reporting stations and roughly the same number spread over the rest of Europe. In addition, "weather ships" stationed in the Atlantic and special aircraft on regular patrol send back systematic reports on weather conditions. From this and other meteorolical data weather forecasts are produced.

The maps which the weather experts study show them many things: places where the air pressure is equal, places of equal temperature, directions of local winds, cloudy or clear skies, rain or snow, the amount of rainfall, and regions where the air pressure is higher or lower than normal.

The weatherman can also tell from looking at the map what is likely to happen under the conditions that exist. He knows that low pressures indicate storms, because cold air is moving in to replace warm rising air that is laden with moisture. High pressures indicate fair weather.

In the Northern Hemisphere, the winds around a high-pressure area blow outward in a direction similar to that followed by the hands of a clock.

In a low-pressure area they blow inward in a counterclockwise direction. Thus the directions the winds will take can be predicted. The weatherman also knows how fast these pressure areas are moving across the country.

Knowing all these things, and having reports of the weather in most parts of the country before him, the weatherman begins to get a pretty good idea of what to say about the weather that's coming to your area!

WHY DO WE HAVE DIFFERENT SEASONS?

Since earliest times, man has been curious about the changing of the seasons. Why is it warm in summer and cold in winter? Why do the days gradually grow longer in the spring? Why are the nights so long in winter?

We all know the earth revolves around the sun, and at the same time it revolves on its own axis. As it moves around the sun, it's also spinning like a top. Now if the axis of the earth (the line from the North Pole through the South Pole) were at right angles to the path of the earth around the sun, we would have no such thing as different seasons, and all the days of the year would be of equal length.

But the axis of the earth is tilted. The reason for this is that a combination of forces is at work on the earth. One is the pull of the sun, the other is the pull of the moon, the third is the spinning action of the earth itself. The result is that the earth goes around the sun in a tilted position. It keeps that same position all year, so that the earth's axis always points in the same direction, toward the North Star.

This means that during part of the year the North Pole tilts toward the sun and part of the year away from it. Because of this tilt, the direct rays of the sun sometimes fall on the earth north of the Equator, sometimes directly on the Equator, and sometimes south of the Equator. These differences in the way the direct rays of the sun strike the earth cause the different seasons in different parts of the world.

When the Northern Hemisphere is turned toward the sun, the countries north of the Equator have their summer season, and the countries south of the Equator have their winter season. When the direct rays of the sun fall on the Southern Hemisphere, it is their summer and it is winter in the Northern Hemisphere. The longest and shortest days of each year are called "the summer solstice" and "winter solstice."

There are two days in the year when night and day are equal all over the world. They come in the spring and fall, just halfway between the solstices. One is the autumnal equinox, which occurs about September 23, and the other is the spring equinox, which occurs about March 21.

WHAT IS THE JET STREAM?

Nowadays, the word "jet" is very much in the news, and you might imagine that the "jet stream" has something to do with jet planes. This isn't the case at all!

The jet stream is part of the system of winds that surround the earth, so let's start with the subject of winds. Winds are currents of air that move parallel to the surface of the earth and close to it.

The movement of winds is chiefly caused by the existence of areas of different pressure, and winds always blow from areas of high pressure to areas of low pressure.

If we look at it from an over-all point of view (not from local regions) we can say that, in general, cold air is transported from the Poles toward the Equator, and warm air from the Equator toward the Poles. This flow doesn't take place in smooth currents, but forms a system of rather turbulent streams. There are various conditions that decide what happens in each specific region. There may be local sources of heat which affect the pressure. The way the land and water and mountains are distributed can decide which way the local winds blow.

Finally, there is the existence of semi-permanent high-pressure areas in certain places. This means that in these regions there tends to be a high-pressure area most of the time. They are called "anticyclones" and wind currents locally are decided by them.

Now, this gives you a general idea of how winds blow and some of the things that affect them. But all of this concerns winds that are quite close to the earth, in the lower layers of the atmosphere. As you know, the earth is surrounded by atmosphere that may go as high as 1,500 miles up. In the higher levels of the atmosphere, different wind conditions exist. Here they usually move with much greater speed than near the surface. At a height of about 9,000 metres, currents of air move with such speed that they have a special name—"the jet stream"! The speed of the jet stream ranges from 100 to 200 miles per hour.

WHERE DOES THE WIND COME FROM?

There are two ways of looking at the wind and where it comes from. One is in terms of your immediate neighborhood, and one is in terms of the world and the big winds that blow over it.

Differences in pressure may exist in a small region around you, and you will have a local wind blowing. If you live near the shore, you have an example of this every day. During the day, the land becomes heated, the air above it rises, and cool winds come in from the water to take its place. At night, the land becomes colder than the water, the warm air rises over the water, and the breeze blows out from the land to take the place of the rising warm air.

What is true in your immediate neighborhood is true on a much larger scale of the winds that blow over the earth. The warmest place on earth is around the Equator. So there is always a belt of warm air rising from this region. This belt of warm air flows out to the north and south and sinks again at certain latitudes, which are called "the horse latitudes." This sinking air flows out along the surface of the earth toward the Equator and the Poles.

If the earth were not rotating, these winds would be north winds or south winds. But the spinning of the earth makes all winds in the Northern Hemisphere deflect to the right and in the Southern Hemisphere to the left. The winds blowing from the horse latitudes toward the Equator are called "the trade winds." Those blowing toward the Poles are called "the westerlies." The United States is largely in the zone of the westerlies.

There are other "prevailing" or common winds in other parts of the world. But as you can see, the wind does come from somewhere — and it comes from there because of very definite reasons caused by the way the air over the earth is heated.

WHAT IS HUMIDITY?

If you put a pitcher of ice water on a table and let it stand a while, what happens? Moisture gathers on the outside of the pitcher. Where does this moisture come from? It comes from the air.

The fact is there is always moisture in the air in the form of water vapor. In the case of the ice pitcher, the vapor condensed on the cold surface of the pitcher and thus became visible. But water vapor in the air is invisible. And the word "humidity" simply means the presence of water vapor in the air. It is found everywhere, even over great deserts.

This means, of course, that we always have humidity, but the humidity is not always the same. We have several ways of expressing the humidity, and two of them are "absolute humidity" and "relative humidity." Let's see what each means.

"Absolute humidity" is the quantity of water vapor in each unit volume of air. There are so many grains per cubic foot of air. But for most practical purposes, this doesn't tell us very much. If you want to know whether you'll feel comfortable or not, the answer "four grains per cubic foot" won't tell you whether the air will feel dry or humid. The more easily moisture from your body can evaporate into the air, the more comfortable you'll be. The evaporative power of the air depends on the temperature, and absolute humidity doesn't indicate anything about the evaporative power of the air.

Relative humidity is expressed as a percentage. "One hundred per cent" stands for air which is saturated or completely filled with water vapor. The higher the temperature, the greater the quantity of water vapor air can hold. Thus, on a hot day, a "90 per cent relative humidity" means an awful lot of moisture in the air—a day that will make you mighty uncomfortable.

WHY DOES IRON GET RUSTY?

When you leave a piece of iron for a few days in a place where it's damp or wet, a covering of rust forms over it just as if someone had come along and painted that reddish color on it.

What is rust? Why does it form on iron and steel? Rust is iron oxide. It is created when iron "burns" by uniting with oxygen dissolved in water.

This means that unless there is moisture in the air, or water is actually present, the oxygen is not dissolved in water and rust cannot begin to form.

When a drop of rain falls on a bright iron surface, the drop will remain clear for a short time. But the iron and the oxygen in the water soon begin to unite and form iron oxide, or rust, inside the drop. The drop will turn a reddish color and the rust is suspended in the water. When the drop evaporates, the rust will remain and form a reddish coat on the iron itself.

Once started, rust will spread even in dry air. This is because the rough spot of rust helps whatever moisture there is in the air to condense; it attracts the moisture and holds it. That's why it's easier to prevent rust from starting than to prevent it from spreading once it has started.

Since iron and steel articles often have to be stored for long periods of time, the problem of preventing rust is an important one. Sometimes such articles are coated with a special paint or a plastic film. But what would you do if you had to keep the insides of battleships rust-free when these ships are not in use? Our Government has solved it by using dehumidifiers. These are machines that draw moist air out of the compartments of the ship and replace it with dry air. Rust never gets a chance to start!

WHAT IS FOG?

A fog is a cloud in contact with the ground. There is no basic difference between a fog and a cloud floating high in the atmosphere. When a cloud is near or on the surface of the earth or sea, it is simply called "fog."

The commonest fogs are those seen at night and in the early morning over the lowlands and small bodies of water. They usually are caused by a cold current of air from above striking down upon the warmer surface of the land or water.

In the autumn they are very common, because the air is cooling faster day by day than the land or the water. On still nights after dark, thin layers of fog often form close to the ground in low places. As the earth cools at night, the lower air gets cooler. Where this cooler air meets the moist warmer air just above, fog forms.

As a general rule, city fogs are much thicker than country fogs. City air is full of dust and soot that mingle with tiny particles of water to form a thicker blanket.

Off the coast of Newfoundland, which is one of the foggiest parts of the world, fogs are formed by the passage of damp, warm air over the cold water flowing south from the Arctic Circle. The chill of the water condenses the moisture of the air into tiny drops of water. These drops are not big enough to fall as rain. They remain in the air as fog.

San Francisco fogs are formed in the opposite way. There a cool morning breeze blows over warm sand dunes, and if rain has moistened the sand the night before, a thick fog bank of evaporated moisture forms.

The reason fogs often seem denser than clouds is that the droplets are smaller in a fog. A large number of small drops absorb more light than a smaller number of large drops (as found in clouds), and thus it seems denser to us.

WHAT IS DEW?

You would imagine that dew is a very simple phenomenon of nature, easily understood and explained. Yet strangely enough, exactly what dew is has long been misunderstood, and whole books have been written on the subject!

Since the days of Aristotle until about 200 years ago, it was believed that dew "fell," somewhat like rain. But dew doesn't fall at all! The most familiar form of dew, seen on the leaves of plants, is now known not to be all dew! So you see, there have been many wrong ideas about dew.

In order to understand what dew is, we have to understand something about the air around us. All air holds a certain amount of moisture. Warm air can hold much more water vapor than cold air. When the air comes in contact with a cool surface, some of that air becomes condensed and the moisture in it is deposited on the surface in tiny drops. This is dew.

The temperature of the cool surface, however, has to drop below a certain point before dew will form. That point is called "the dew point." For example, if you place water in a glass or a polished metal container, dew may not collect on the surface. If you place some ice in the water, dew may still not collect until the surface of the glass or container is brought down to a certain point.

How does dew form in nature? First, there has to be moisture-laden warm air. This air must come into contact with a cool surface. Dew doesn't form on the ground or sidewalk, because it still remains warm after having been heated by the sun. But it may form on grasses or plants which have become cool.

Then why did we say that the dew seen on plants is really not dew? The reason is that while a small part of the moisture seen on plants in the morning is dew, most of it—and in some cases all of it— has really come from the plant itself! The moisture comes out through the pores of the leaves. It is a continuation of the plant's irrigation process for supplying the leaves with water from the soil. The action starts in the daytime, so that the surface of the leaf should be able to withstand the hot sun, and it simply continues into the night.

In some places in the world, enough dew is deposited every night for it to be collected in dew ponds and used as a water supply for cattle!

WHY DO SNOWFLAKES HAVE SIX SIDES?

One of the most beautiful objects formed by nature is a snowflake. It would take most of us a long time to "design" a shape as beautiful as a single snowflake. Yet in an ordinary snowstorm, billions upon billions of snowflakes fall to the earth—and no two are exactly alike!

Snow, as you may know, is just frozen water. In fact, you may ask why snow is white if it's just frozen water. Shouldn't it be colorless? The white appearance is caused by the fact that the many surfaces in all the ice crystals that make up a snowflake reflect light, and we therefore see it as white.

When water freezes, it forms crystals. This simply means that the molecules come together in a special arrangement, or geometrical form, and we call this "a crystal."

It so happens that a water molecule consists of three units—two atoms of hydrogen and one of oxygen. So when it crystallizes, it has to form either three-sided or six-sided figures.

The water that freezes to form snow is in the form of water vapor in the atmosphere. As it freezes, the crystals that form are so small that they are invisible. But when snow is being formed, these crystals are carried up and down in the atmosphere by air currents.

As they move up and down, a group of crystals begin to collect around something. It might be around a speck of dust, or around a tiny drop of water. The group of crystals gets larger and larger, so that soon there might be hundreds of crystals gathered around one nucleus.

When such a group becomes large enough, it begins to float down toward the ground and we call it "a snowflake." Some snowflakes are more than 3 centimetres in diameter! The size of a snowflake depends on the temperature. The colder the temperature, the smaller the snowflakes that will form.

Did you know that in many parts of the world snow has fallen that has been blue, green, red, and even black? This is due to the presence of certain fungi or dust in the air around which the snowflakes formed.

WHY DOES FROST FORM ON WINDOWS?

Children who live in places where the winters get cold love to see frost on the windows. Some of the patterns are quite beautiful and look like intricate designs on trees or leaves.

For this frost to form on the windowpanes—as well as on trees and grass —certain conditions are necessary. Frost is made up of tiny crystals of frozen water. It forms when air that has a lot of moisture in it is cooled below the freezing temperature of water. This temperature, which we call "the freezing point," is 32 degrees Fahrenheit and zero degrees centigrade, at sea level.

When air becomes cooler, it cannot hold as much water as before. The excess water condenses on such objects as the windowpane. Now, if the temperature falls below 0 degrees centigrade, this water becomes crystallized. In other words, it freezes into a coating of interlocked crystals of water.

What causes the patterns to appear in the frost on the windowpanes? For one thing, the tiny crystals have a certain structure which gives them a pattern. In addition, there may be tiny scratches in the glass, dust particles, air currents—all of which help create the designs that "Jack Frost" makes on your windows.

White frost, which is often called "hoarfrost," is of two kinds: granular and crystalline. Granular frost is simply frozen fog. The crystalline frost, which we have described, is formed directly from the water vapor in the air. It goes right from being a gas to being a solid, without going through the liquid state.

Frost, as you know, can be a serious danger for the farmer by killing buds or ripening fruit. Actually, it is not the frost itself, but the freezing of the plant juices that is harmful. So farmers have had to develop ways of preventing frost to save their crops. One way is to cover the plants with a light cloth to prevent radiation of heat. Smudge pots in orchards cover the trees with thick smoke, and this also helps the plants hold in their heat.

So while you enjoy seeing the work of "Jack Frost," remember that it may mean serious damage to millions of pounds worth of crops.

HOW DOES WATER CHANGE TO ICE?

If you've ever noticed a pond, lake, or river freeze, you've seen a sheet of ice begin to form over the top of the water.

Do you realize that if ponds, lakes, and rivers froze from the bottom up, instead of from the top down, many important things about our life would be quite different? Not only would it change the climate of the world, but certain creatures who live in the water would disappear altogether!

Here is how the water in a pond changes into ice: When the air above the pond grows cold, it cools off the top layer of water, too. This coldness makes the water heavier than the warmer layers underneath, and the cold water sinks down. This process goes on and on until all the water in the pond has reached a temperature of about 4 degrees Centigrade.

But our temperature is still dropping! When the top layer of water becomes colder than 4 degrees, it remains on top. The reason is that water cooled to below 4 degrees actually becomes lighter!

We now have the top layer of water ready to start freezing. So when the temperature remains at the freezing point of 0 degrees, or if it goes below that, tiny crystals begin to form.

Each of these crystals has six rays, or points. As they join together they form ice, and soon a whole sheet of ice appears on top of the water. Sometimes the ice is clear, sometimes it's cloudy. Why? The reason is that when each drop of water freezes, it sets free a tiny bubble of air. This bubble sticks to the arms of the crystal. As more crystals form, the bubble remains caught and we have cloudy ice.

If the water under the ice is moving, the little air bubbles are grouped together into clear ice.

Water is one of the few substances that do not shrink when changed from liquid to solid. When water is frozen into ice it expands by one-ninth, so that nine litres of water give you ten litres of solid ice! When automobile radiators and water lines crack in winter, it's because the water freezes and there is no room for the ice!

WHAT IS A STORM?

Even though man has become a powerful creature, able to control mighty forces, nature can still strike terror into his heart when she whips up a storm! What is a storm?

Whenever there is something taking place in the weather of a violent nature, it is a storm. At sea, a storm may be a strong wind or gale. Inland, a storm usually means there is a weather situation that is marked by heavy rain, and often by lightning, thunder, and strong winds.

A storm in the latitudes where the United States lies usually covers an area hundreds of miles across. It represents vast circular whirls of air rotating about a central point of low atmospheric pressure.

Such storms begin where cold dry masses of air moving southward from Arctic regions are met by warm moist air masses moving northward from the tropics. At certain places, great tongues of the warm air thrust their way into the cold. The tip of such a warm air tongue becomes a spot of low atmospheric pressure, toward which the winds blow, and the storm area develops around it.

Where the cold and warm air masses actually meet, they mix only slightly. The lighter warm air climbs up and over the cold air along a sloping surface. This cools the warm moist air, it becomes saturated, clouds form, and the result may be rain or snow.

In the Northern Hemisphere, the earth's rotation causes the winds to be deflected toward the right, so the "whirl" of the storm is counterclockwise. In fact, it's like a whirlwind on a huge scale.

Typhoons and hurricanes north of the Equator usually originate in late summer or fall over warm tropical waters. They move westward and northwestward in a path that curves to the right. A tornado is a violent whirlwind. It begins as a black, funnel-shaped cloud that accompanies a larger thunderstorm area. The tip of the funnel may be only one hundred metres wide but it destroys whatever it touches. The destruction is caused by the terrific speed of the wind and the terrific reduction in atmospheric pressure. Walls of houses are sucked out and the buildings collapse! Tornadoes are so destructive that in regions where they occur often, people have built special places to hide from their danger.

WHY DOES THUNDER FOLLOW LIGHTNING?

Lightning and thunder must have been among the first things about nature that mystified and frightened primitive man. When he saw the jagged tones of lightning in the sky and heard the claps and rumbles of thunder, he believed the gods were angry and that the lightning and thunder were a way of punishing man.

To understand what lightning and thunder actually are, we must recall a fact we know about electricity. We know that things become electrically charged—either positively or negatively. A positive charge has a great attraction for a negative one.

As the charges become greater, this attraction becomes stronger. A point is finally reached where the strain of being kept apart becomes too great for the charges Whatever resistance holds them apart, such as air, glass, or other insulating substance, is overcome or "broken down." A discharge takes place to relieve the strain and make the two bodies electrically equal.

This is just what happens in the case of lightning. A cloud containing countless drops of moisture may become oppositely charged with respect to another cloud or the earth. When the electrical pressure between the two becomes great enough to break down the insulation of air between them, a lightning flash occurs. The discharge follows the path which offers the least resistance. That's why lightning often zigzags.

The ability of air to conduct electricity varies with its temperature, density, and moisture. Dry air is a pretty good insulator, but very moist air is a fair conductor of electricity. That's why lightning often stops when the rain begins falling. The moist air forms a conductor along which a charge of electricity may travel quietly and unseen.

What about thunder? When there is a discharge of electricity, it causes the air around it to expand rapidly and then to contract. Currents of air rush about as this expansion and contraction take place. The violent collisions of these currents of air are what we hear as thunder. The reason thunder rolls and rumbles when it is far away is that the sound waves are reflected back and forth from cloud to cloud.

Since light travels at about 186,284 miles (299,795 kilometres) per second and sound at about 335 metres per second through air, we always see the flash first and then hear the thunder later.

WHAT IS A RAINBOW?

A rainbow is one of the most beautiful sights in nature, and man has long wondered what makes it happen. Even Aristotle, the great Greek philosopher, tried to explain the rainbow. He thought it was a reflection of the sun's rays by the rain, and he was wrong!

Sunlight, or ordinary white light, is really a mixture of all the colors. You've probably seen what happens when light strikes the beveled edge of a mirror, or a soap bubble. The white light is broken up into different colors. We see red, orange, yellow, green, blue, and violet.

An object that can break up light in this way is called "a prism." The colors that emerge form a band of stripes, each color grading into the one next to it. This band is called "a spectrum."

A rainbow is simply a great curved spectrum, or band of colors, caused by the breaking-up of light which has passed through raindrops. The raindrops act as prisms.

A rainbow is seen only during showers, when rain is falling and the sun is shining at the same time. You have to be in the middle, the sun behind you, the rain in front of you, or you can't see a rainbow! The sun shines over your shoulder into the raindrops, which break up the light into a spectrum, or band of colors. The sun, your eyes, and the center of the arc of the rainbow must all be in a straight line!

If the sun is too high in the sky, it's impossible to make such a straight line. That's why rainbows are seen only in the early morning or late afternoons. A morning rainbow means the sun is shining in the east, showers are falling in the west. An afternoon rainbow means the sun is shining in the west and rain is falling in the east.

Superstitious people used to believe that a rainbow was a sign of bad luck. They thought that souls went to heaven on the bridge of a rainbow, and when a rainbow appeared it meant someone was going to die!

WHY IS IT HOT AT THE EQUATOR?

Every time you look at a map or a globe, the Equator shows up as such a prominent feature that it's almost hard to believe it's imaginary. The Equator is only an imaginary line, and you could cross it back and forth without knowing you've passed it.

This may explain why sailors like to remind themselves that they're "crossing the line," as they call it, by making quite a ceremony of it. The word "Equator" comes from a Latin word meaning "to equalize." And this is what the Equator does. It divides the earth into the Northern and Southern Hemispheres. It is the imaginary line that encircles the earth midway beween the North and South Poles.

Imaginary lines, encircling the earth parallel to the Equator are called "parallels." The Equator is the zero line, and lines above and below it measure latitude for locating points on the earth's surface.

The earth, as you know, is also divided on maps into regions. Starting at the top or north, we have the Arctic Region, the North Temperate Region, the Tropical Region, the South Temperate Region, and the Antarctic Region.

The Tropical Region, or the Equatorial Region, extends beyond the Equator to 23½ degrees north latitude and to 23½ degrees south latitude. Within this region, the rays of the sun come down vertically, and therefore it is always hot here.

Let's see why this is so: The earth, as you know, has its axis tilted to its path around the sun. The Equator, therefore, is tilted to this path, too, and that tilt is exactly 23½ degrees. Because of this tilt, as the earth goes around the sun, the direct rays from it sometimes fall on the earth north of the Equator, sometimes directly on the Equator, and sometimes south of the Equator. The sun, however, cannot be directly overhead more than 23½ degrees from the Equator.

This explains why the Equatorial Region is the only place on earth where the sun's rays come down vertically. You can understand why, since this happens the year round, it's always pretty hot near the Equator!

IS THE SOUTH POLE AS COLD AS THE NORTH POLE?

To most of us, the regions of both the North and South Poles are lands of great mystery. We have a vague idea of what they're like, and we imagine that they must be very similar to each other.

The strange thing is that differences between the Antarctic region (South Pole area) and the Arctic region (North Pole area) are greater than their similarities! The South Pole area consists chiefly of a continent called Antarctica. This ice-and-snow-covered continent is nearly twice as large as the United States. By contrast, the North Pole region consists of the Arctic Ocean surrounded by the margins of North America, Europe, and Asia.

Another big difference is that man, animals, and plants have slowly migrated northward to the North Pole region, as they have adapted themselves to the polar environment. But the South Pole region, separated by hundreds of miles of ocean from all continents except South America, has no land animals and no native population. The plant life is so scarce there that the only things growing are lichens, mosses, grasses, and a few flowering plants.

By the way, one of the reasons why the penguin can continue to live in this area so happily is that it has no land enemies to contend with.

What about the climate in the Antarctic region? It has two chief characteristics: low temperatures even in summer, and the world's greatest blizzards in winter. In the North Pole area, air currents rise from the surrounding waters and help raise the temperature a bit. But in Antarctica, which has a huge icecap spreading over most of it, large, cold, high-pressure air masses develop, and so the climate is much more severe than in the North Pole region.

Even during the summer months, the average temperature in Antarctica is below freezing! Now and then, during some summer days, the temperature may rise to 4 degrees, but on the other hand temperatures below zero may also occur right in the middle of the summer. And in the winter, the temperature at the South Pole averages from 23 to 35 degrees below zero!

WHY IS A DESERT DRY?

What is a desert? A desert is a region where only special forms of life can exist. All deserts have a shortage of moisture, which means the life that exists in them must be able to get along with almost no water.

The amount of rainfall largely controls the amount and kinds of plant life in a region. Forests grow where there is much rain. Grassland grows where the rainfall is less. Where there is still less rain, only scattered, specialized desert plants can live.

The hot deserts near the Equator, such as the Sahara in Africa, lie in

subtropical land where the air settles downward, becoming warmer and drier as it does so. Lands in these areas are dry, even though they are next to the ocean. The same is true of deserts in northwest Africa and western Australia.

Deserts farther away from the Èquator are generally caused by the great distance from the sea and its moist winds, and by the mountains between the desert and the sea. These mountain barriers may catch rainfall on their seaward side but the interior, leeward region remains dry.

This is known as "the rain shadow" effect. The deserts of Central Asia lie in the rain shadow of the great Himalayan ranges and the plateau of Tibet. The deserts of the Great Basin, in Western United States, lie in the rain shadow of high mountain ranges on their west, such as the Sierra Nevada.

Deserts differ greatly in appearance. Where sand is abundant, the winds may build sand hills or dunes. These are sand deserts. Rock deserts consist mostly of bare rock, which forms fantastic cliffs and hills, or rough, jagged plains. Other deserts, like much of Southwestern United States, include barren rocky mountains and dry plains of soil and gravel. The wind sweeps away finer soil and the stones which are left form a gravelly surface called "a desert pavement."

Most deserts have some sort of plant and animal life. Desert plants often have little or no leaf surface to reduce evaporation of water from the plant. Or they have thorns or spines to discourage animals from eating them. Animals which can live in deserts can go for long periods without water and get liquid from plants or night dew.

WHAT IS SMOKE?

Smoke is the result of incomplete combustion of certain fuels. This means that if most of our common fuels were able to burn completely, we would have no smoke!

Most fuels consist of carbon, hydrogen, oxygen, nitrogen, a little sulphur, and perhaps some mineral ash. Now, if these fuels would burn completely, the final product would be carbon dioxide, water vapor, and free nitrogen, all of which are harmless. If sulphur is present, small quantities of sulphur dioxide are also given off, and when this comes in contact with air and moisture, it becomes a corrosive acid.

For complete combustion, a fuel must have enough air for full oxidation at a high temperature. These conditions are difficult to obtain, especially with solid fuels, and the result is smoke. Anthracite and coke can be burned without producing smoke because they have no volatile matter.

But bituminous coals decompose at rather low temperatures so that gases and tarry matter are freed; they combine with dust and ash and produce smoke.

The air in any city is full of suspended solid particles, but not all of this is smoke. It may contain dust, vegetable matter, and other materials. All of these gradually settle under the force of gravity. In small towns or suburbs, probably about 70 to 90 tonnes of these deposits settle down per square mile during a year. In a big industrial city, the deposits may be 10 times as great!

Smoke can do a great deal of harm. It damages health, property, and vegetation. In big industrial towns, it lowers the intensity of the sunshine, especially the ultraviolet rays which are essential to health.

If the wind didn't spread the smoke, big industrial towns would probably have fog every day. In fact, where smoky fog occurs, it often happens that the death rate goes up from lung and heart diseases.

The effect of smoke on vegetation is especially harmful. It interferes with the "breathing" of plants and screens off needed sunlight. Quite often, the acid in the smoke destroys plants directly!

Today, many cities are waging active campaigns to cut down on smoke or to prevent it from doing damage.

WHAT IS SMOG?

In Britain determined efforts have been made to reduce the harmful effects of fog by controlling smoke from domestic coal fires and factory chimneys. In some areas coal fires are banned.

In some cities the combination of different industrial gases released into the air makes up a kind of fog we call "smog." It makes people cough when they breathe it. If certain fumes and fine particles are present in the smog, it can become poisonous.

Now, dust is present in the air at all times. Dust is tiny particles of solid matter that can be carried in suspension by air. Dust may come from soil blowing, ocean spray, volcanic activity, forest fires, the exhaust from automobiles, and from industrial combustion processes. The latter is what you see pouring out of factory chimneys.

The amount of dust in the air is almost unbelievable. It is estimated that over the United States about 39,000,000 tonnes of dust settle every year! Of this amount, about 28,000,000 tonnes are from natural sources. That leaves about 11,000,000 tonnes of dust that are the result of human activities!

Naturally, the amount of dust is greatest in big industrial cities. For example, here is roughly how much dust falls per square mile each month in some big cities: Detroit—65 tonnes; New York—63 tonnes; Chicago—55 tonnes; Pittsburgh—42 tonnes; and Los Angeles—30 tonnes. In a section of the city where there are many industrial buildings, it might be as much as 180 tonnes per square mile each month.

This is such an important health problem that many cities are carrying on intensive campaigns to reduce the amount of industrial dust in the air. Dust-producing machinery is built with hoods to keep the dust down. Ventilation systems, blower fans, and electrical devices that cause the dust to settle are also used. In some cases, wet drilling is done and water sprays are used, too. But the problem of dangerous dust in the air—or "smog"—has not yet been licked.

WHAT IS GAS?

Centuries ago, at a place called Delphi in Greece, a shepherd discovered that something arose from the ground which made his sheep act queerly and caused people to become light-headed and talk strangely. The Greeks thought this was the spirit of a god and built a temple there. This "spirit" was natural gas.

Today there are three chief types of gas: natural gas, coal gas, and water gas. Natural gas fields exist in many parts of the world. The gas has accumulated in these areas underground as the result of changes in the forming of the earth's crust. Long pipelines bring this gas under pressure to cities many hundreds of miles away, where much of it is used in iron and steel plants and by utility companies to make light and power.

Coal gas is made from powdered coal which is heated in great closed ovens from which air is shut out. When the heat under the ovens reaches a certain point, the coal becomes pasty and gives up its gases, which are carried away through pipes.

The gas is collected in a large container where some of the impurities are removed. It is then passed through water-cooled pipes into a "scrubber," where other impurities are taken out. Finally the pure coal gas is sent through a great meter which measures it. From the meter it passes into storage holders which are connected by pipelines with homes and factories where the gas is to be used.

The thick, black coal tar that is removed from the gas contains many valuable byproducts which are separated and made into perfumes, dyes, drugs, and oils. The substance that remains in the gas ovens is called "coke."

Today, of course, the use of gas for lighting purposes has almost disappeared. More than 80 per cent of the gas made today is used to produce the heat necessary in cooking and heating in homes and factories. Gas is a clean fuel, which makes it very desirable. It is easy to control, there is no storage expense, and no cost of removing ashes.

Today, coffee is roasted, food is cooked and pies and bread are baked by gas fires. There are even refrigerators run by gas. In modern laundries, steam is often made by gas. The use of gas for fuel is one way of keeping our cities relatively clean and smokeless.

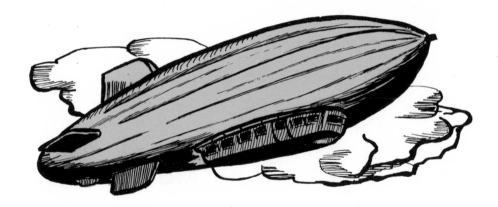

WHAT IS HELIUM?

The discovery of helium was like a scientific detective story!

In 1868, a British scientist named Sir Norman Lockyer was studying the sun with an instrument called "the spectroscope." This instrument enables scientists to identify elements, because each element produces certain lines in a spectrum.

A mysterious line appeared in the spectrum he was looking at, and it could only come from a new element, an element that wasn't even known to exist on earth! The new element was named "helium," from the Greek word *helios,* meaning "sun."

Then scientists set out to see if they could find this element on the earth, too. In time, after many experiments, they discovered that there was helium in our atmosphere. The amount is so small that out of 247,350 cubic metres of air, there is only one cubic metre of helium!

Other experiments were made that led to the discovery that radium gives off helium and that when radium sends out rays, one form of these is "alpha rays," atoms of helium moving at great speed.

Helium was found to be a very useful element. It is so light that it has great lifting power. And since helium will not catch fire, it's perfect for using in dirigibles, army and navy blimps, weather balloons, and so on.

The U.S. Government felt that helium was so important that a natural source of helium had to be found. In certain parts of the country, such as Texas, New Mexico, and Kansas, there are natural gas wells. It was found that this gas contained about one or two per cent helium.

Since there is no other source of helium to equal this, the United States Government is the only government in the world which has a plentiful supply of helium! At first the cost of helium was over $70,000 a cubic metre. Today it sells for a small fraction of that price.

Did you know helium is used in medicine, too? It is used to help people who have asthma breathe easier. Also, when divers and workers in tunnels come up, they are given a mixture of helium and oxygen to breathe so they won't get the "bends"!

HOW BIG IS AN ATOM?

Let us begin by saying that anything we know about the atom today might be changed tomorrow. Science is constantly learning new things about the atom as atom-smashing machines are built.

Oddly enough, the word "atom" comes from the Greek and means "not divisible." The ancient Greeks thought an atom to be the smallest possible particle of any substance.

Yet today we have found more than 20 different particles in the core of the atom! Scientists believe the atom is made of electrons, protons, neutrons, positrons, neutrinos, mesons, and hyperons. Electrons are particles that carry a tiny negative charge of electricity. The proton, about 1,836 times as heavy as the electron, carries a positive charge of electricity. The neutron, still heavier, carries no electric charge at all. The positron, about the size of the electron, carries a positive charge. The neutrino, about one two-thousandth the size of the electron, has no charge. Mesons may be either positively or negatively charged. Hyperons are larger than protons.

How all these particles or charges are held together to make up the atom is still not known to us. But these atoms make up the elements and they differ from each other. One way they differ is by weight, and thus elements are classified according to atomic weights. For example, hydrogen is "1" on this table and iron is "55." This means that an atom of iron is 55 times as heavy as an atom of hydrogen.

But these weights are very small. A single atom of hydrogen only weighs about one million-million-million-millionth of a gram! To give you another idea of how small atoms are, let's see how many atoms there would be in one gram of hydrogen. The answer is about 6 followed by 23 zeros. If you started to count them and counted one atom per second, it would take you ten thousand million million years to count all the atoms in just one gram of hydrogen!

WHAT IS ATOMIC ENERGY?

Atomic energy is energy obtained from the atom. Every atom has in it particles of energy. Energy holds the parts of an atom together. So in atomic energy the core of an atom is the source of the energy, and this energy is released when the atom is split.

But there are actually two ways of obtaining energy with atoms. One is called "fusion" and one is called "fission." When fusion takes place, two atoms are made to form one single atom. The fusion of atoms results in the release of a tremendous amount of energy in the form of heat. Most of the energy given off from the sun comes from fusion taking place in the sun. This is one form of atomic energy.

Another form of atomic energy comes from the fission process. Fission happens when one atom splits into two. This is done by bombarding or hitting atoms with atomic particles such as neutrons (one of the particles that make up the atom).

An atom doesn't split every time it is bombarded by neutrons. In fact, most atoms cannot be made to split. But uranium and plutonium atoms will split under proper conditions.

One form of uranium called "U-235" (it is known as an "isotope" of uranium), breaks into two fragments when it is struck with neutrons. And do you know how much energy this gives? One kilogram of U-235 gives much more than 1,000,000 times as much energy as could be obtained by burning a kilogram of coal. A tiny pebble of uranium could run an ocean liner or an airplane or even a generator. So you see, atomic energy may well be the chief source of energy for man in the future.

WHAT IS RADIUM?

Radium is a radioactive element. Let us see what "radioactive" means.

Elements are made up of atoms. Most atoms are stable, which means they do not change from year to year. But a few of the heaviest atoms break down and change into other kinds. This breakdown or decay is called "radioactivity."

Each radioactive element decays or disintegrates by giving off rays at a certain rate. This rate cannot be hurried or slowed by any known method. Some change rapidly, others slowly, but in all cases the action cannot be controlled by man.

In the case of radium, this decay would go on and on until the radium would be finally changed into lead. For example, half a gram of radium would change to atoms of lower atomic weight in 1,590 years. After another 1,590 years, half of the remaining radium would change; and so on until it all became lead.

Radium was discovered by Madame Curie and her husband, Pierre Curie. They were refining a ton of pitchblende, which is an ore that contains uranium. They knew the uranium was giving off invisible rays, but they felt there must be some other substance there, too, much more powerful.

First they found polonium, another radioactive element, and finally they succeeded in isolating a tiny speck of radium.

Radium gives off three kinds of rays, called *alpha, beta,* and *gamma* rays. *Alpha* rays are fast-moving particles of the gas helium. *Beta* rays are fast-moving electrons. And *gamma* rays are like X-rays but usually more penetrating. Whenever one of these rays is ejected, the parent atom from which it comes changes from one element to another. This change is called "atomic transmutation."

The largest deposit of radium-bearing pitchblende ever found is in the Great Bear Lake region in Canada.

WHAT IS RADIOACTIVITY?

Hardly anyone can grow up in the world today without hearing about—and worrying about—radioactivity. We know that testing of atom bombs creates radioactivity, which is why it is one of the greatest problems facing mankind today. But just what is radioactivity—and why is it harmful to man?

Let's start with the atom. Every kind of atom is constructed somewhat like our solar system. Instead of the sun there is a nucleus, and instead of planets there are electrons revolving around it. The nucleus is made up of one or more positively charged particles.

Radioactivity occurs when something happens to cause the atom to send off one or more particles from its nucleus. At the same time, the atom may send out energy in the form of rays (gamma rays).

Now some elements are naturally radioactive. This means the atoms are constantly discharging particles. When this happens, we say it is "disintegrating." When particles are sent off, the element undergoes a change. In this way, radium—which is naturally radioactive—sends off particles and disintegrates into other elements until it becomes lead.

Scientists have now learned how to produce artificial radioactivity. By bombarding the atoms of certain elements with particles, they could make those atoms begin to disintegrate and thus become radioactive. The bombarded atoms would thus send off energy. That's why these machines are called "atom smashers."

Why is radioactivity dangerous to man? Well, just picture these flying particles coming from the smashed atoms. When these particles strike other atoms, they can cause them to break up, too, and change their chemical character. Now, if these particles strike living cells in the body, they certainly can cause changes there! They can burn and destroy the skin, destroy red blood cells, and cause changes in other cells.

So while radioactivity can be useful to man in many ways, it can also be dangerous and destructive.

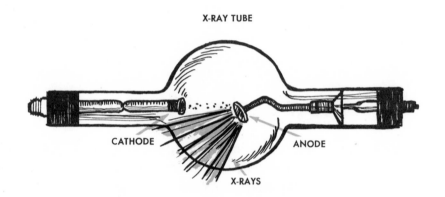

X-RAY TUBE

CATHODE   ANODE

X-RAYS

WHAT ARE X-RAYS?

X-rays were discovered in Germany in 1895 by Wilhelm Roentgen, and thus are sometimes called "Roentgen rays."

They are penetrating rays similar to light rays. They differ from light rays in the length of their waves and in their energy. The shortest wave length from an X-ray tube may be one fifteen-thousandth to one-millionth of the wave length of green light. X-rays can pass through materials which light will not pass through because of their very short wave length. The shorter the wave length, the more penetrating the waves become.

X-rays are produced in an X-ray tube. The air is pumped from this tube until less than one hundred-millionth of the original amount is left. In the tube, which is usually made of glass, there are two electrodes. One of these is called "the cathode." This has a negative charge. In it is a coil of tungsten wire which can be heated by an electric current so that electrons are given off. The other electrode is "the target," or "anode."

The electrons travel from the cathode to the target at very great speeds because of the difference between the cathode and the target. They strike the target at speeds that may vary from 60,000 to 175,000 miles per second.

The target is either a block of tungsten or a tungsten wheel, and it stops the electrons suddenly. Most of the energy of these electrons is changed into heat, but some of it becomes X-radiation, and emerges from a window at the bottom as X-rays.

Have you ever wondered how X-ray pictures are taken of bones in your body? The X-ray "picture" is a shadowgraph or shadow picture. X-rays pass through the part of the body being X-rayed and cast shadows on the film. The film is coated with a sensitive emulsion on both sides. After it is exposed, it is developed like ordinary photographic film. The bones and other objects the X-rays do not pass through easily cast denser shadows and so show up as light areas on the film.

Today, X-rays play an important part in medicine, science, and industry, and are one of man's most helpful tools.

WHAT ARE COSMIC RAYS?

You have read, of course, that when a satellite is sent up into the air it carries all kinds of instruments and measuring devices. Did you notice that in almost every case there is some detecting or measuring instrument for cosmic rays? These rays are still as exciting and mysterious as anything you might find in science fiction!

About 60 years ago, scientists noticed a strange occurrence. They found that a sample of air in a closed container showed a small amount of electrical conductivity. Even when they surrounded the container with thick shields, this was still true. It meant that some kind of radiation was entering the container, radiation more penetrating than any known before!

Where was this mysterious radiation coming from? All kinds of experiments were made to get the answer. First, they proved that it wasn't coming from land, because it was over the sea, too. Since it was the same night and day, it wasn't coming from the sun. And by going up in a balloon to great altitudes, it was shown to be everywhere in space, or "cosmic"—which means "universal."

What actually are cosmic rays? They are atomic particles. They travel in space outside the earth's atmosphere at speeds nearly equal to that of light. Some of them happen to approach the earth and enter our atmosphere.

These atomic particles, called "primary cosmic rays," collide with atoms in the air. These collisions create new particles which also travel at great speeds and in the same direction as the primary particles. These new particles are called "secondary cosmic rays." They in turn collide with other atoms and create more new particles. Thus, a great shower of radiation bombards the earth. One proton coming from outer space may create enough radiation in this way to cover 90 square metres.

As far as we know, this bombardment of cosmic rays is harmless when it reaches the earth, because, after all, it has been going on for billions of years and has not affected life on earth.

Science still cannot explain where cosmic rays originate, though now that we are penetrating outer space, the mystery may eventually be solved.

WHAT CAUSES A MIRAGE?

Imagine a wanderer in the desert, dying of thirst. He looks off into the distance and sees a vision of a lake of clear water surrounded by trees. He stumbles forward until the vision fades and there is nothing but the hot sand all around him.

The lake he saw in the distance was a mirage. What caused it? A mirage is a trick Nature plays on our eyes because of certain conditions in the atmosphere. First we must understand that we are able to see an object because rays of light are reflected from it to our eyes. Usually, these rays reach our eye in a straight line. So if we look off into the distance, we should only see things that are above our horizon.

Now we come to the tricks the atmosphere plays with rays of light. In a desert, there is a layer of dense air above the ground which acts as a mirror. An object may be out of sight, way below the horizon. But when rays of light from it hit this layer of dense air, they are reflected to our eyes and we see the object as if it were above the horizon and in our sight. We are really "seeing" objects which our eyes cannot see! When the distant sky is reflected by this "mirror" of air, it sometimes looks like a lake, and we have a mirage.

On a hot day, as you approach the top of a hill, you may think the road ahead is wet. This is a mirage, too! What you are seeing is light from the sky that has been bent by the hot air just above the pavement so that it seems to come from the road itself.

Mirages occur at sea, too, with visions of ships sailing across the sky! In these cases, there is cold air near the water and warm air over it. Distant ships, that are beyond the horizon, can be seen because the light waves coming from them are reflected by the layer of warm air and we see the ship in the sky!

One of the most famous mirages in the world takes place in Sicily, across the Strait of Messina. The city of Messina is reflected in the sky, and fairy castles seem to float in the air. The Italian people call it *Fata Morgana,* after Morgan Le Fay, who was supposed to be an evil fairy who caused this mirage.

WHAT IS LIGHT?

Without light we couldn't see the world around us, yet we still don't know exactly what light is!

We know light is a form of energy. Its speed can be measured and the way it behaves is known to us. We also know that white light is not a special kind of light—it is a mixture of all colors. We call this "the spectrum."

We also know that color is not in the objects seen—it is in the light by which they are seen. A piece of green paper looks green because it absorbs all the colors except green, which it reflects to the eyes. Blue grass allows only blue light to pass through it; all other colors are absorbed in the glass.

Sunlight is energy. The heat in rays of sunlight, when focused with a lens, will start a fire. Light and heat are reflected from white materials and absorbed by black materials. That's why white clothing is cooler than black clothing.

But what is the nature of light? The first man to make a serious effort to explain light was Sir Isaac Newton. He believed that light is made up of corpuscles, like tiny bullets that are shot from the source of the light. But some of the things that happen to light couldn't be explained according to this theory.

So a man called Huygens came up with another explanation of light. He developed the "wave" theory of light. His idea was that light started pulses, or waves, the way a pebble dropped into a pool makes waves.

Whether light was waves or corpuscles was argued for nearly 150 years. The wave theory seemed to be the one that most scientists accepted. Then something was discovered about the way light behaves that upset this theory.

Where does science stand today about light? Well, it is now believed that light behaves both as particles and as waves. Experiments can be made to prove that it is one or the other. So there just doesn't seem to be a single satisfactory answer to the question of what is light.

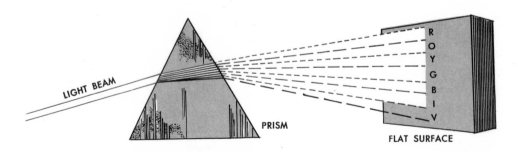

LIGHT BEAM

PRISM

R
O
Y
G
B
I
V

FLAT SURFACE

WHAT IS COLOR?

When Sir Isaac Newton passed a beam of sunlight through a glass prism, he proved that sunlight is made up of colors. As the light was bent by the prism, it formed a spectrum.

Most people can see six or seven colors in the spectrum, but with instruments, more than 100 colors can be seen in it. But white light is really made up of three basic colors which are called "the primary colors." They cannot be made from any other colors. The primary colors of light are orange-red, green, and violet-blue.

In the spectrum, we can also see three mixed colors with the naked eye. These are called "secondary colors." They are green-blue (turquoise), yellow, and magenta red. You can make the secondary colors by mixing other colors together.

Colors consist of wave lengths to which the human eye is sensitive. Insects and many other creatures respond to other wave lengths and see other colors.

Light or color wave lengths are very short.

Paint colors are substances, and they are exactly the opposite from light colors. The secondary colors in light are the primaries in paint. This means that in paint the primary colors are yellow, green-blue (turquoise), and magenta red; and the secondary colors are orange-red, green, and violet-blue.

A color that is brilliant and has no black or white paint in it is called "a hue." Yellow, red, blue, green, etc., are hues. A color that is mixed from a hue and black is called "a shade." Deep brown is a shade. A color that is made with a hue and white is "a tint." Pink and ivory are tints. A color that is a mixture of pure hue, black, and white is "a tone." Tan, beige, straw, and grey are tones.

Red paint inside the can doesn't look red——it looks black! Where there is no light there is no color. Not only do we not see color in a dark room, the color is not there! The color of an object depends on the material of the object and the light in which the object is seen. An orange-red sweater looks orange-red because the dye with which the wool was treated reflects the orange-red part of the light and absorbs the violet-blue and green parts of the light.

HOW FAST DOES SOUND TRAVEL?

Every time a sound is made, there is some vibrating object somewhere. Something is moving back and forth rapidly. Sound starts with a vibrating object.

But sound must travel in something. It requires something to carry the sound from its source to the hearer. This is called "a medium." A medium can be practically anything—air, water, objects, even the earth. The Indians used to put their ears to the ground to hear a distant noise!

No medium—no sound. If you create a vacuum, space containing no air or any other substance, sound cannot travel through it. The reason for this is that sound travels in waves. The vibrating objects cause the molecules or particles in the substance next to them to vibrate. Each particle passes on the motion to the particle next to it, and the result is sound waves.

Since the mediums in which sound travels can range from wood to air to water, obviously the sound waves will travel at different speeds. So when we ask how fast does sound travel, we have to ask: In what?

The speed of sound in air is about 335 metres per second (750 miles per hour). But this is when the temperature is 0 degrees centigrade. As the temperature rises, the speed of sound rises.

Sound travels much faster in water than in air. When water is at a temperature of 8 degrees centigrade, sound travels through it at about 1,435 metres per second, or 3,210 miles per hour. And in steel, sound travels at about 5,000 metres per second, or 11,160 miles per hour.

You might imagine that a loud sound would travel faster than a weak sound, but this isn't so. Nor is the speed of sound affected by its pitch (high or low). The speed depends on the medium through which it is traveling.

If you want to try an interesting experiment with sound, clap two stones together when you are standing in the water. Now go under water and clap those two stones together again. You'll be amazed how much better sound travels through water than through air!

WHAT IS THE SOUND BARRIER?

The name "sound barrier" is actually a wrong way to describe a condition that exists when planes travel at certain speeds. A kind of "barrier" was expected when planes reached the speed of sound — but no such barrier developed!

In order to understand this, let's start with a plane traveling at ordinary low-speed flight. As the plane moves forward, the front parts of the plane send out a pressure wave. The pressure wave is caused by the building-up of particles of air as the plane moves forward.

Now this pressure wave goes out ahead of the plane at the speed of sound. It is, therefore, moving faster than the plane itself, which, as we said, is moving at ordinary speed. As this pressure wave rushes ahead of the plane, it causes the air to move smoothly over the wing surfaces of the approaching plane.

Now let's say the plane is traveling at the speed of sound. The air ahead receives no pressure wave in advance of the plane, since both the plane and the pressure wave are moving forward at the same speed. So the pressure wave builds up in front of the wing.

The result is a shock wave, and this creates great stresses in the wing of the plane. Before planes actually flew at the speed of sound and faster, it was expected that these shock waves and stresses would create a kind of "barrier" for the plane — a "sound barrier." But no such barrier developed, since aeronautical engineers were able to design planes to overcome it.

Incidentally, the loud 'boom" that is heard when a plane passes through the "sound barrier" is caused by the shock wave described above — when the speed of the pressure wave and the speed of the plane are the same.

WHAT CAUSES AN ECHO?

Today, when you have a question about anything in nature, you expect to get a true, scientific answer. But in ancient times, people would make up legends to explain things. The legend that the early Greeks had to explain an echo is very charming. Would you like to know it? Here it is.

There was once a lovely nymph called Echo who had one bad fault—she talked too much. To punish her, the goddess Hera forbade her ever to speak without first being spoken to, and then only to repeat what she had heard. One day, Echo saw the handsome youth Narcissus. She fell in love with him at once, but he did not return her love. So Echo grew sadder and sadder and pined away, until nothing was left of her but her voice! And it is her voice which you hear when you speak and your words are repeated.

That sad legend doesn't really explain an echo, of course. To understand what causes an echo, you have to know something about sound. Sound travels at a speed of about 335 metres per second in the open air. It travels in waves, much like ripples made by a pebble thrown into water. And sound waves go out in all directions from the source, like the light from an electric bulb.

Now, when a sound wave meets an obstacle, it may bounce back, or be reflected, just as light is reflected. When a sound wave is reflected in this way, it is heard as an echo. So an echo is sound repeated by reflection.

Not all obstacles can cause echoes, however. Some objects absorb the sound instead of reflecting it. This means the sound doesn't bounce back. There is no echo. But usually, smooth, regular surfaces, such as a wall, a cliff, a side of a house, or a vaulted roof, will produce an echo.

Did you know that clouds reflect sounds and can cause echoes? In fact, when you hear the rumbling of thunder, it's because the first sharp clap is being reflected again and again by the clouds.

WHAT IS ENERGY?

As you know from reading the news columns, the greatest goal of science today is to obtain energy from the atom to enable man to live a life of peace and plenty. The mere idea that this can be done is one of the greatest steps forward in the history of human thought!

Albert Einstein was the first man to set up a theory that measured matter in terms of energy. In other words, he showed that matter could be changed into energy. This changed our whole way of looking at the physical world. Matter became secondary; energy became the most important thing in the physical world.

What is energy? Energy is the ability to do work. Energy is that which stands back of forces, and makes the forces possible. Let's try to understand this by considering the automobile.

To make the motor go, a force must be used. Something must provide that force. That something is energy. Where does it come from? It comes from the petrol, and the energy is let loose by burning the petrol in the cylinder. This energy puts certain forces into operation, forces which produce motion through the gears and wheels of the car. The result is that the engine does work, and energy has made it possible.

There are two kinds of energy, potential and kinetic. First let's understand potential energy. In the case of petrol, the molecules are held together by electrical forces. Energy is stored in these molecules, potential energy. When the petrol explodes, that potential energy is used up.

Another example of potential energy is a suspended weight. There is stored-up energy in the weight which we can release just by letting it drop. Water at the top of a falls or behind a dam also has potential energy.

Now suppose the weight drops, or the water goes down over the falls. The mere fact that it is moving at a certain speed enables it to do work, and this energy is called "kinetic energy." It is energy that is derived from the weight of a moving body and its speed. As a body falls, it loses potential energy and gains kinetic energy. But the amount gained is exactly equal to the amount lost. In fact, the total amount of energy in the universe is always the same. We can't create it or destroy it. What we do, whether we use falling water, coal, or the atom, is change it from one form to another.

WHAT IS HEAT?

At one time it was believed heat was a kind of fluid that passed from hot bodies into cold ones. This imaginary fluid was called "caloric."

Today we know that heat is the constant motion of atoms and molecules in objects. In the air, for instance, the atoms and molecules move about freely. If they move rapidly, we say that the temperature of the air is high or that the air is hot. If they move slowly, as on a cold day, we feel the air to be cool.

Atoms and molecules can't move about as freely in liquids and solid objects, but motion is present.

Even at the temperature of melting ice, the molecules are in constant motion. A hydrogen molecule at this temperature moves with a speed of 1,950 metres per second. In 16 cubic centimetres of air, a thousand million million collisions per second occur among the molecules every second!

Heat and temperature are not the same thing. A large gas burner may be no "hotter" than a small burner, but it may supply more heat because it burns more gas. Heat is a form of energy, and when we measure heat we measure energy. Quantity of heat is measured in calories. A calorie is the amount of heat energy required to raise the temperature of one gram of water one degree centigrade. But the temperature of a body only indicates the level to which the heat energy that it contains brings it. Temperature is indicated by a thermometer and is expressed in degrees.

When two bodies are brought together and there is no passage of heat energy from one to the other, we say that they are at the same temperature. But if heat energy is lost by one (its molecules are slowed down), while this same energy is gained by the other (its molecules move faster), we say that heat has passed from the hotter to the colder body, and that the first body was at a higher temperature than the second.

WHAT IS FIRE?

The scientific name for burning is "combustion." There are many different kinds of combustion, but in most cases a very simple thing has to take place. Oxygen from the air has to combine with some material that can burn.

This reaction produces heat. If the process takes place rapidly, we may see flames or an intense glow or actually feel the combustion, as in an explosion. When wood or paper combine with oxygen, we usually have flames. But we also have combustion in the engines of our automobiles. The gasoline burns with oxygen taken from the air.

In the automobile engine the combustion proceeds so rapidly that we call it an explosion. At the opposite end, we have a kind of combustion that

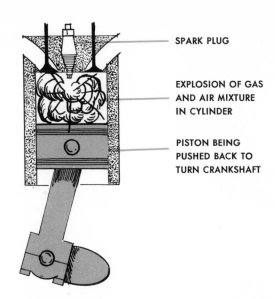

SPARK PLUG

EXPLOSION OF GAS
AND AIR MIXTURE
IN CYLINDER

PISTON BEING
PUSHED BACK TO
TURN CRANKSHAFT

goes on so slowly that we may not notice it for years. For instance, when iron rusts, a slow burning process is actually taking place!

When slow combustion takes place and the heat that results cannot escape into the air, the temperature may reach a point where active burning begins. This is called "spontaneous combustion." Spontaneous combustion might occur in a heap of oily rags left in some closed place. The oil will undergo slow oxidation or burning which results in heat. Since the heat cannot escape, it accumulates. Eventually there will be enough heat to cause the cloth to burst into flames.

Oxygen, which is necessary in combustion, is one of the most common elements in nature. The air which surrounds us contains approximately 21 per cent of oxygen. This oxygen is always ready to enter the combustion process.

However, materials which are "combustible" are as necessary as oxygen for combustion to take place. We call these materials "inflammable." Inflammable materials which are planned to be used for combustion are known as "fuels." For instance, wood, coal, coke, fuel oil, kerosene, and certain gases are common fuels.

During combustion, two atoms of oxygen from the air combine with one atom of carbon from the fuel to form a molecule of a new substance called "carbon dioxide." Did you know that the combustion process which goes on in our body to generate heat and energy creates carbon dioxide which we breathe out?

WHY DO HOT THINGS BURN YOU?

The fact that fire and hot things cause a painful sensation which we call "burning" is really something we all have to discover for ourselves! A baby doesn't know it—and so it burns itself. Only experience seems to be able to teach us this lesson.

In a block of hot iron, the atoms vibrate rapidly, perhaps a million times each second! If you were to touch the tip of your finger to such a block, you would suffer pain because the fast-moving particles of the iron would cause the molecules in your skin to go into sudden and violent motion. You would simply feel this violent motion as pain, and this is why hot things burn you.

You may wonder how fast the molecules must move in order to cause such a sensation in your skin. Well, maybe this will give you an idea. At the temperature of melting ice, which certainly isn't hot, a hydrogen molecule moves with a speed of over 1,700 metres per second!

Skidding indicates the absence of friction.

WHAT IS FRICTION?

Friction is the resistance offered to the movement of one material against another. It could be any two materials you can think of.

Many of the jobs and activities we carry on in life would be impossible without friction. Without friction, the belts of machines would slip, nails and screws wouldn't hold, feet would not grip the floor or pavement, wheels would spin without making things move! Yet in many cases, especially in machines, we actually try to reduce friction as much as possible.

In the case of solid things, friction is caused mainly by unevenness in surfaces that touch each other. The smoother these surfaces, the less friction. Interestingly enough, friction between unlike materials is less than that between substances of the same kind. When we lubricate the surfaces, as when we oil the bearings of machines, we reduce friction by substituting liquid friction for solid friction.

Friction between solids is of two kinds—sliding and rolling. Rolling friction is less than sliding friction. That's why the wheel was one of man's greatest inventions. It made it possible to substitute rolling friction for sliding friction in pulling loads.

Here is a way to realize what a big difference this makes. Let's take a large stone on a rough surface. It would take perhaps a dozen men to drag it over the surface with sliding friction. Now, if we put the same stone on rollers, it might take six men to pull the same stone over the rough surface. Now, if we put the stone in a cart with two wheels, only four men might be needed. We would have sliding friction at the axle, and rolling friction over the rough surface. Now, if we grease the axle and make the road smooth, two men can pull the cart. By using wheels with ball bearings, only one man can move the same stone easily!

Air and water also create friction. We streamline airplanes to reduce air resistance, and boats are shaped the way they are to cut down water friction.

HOW DOES A BODY FALL THROUGH SPACE?

Gravitation is the force which pulls every object in the universe toward every other object in the universe. It is the force that makes a body fall through space toward the earth.

It was not until the time of Galileo (1564-1642) that any effort was made to measure the effect of gravity. It was believed until that time that the speed with which a falling object struck the ground from any height depended on the weight of the object.

Galileo dropped objects of different weights from the leaning tower of Pisa to show how the "force" of gravity caused them to fall. He showed that a heavy weight and a light weight when dropped together reached the ground at the same time.

Galileo also rolled a ball down a slope slowly enough to measure its position at definite times. He found that the increase in the speed of the ball was proportional to the time it was rolling. This means that, at the end of two seconds, it was traveling twice as fast as at the end of one second and, at the end of three seconds, it was traveling three times as fast, and so on.

He also found that the distance it traveled was proportional to the square of the time it spent traveling. (The square of a number is the number multiplied by itself.) So at the end of two seconds, it was four times as far as at the end of one second. At the end of three seconds, it was nine times as far away, and so on.

Sir Isaac Newton made the next great discoveries about gravitation. Newton assumed that the force which attracts any body toward the earth should grow less as the distance grows greater. Out of his studies and the observations of others came Newton's Law of Universal Gravitation. The basic idea of this law is that if the mass (amount of matter) of one of the two attracting bodies is doubled, the gravitational attraction will also be doubled; but if their distance apart is doubled, the force will be only one-fourth as great.

Albert Einstein attempted to answer the question "What is gravity?" by explaining that it is due to the shape of four-dimensional space-time. This is a very complicated theory requiring scientific training to understand. His latest theory related the gravitational 'field" to the electric, magnetic, and electromagnetic fields. But we can say that actually no one has yet been able to explain exactly what gravity is to everyone's satisfaction.

We do know, however, that the acceleration (increase in speed) caused by gravity is 10 metres per second each second. That means the speed of a falling body is increased 10 metres per second for each second it is falling. At the end of one second, it is dropping at a speed of 10 metres per second; at the end of two seconds, 20 metres per second; and so on. At the end of the first second, a falling object will be 5 metres down; at the end of two seconds, 20 metres, and at the end of 3 seconds, 45 metres.

WHAT IS EINSTEIN'S THEORY OF RELATIVITY?

When this theory was first published, it was said that it could be understood by only a dozen or so scientists in the whole world! So obviously, we cannot even begin to try to explain it in any technical detail in this book. But it should be useful to have a general idea of what Einstein was dealing with, the problem he was concerned with.

Everybody knows from experience that all motion is "relative." This means that it can only be measured in relation to something else. For example, you're sitting in a railroad train and you look out the window. As you see things moving by quickly, you know you're in motion. But there's a man sitting opposite you, and relative to him you're not moving at all!

So the existence of motion can have meaning only when it is considered relative to something which is fixed. That's the first basic part of Einstein's theory. We may state it as: The motion of a body traveling at uniform speed through space cannot be detected by observation made on that body alone.

The second basic part of Einstein's theory said that the only absolute unchanging quantity in the universe was the speed of light. Now, we know this to be about 186,000 miles per second. But it is really a fantastic idea to be able to imagine that this cannot change. Here is why this is so strange: If a car is going at 60 miles an hour, we mean that its speed, measured by a someone standing still, is 60 miles per hour. If it passes a car traveling in the same direction at 40 miles per hour, it passes it at a speed of 20 miles per hour. And if the second car, instead of traveling in the same direction, were coming to meet it, they would pass each other at a speed of 100 miles per hour.

Now, according to Einstein, if the speed of a ray of light were measured in the same way (for example, if we were racing in one direction and it was going the opposite way), it wouldn't make any difference! That ray of light would still pass at about 186,000 miles per second. This is only the rough, general idea of what Einstein was dealing with in his theory of relativity. Among other things he dealt with were mass and energy and how they can be transformed into each other.

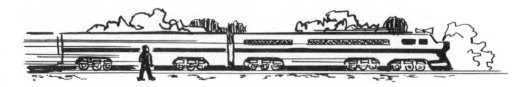

WHAT IS OXYGEN?

Every now and then you read about something that man "couldn't live without." Well, one thing you can be sure is absolutely necessary to life is oxygen. Without oxygen, a human being cannot live more than a few minutes.

Oxygen is an element, the most plentiful element in the universe. It makes up nearly half of the earth's crust and more than one-fifth of the air. Breathed into the lungs, it is carried by the red blood corpuscles in a constant stream to the body cells. There it burns the food, making the heat needed to keep the human engine going.

Oxygen combines very easily with most elements. When this takes place, we call the process "oxidation." When this oxidation takes place very quickly, we have "combustion." In almost all oxidations, heat is given off. In combustion, the heat is given off so fast that it has no time to be carried away, the temperature rises extremely high, and a flame appears.

So at one end we have combustion, the fast oxidation that produces fire and at the other end we have the kind of oxidation that burns the food in our body and keeps the life process going. But slow oxidations, by the oxygen of the air, are found everywhere. When iron rusts, paint dries, alcohol is changed into vinegar, oxidation is going on.

The air we breathe is a mixture chiefly of nitrogen and oxygen. So we can prepare pure oxygen from the air. It is done by cooling the air to very low temperatures until it becomes liquid. This temperature is more than 180 degrees below zero centigrade. As soon as the liquid air warms up a little above that temperature, it boils. The nitrogen boils off first and oxygen remains. Many a life has been saved by giving people oxygen to make breathing easier when their lungs were weak.

WHAT IS WATER?

When scientists wonder whether there is life on other planets, they often ask this question: "Is there water there?" Life as we know it would be impossible without water.

Water is a tasteless, odorless, colorless compound that makes up a large proportion of all living things. It occurs everywhere in the soil, and exists in varying amounts in the air.

Living things can digest and absorb foods only when these foods are dissolved in water. Living tissue consists chiefly of water. What is water made of? It is a simple compound of two gases: hydrogen, a very light gas; and oxygen, a heavier, active gas.

When hydrogen is burned in oxygen, water is formed. But water does not resemble either of the elements which compose it. It has a set of properties all its own.

Water, like most other matter, exists in three states: a liquid state, which is the common form; a solid, called "ice"; and a gas, called "water vapor." In which one of these forms water shall exist depends ordinarily on the temperature.

At 0 degrees centigrade, or 32 degrees Fahrenheit, water changes from the liquid to the solid state, or freezes. At 100 degrees centigrade, or 212 degrees Fahrenheit, it changes from the liquid to the gaseous state. This change from liquid, visible water to the invisible water gas is called "evaporation."

Thus, if a piece of ice is brought into a warm room, it starts to become liquid or melt. If the room is warm enough, the little puddle of water formed from the melting ice finally disappears. The liquid is changed into water vapor. When water is cooled, it expands just before it reaches the freezing point.

Water as it occurs in nature is never pure in the true sense. It contains dissolved mineral material, dissolved gases, and living organisms.

HOW IS SOIL FORMED?

If the surface of our earth were not covered with soil, man would perish. Without soil, plants could not grow and human beings and other animals would have no food.

Soil is the loose, powdery earth in which plants grow. It is made up of very small pieces of rock and decayed plant and animal materials. The small pieces or particles of rock were once parts of larger rocks. The plant and animal materials come from plant and animal bodies.

No rock is so hard that it cannot in time be broken into pieces. The crumbling and wearing away of rock, which is called "weathering," goes on all the time and is done in many ways. Glaciers push great piles of rocks ahead of them as they move along and this pushing and grinding help crumble the rocks.

Water with chemicals in it will dissolve and wear away some kinds of rocks. Changes in temperature often help break rocks into small pieces. The heating and cooling of rocks may cause cracks to appear. Water gets into the cracks, freezes, and cracks the rocks even more. Even plant roots may cause rocks to break. Sometimes the seeds of trees fall into cracks in rocks, the seeds sprout, and as the roots of the plant grow, they help split the rock. Wind also helps crumble rocks by hurling sand against the rocks.

But this is only the beginning of soil-making. To make real soil, the sand or fine particles of rock must have "humus" added to it. Humus is an organic material that comes from plants and animal bodies. The bodies of almost all dead land plants and animals become a part of soil, through the work of bacteria.

Bacteria cause the plants and animals to decay and make the soil fertile. Earthworms and many kinds of insects help to make the soil rich. The richest layer of soil is at the top and is called "topsoil." This has much humus in it. The next layer, which is called "subsoil," contains mostly bits of rock. The layer beneath is bedrock, which is under the soil everywhere.

PLANTS

TOP SOIL

SUBSOIL

BEDROCK

WHY ARE THERE DIFFERENT KINDS OF SAND?

When a solid rock is exposed to the action of the wind, rain, and frost, and broken up into smaller particles, if the particles are small enough (between 0.05 millimetres in diameter and 2.5 millimetres in diameter), these particles are called "sand".

Since sand is formed of small grains of the minerals making up the rocks, any of these minerals may be found in sand. The principal mineral found in sand is quartz, because it is very hard and is quite abundant. Some sands have as much as 99 per cent pure quartz. Other minerals sometimes found in sand are feldspar, calcite, mica, iron ores, and small amounts of garnet, tourmaline, and topaz.

Sand is found wherever rocks have been exposed to the weather. One of the principal sand-forming regions is the beach of a sea. There the action of the tide upon the rocks, the action of wind-blown sand rubbing against the rocks, and the dissolving of some of the minerals in the rocks by the salt water all combine to make sand.

The loose sand along the beaches is picked up by the wind and carried inland. Sometimes, so much sand is moved in this way that a whole forest may be covered by sand dunes.

What about the sand often found in deserts? Most of the loose sand there has been brought to this place by wind. In some cases, the desert sands may have been formed by the decay of rocks. In still other cases, the desert was once really a sea bottom and the water retreated thousands of years ago, leaving the sand.

Sand is a very useful substance. It is used a great deal in modern building. When mixed with cement and water, it forms a sticky, mudlike paste called "mortar," which hardens quickly into a solid mass called "concrete." It is also used in making glass, in sandpaper, and as a filter in helping keep water pure.

WHAT DOES ASPHALT COME FROM?

The chances are you've walked, driven, bicycled on asphalt pavements, and seen them all your life. But did you know that asphalt was also known and used in ancient times? Asphalt has a waterproofing quality and it was known to the early Babylonians who called it "pitche" and "slime." It was known much later to the Romans who called it "bitumen." They lined reservoirs and swimming pools with asphalt to keep them from leaking.

Asphalt is a dark brown to black mineral substance found in the earth in liquid, solid, and partly solid forms. It is also a natural part of most crude oils. Asphalt softens when warmed. It becomes liquid when heated, and then hardens when cooled. Chemically, asphalt is a combination of hydrogen and carbon.

There are two kinds of asphalt—natural asphalt and petroleum asphalt. Natural asphalt comes from deposits found on or near the surface of the earth. Petroleum asphalt is separated from crude oil by modern refining methods.

Natural asphalt was formed in the early ages by oil being forced to the surface through sand beds and rock formations. The purest asphalt was trapped in the rocks where it was protected. It oozed out as almost pure liquid asphalt.

One of the largest known lakes of natural asphalt is on the island of Trinidad in the West Indies. It covers about 40 hectares and is more than 30 metres deep. When the streets of Washington, D.C., were paved in 1876, most of the asphalt came from this source in Trinidad.

Asphalt cement is the name for modern paving asphalt. Asphalt cement is used in paving to hold sand and stone tightly together, and to prevent water from entering the pavement. It has rubberlike qualities which cause it to bend under an extra heavy blow rather than break like a rock. The heavy-duty asphalt pavements are built for airfields where planes may weigh 140,000 kilograms and for roads with trucks of 45,000 kilograms.

HOW IS COAL FORMED?

Coal has been made at several different times in the earth's long history. The greatest period of coal formation is called the Pennsylvanian period, which started about 250,000,000 years ago and lasted some 35,000,000 years. Most of the other coal was formed in periods from 1,000,000 to 100,000,000 years ago.

What took place during these periods and how was the coal formed? Coal is found in the earth in flat layers many miles wide, sometimes more than 3 metres thick, buried between other layers of rock. Coal is the remains of ancient trees and plants that grew in great swampy jungles in warm, moist climates during those periods hundreds of millions of years ago.

Fast-growing rushes and giant tree ferns grew in these swamps. In time, they died and fell into the quiet swamp waters. This protected them against rotting, which would soon destroy them if they were exposed to the air. Bacteria changed some parts of the wood to gases which escaped, leaving behind a black mixture, mostly carbon, which was to become a coal seam.

Long years of lush growth caused the layer of decaying vegetation to become several metres thick. Sooner or later, this process was brought to an end by the sinking of the earth's surface. This resulted in thick layers of mud and sand being washed in on top of the vegetation.

In time, the increasing pressure from the overlying mud and sand squeezed out most of the liquid, leaving behind a pasty mass which slowly hardened into coal. This process was in some places repeated many times. As the layer of sediment built up until it was close to the water level, another swamp was formed. A layer of vegetable matter was formed in this again, and then it sank again. In this way, seams of coal were formed, separated from the others by mud and sand which in time turned to rock.

The change from wood to coal takes thousands of years. But the proof that coal came from plants is easily seen. Sometimes, perfect impressions of ferns are found within the coal, or patterns of bark, and even fossil tree stumps are seen within the coal.

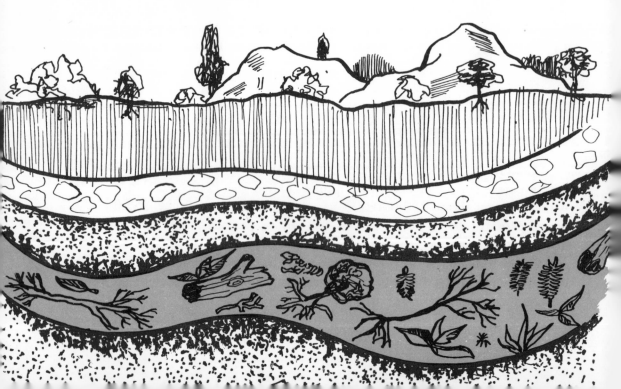

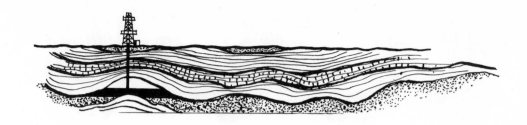

WHAT IS PETROLEUM?

Petroleum is one of the great servants of mankind. It provides light, heat, and power for automobiles, tractors, planes, and ships. Without it, nearly all our machines would stop because of friction.

From petroleum come motor-spirit, paraffin, fuel and lubricating oils, greases, wax, asphalt, and many other products. What is petroleum? The word comes from the Latin and means "rock oil." How was it created? Scientists believe that petroleum was formed from plants and animals that lived ages ago in and around warm seas that covered much of the earth.

As the plants and animals died, they piled up on the sea bottom. In time, millions of tonnes of sand and mud covered them. Under pressure, the mud and sand changed to rock. The plants and animals turned to a dark liquid trapped in the pores of the rocks. Upheavals of the earth's crust caused parts of the old sea floor to become dry land. Some of the liquid oozed to the surface of the earth where men first noticed it.

Petroleum, or crude oil, has been used for thousands of years. Ancient peoples, including the Chinese and Egyptians, used it as a medicine. In India, it was being burned long before the beginning of the Christian Era.

It was used in ancient days to make torches and, in its heavier forms of pitch and asphaltum, to bind bricks, to waterproof baskets and seal the seams of wooden ships. The American Indians used petroleum for many purposes, and when the white men came to America, they imitated the practice of the Indians and used this "mineral oil" for medicinal purposes.

Crude petroleum, as it comes from the well, is of little use. It must be refined. The basic refining process, distillation, is based on the fact that petroleum is a mixture of many solids, liquids, and gases.

By means of heat, distillation separates the different things nature put into crude oil. This is possible because each part of the mixture boils, or changes to a gas, at a different temperature. The first thing that comes off is motor-spirit, then paraffin, then gas, oil, and lubricating oils.

WHAT IS A MINERAL?

A "mineral" is any substance found in the earth's crust that does not come from a living thing.

Sometimes petroleum, coal, and limestone are called minerals, but since they were made from plants or animals which lived on the earth a long time ago, they are not really minerals.

Minerals are usually divided into two groups, metallic and nonmetallic. Examples of metallic minerals are hematite (iron), bornite (copper), and bauxite (aluminum). The non-metallic minerals include quartz, asbestos, and calcite. Minerals are usually found in forms called "crystals."

It is easy to confuse minerals and rocks, but there is a difference. A mineral has a definite composition. The chemical make-up of a mineral is almost always the same, no matter where it is. So a mineral found in any part of the world will have the same luster, hardness, and other properties.

Rocks, however, are made up of mixtures of several minerals. For example, granite is a rock made up of minerals like quartz, feldspar, mica, and others. But a piece of granite found in one place might have different amounts of these minerals from a piece of granite in another place.

Minerals are found in many places. They may be found in rocks or in sands and gravels. And they are formed in many different ways. Many minerals crystallized or hardened years ago from a very hot, melted mass of rock, called "a magma." Diamond, mica, and feldspar are examples of minerals that formed from molten magma.

Certain minerals, chiefly because of their beauty and scarcity, are very valuable. These are called "gems." Some examples of valuable gem minerals are diamond, garnet, topaz, and zircon.

Some minerals, on the other hand, are found almost everywhere. The most common mineral is quartz. There are about 200 different kinds of quartz and it is found in almost every part of the earth.

WHAT IS SILVER?

The mining of silver has been carried on from ancient times. In Europe, kings depended on it as their source of wealth. In fact, when the Spanish silver mines began to run low, the King of Spain was delighted that the discovery of America led him to obtain the great silver mines of Mexico and Peru. The mines at Potosi in Peru produced $4,000,000 worth of silver every year for 250 years for the kings of Spain!

During the gold rush days in California, people cursed the "black earth" that stuck to their gold dust. It was only by accident that they discovered it was silver ore!

Silver is one of the most widely distributed of all metals. Sometimes it is found in solid pieces, and in Norway a piece of solid silver was once found that weighed three-quarters of a ton! But usually silver comes in ores from which it must be separated.

In this ore, silver is usually combined with sulphur as silver sulphide, or is a part of other sulphides, chiefly those of copper, lead, or arsenic. In the United States, it is found mostly in connection with lead. In fact, silver occurs in so many combinations that there are a great many different methods of separating it from the other elements.

Today, the world produces almost 850,500,000 grams of pure silver a year. Mexico, United States, and Canada are the chief silver-producing countries.

Silver is too soft to be used in its pure state, so it is combined with other metals. Silver coins, for instance, contain 90 per cent silver and 10 per cent copper. The sterling silver of which jewelry and silverware are made contains 92.5 per cent silver and 7.5 per cent copper.

The name "sterling," by the way, has a curious origin. It comes from a North German family called Easterling. The Easterlings were such honest traders that King John of England gave them the job of making the English coins in 1215. They did it so well and truly that their name is still used as a sign of solid worth. All sterling silver is stamped with a hallmark, either the word "sterling" or a symbol, depending on the country.

Pure silver doesn't tarnish in pure air. When it turns black, that's a sign there is sulphur in the air, as from city smoke or oil wells. Next to gold, silver is the easiest metal to work. Thirty grams of silver can be drawn into a wire more than 30 miles long! It is also the most perfect known conductor of electricity and heat.

WHAT IS QUICKSILVER?

"Quicksilver" is a popular name for mercury. It is an unusual metallic element because it is liquid at room temperature.

Mercury freezes at −39 degrees centigrade and boils at 357 degrees centigrade. It is 13.6 times heavier than water. Its surface tension is such that it does not wet many objects. Instead, it tends to break up into small globules, or round particles, and run away.

In nature, mercury is usually found combined in the red mineral cinnabar. Cinnabar is found in many kinds of rocks, but nearly always in rocks of volcanic origin. It is supposed to have been deposited by volcanic action.

Mercury is easily turned into vapor. To get pure mercury from its ore, it is only necessary to heat the ore to about 482 degrees centigrade. The vapor is caught and condensed to obtain mercury.

Various forms of mercury have long been used by man. Before the time of written history, cinnabar was used in making red pigments. As early as 415 B.C., mercury was reduced from its ores and used for gilding and for medical purposes. When the alchemists were trying to make precious metals, they thought mercury was almost a magic material. It was commonly used in their experiments and in their mysterious ceremonies.

In modern times, the most important use of mercury has been in medicines. Although mercury and its compounds are poisonous, it is used in drugs and disinfectants. About one-third of the total production of mercury each year is used for medicinal purposes.

Of course, most of us know mercury because it is used in thermometers. The reason for this is that mercury reacts very quickly and evenly to changes in temperature. Today, mercury is also used in paints, dental preparations, chlorine, caustic soda, and electrical equipment.

WHAT IS QUARTZ?

Many people see and use quartz every day without knowing that it is quartz they are using. Quartz is one of the most widely distributed and most useful minerals known.

Another name for quartz is "silica." It is made up of silicon and oxygen, and it is harder than steel and clearer than glass!

When quartz is pure, it is colorless or white, but when mixed with impurities it may be various shades of red, yellow, brown, green, blue, lavender, or black. Quartz is sometimes found in large, clear six-sided crystals with pyramidlike ends called "rock crystals."

Some of the most abundant rocks are composed largely of quartz. Sandstone consists of grains of quartz held together by a cementing substance. Quartz forms a large part of the rock we call granite. White sand is almost pure quartz and all sand consists largely of quartz!

Even many of our semi-precious stones are only quartz colored by small quantities of other substances. Agate, amethyst, and onyx are examples.

Quartz is used in the manufacture of optical instruments and glass. Thin slices cut from pure quartz crystals are used in radio broadcasting to keep the stations on their proper wave lengths.

When pure rock crystal is melted at a very intense heat, we get fused quartz. This is a very valuable and useful substance. It has a very high melting point, 1,710 degrees centigrade, it expands and contracts less than any other known material, and it is more transparent than glass!

As you might expect, a substance that behaves in this way is invaluable material for laboratory utensils. A dish made of fused quartz may be heated red-hot and plunged into ice water without being harmed in any way.

Light and radiant heat waves travel through it very easily. Since health-giving ultraviolet rays, which are absorbed by glass, will go through fused quartz, sanatoria are sometimes roofed with panes of fused quartz, and special quartz lamps are used to give artificial sun treatments.

WHY IS GOLD PRECIOUS?

As far back as man has been known to exist, he has considered gold precious. It was probably the first metal known to man.

One reason primitive man was drawn to gold was that it can be found in the free state, which means gold can be found in small lumps (called "nuggets") uncombined with other metals or rocks. Since it has a bright yellow color and a shiny appearance, even the earliest man liked to possess it and make ornaments out of it.

The value of gold increased when people realized that it is the most easily worked of all metals. A nugget of gold is easily hammered thin and is flexible enough to bend without breaking. This means that early man could fashion gold into any shape he wished. At one time, for instance, it was used for hoops to bind the hair. Out of this came the idea of crowns and coronets made of gold.

The supply of gold that can be obtained easily from the earth is very limited. Soon people who couldn't find their own gold offered to exchange other things in return for some gold. That's how gold came to be a medium of exchange. While other commodities were perishable, gold was not, so it became a means of storing value for the future, and a measure of value, as well.

Centuries later, gold was made into coins as a convenient way of indicating the weight and fineness of the metal, and thus its value.

Later on, bankers would keep the gold itself in their vaults for safety's sake, and give a written pledge to deliver the gold on demand. From this practice, governments began to issue currency, or money, that was also simply a pledge to deliver a certain amount of gold on demand. By the way, about one-half of all the known mined gold in the world today is owned by the United States Treasury!

WHAT IS MICA?

Did you ever find a piece of mica and take it apart with your fingernails? Perhaps you called it "isinglass." "Isinglass" is really the name for sheets of mica.

Mica is actually a mineral. In fact, we use the name "mica" to describe a whole family of rock-forming minerals. The mica minerals are muscovite, phlogopite, biotite, and lepidolite. If you had trouble even pronouncing them, you can see why we prefer to call them "mica"!

All these minerals look much alike, though they are formed from different metals. All micas can be split into thin sheets. They are very soft and can be scratched easily with a fingernail. All of the micas form the same kind of crystals. In color, they range from colorless through shades of yellow, green, red, brown, and black.

Micas are found in many of the rocks of the earth's crust. They are an important part of a large group of igneous rocks, which means rocks that were formed from the cooling of hot, molten material. Sometimes other minerals change to mica through a process called "metamorphism," which means change caused by pressure, heat, and water.

Mica has to be mined, and the important mica-producing areas of the world are the Appalachian and Rocky Mountains, Canada, India, Madagascar, the Soviet Union, Brazil, and the Union of South Africa.

To prepare mica for commercial use, it is split into sheets of the desired thickness, and then trimmed to size. Micas are very good insulators; they do not conduct heat or electricity. So you can see how useful micas can be in the manufacture of electrical equipment and in fireproofing materials. You probably have mica in your home right now in your electric toaster, electric iron, and in lamp sockets.

Did you know that before glass became commonly used, sheets of mica were used as windows?

WHAT IS A GEM?

Gems have always had a special fascination for mankind. For thousands of years, gems were worn as charms, or amulets, to protect people from demons and diseases. Some gems were believed to have the power of enabling their owners to foretell the future. Other gems were supposed to be able to tell whether a person was guilty or innocent of a crime.

In ancient times, gems were distinguished only by their colors. The name "ruby" was given to all precious stone of a red hue. All green stones were called "emeralds." And all those of blue were called "sapphires."

Later on it was discovered that some gems were harder than others and endured longer. So it came about that the value of a gem depended not only on its color, brilliancy, and rarity, but also on its hardness. Diamonds for instance, are today considered the most precious of gems because, besides their beauty, they are the hardest of all stones.

All the gems are called "precious stones." But strictly speaking, the word "precious" is used only for the four most valuable stones: the diamond, the ruby, the emerald, and the sapphire. The other valuable stones are "semi-precious," and these include opals, amethysts, and topazes. Many of the precious and semi-precious stones are close relations.

The diamond, the most precious gem, is also the simplest. It is composed of one element, pure carbon. Rubies and sapphires are varieties of a substance called "corundum." Rubies have their carmine color because of small quantities of iron in the corundum. And the presence of various oxides make sapphires bright blue or velvet blue.

A great many of the most beautiful gems are made of combinations of a substance called "silicate." Topaz and tourmaline are members of the silicate group. Garnets and jade are also silicates. Some of the less costly gems belong to the quartz group, which is pure silica. Amethyst is one of these. The opal is silica containing five to ten per cent of water. The opal, by the way, is one of the few precious stones which are supposed to bring evil to those who possess it. Even today, many people will not wear opals because of this ancient superstition.

Science today is beginning to learn how to manufacture precious stones artificially. This includes diamonds, emeralds, rubies, and sapphires. These are not imitations; they are actually the same as the natural stone, only they are being produced in laboratories!

HOW HARD IS A DIAMOND?

If you had a piece of putty and wanted to make it hard, what would you do? You'd squeeze it and press it, and the more you squeezed and pressed, the harder it would become.

Diamonds were made in the same way by nature. A hundred million years ago, the earth was in its early cooling stages. At that time, there existed beneath the ground a mass of hot liquid rock. This was subjected to extreme heat and pressure. Carbon which was subjected to this pressure became what we called "diamonds."

Diamonds are the hardest natural substance known to man. But it is not very easy to measure "hardness" exactly. One way it is done is by using the scratch test, scratching it with another hard substance. In 1820, a man called Mohs made up a scale of hardness for minerals based on such a test. On his scale, this is the way the minerals ranked in hardness: 1. Talc. 2. Gypsum. 3. Calcite. 4. Fluorite. 5. Aphatite. 6. Feldspar. 7. Quartz. 8. Topaz. 9. Corundum. 10. Diamond.

But all this measured was how they compared to each other. For example, it has been found that even though corundum is 9 on the scale and diamond is 10, the difference between them in hardness is greater than the difference between 9 and 1 on the scale. So diamonds are the champions for hardness with no competition!

Since diamonds are so hard, how can they be shaped and cut? The only thing that will cut a diamond is another diamond! What diamond cutters use is a saw with an edge made of diamond dust.

In fact, diamond grinding and cutting wheels are used in industry in many ways, such as to grind lenses, to shape all kinds of tools made of copper, brass, and other metals, and to cut glass. Today, more than 80 per cent of all diamonds produced are used in industry!

WHAT IS RUBBER?

Rubber is as old as nature itself. Fossils have been found of rubber-producing plants that go back almost 3,000,000 years! Crude rubber balls have been found in the ruins of Incan and Mayan civilizations in Central and South America that are at least 900 years old.

In fact, when Columbus made his second voyage to the New World, he saw the natives of Haiti playing a game with a ball made from "the gum of a tree." And even before that, the natives of Southeastern Asia knew of rubber prepared from the "juice" of a tree and they used it to coat baskets and jars to make them waterproof!

Rubber has been found in more than 400 different vines, shrubs, and trees. But the amount of rubber found in each varies greatly and it doesn't pay to extract the rubber from such plants as dandelion, milkweed, and sagebrush.

Rubber is a sticky, elastic solid obtained from a milky liquid known as "latex," which is different from sap. The latex appears in the bark, roots, stem, branches, leaves, and fruit of plants and trees. But most of it is found in the inner bark of the branches and trunk of the rubber tree.

Latex consists of tiny particles of liquid, solid, or semi-fluid material which appear in a watery liquor. Only about 33 per cent of the latex is rubber; the rest is mostly water. The rubber particles in the latex are drawn together and a ball of rubber is formed.

Rubber grows best within 10 degrees of the Equator, and the area of about 700 miles on each side of the Equator is known as "the Rubber Belt." The reason for this is that the rubber tree needs a hot, moist climate and deep, rich soil. The best and most rubber comes from a tree called *Hevea brasiliensis*. As the name suggests this tree was first found in Brazil. Today almost 96 per cent of the world's supply of natural rubber comes from this tree, but now this tree is cultivated in many parts of the world within the Rubber Belt.

The first white men to manufacture rubber goods were probably the French, who made elastics for garters and suspenders some time before 1800.

WHAT IS CHALK?

Practically no one can grow up in the world today without coming into contact with chalk at some time in his life. In millions of classrooms around the world, children step up to blackboards to write things with chalk. And, of course, what could teacher do without chalk to help her?

Did you know that chalk was originally an animal? The waters of our oceans are covered with many forms of very tiny plants and animals. One of these is a one-celled animal called "Foraminifera." The shells of these creatures are made of lime.

When these animals die, their tiny shells sink to the floor of the ocean. In time, a thick layer of these shells is built up. Of course, this takes millions of years to accomplish. This layer gradually becomes cemented and compressed into a soft limestone which we call chalk.

As we know, various disturbances in the surface of the earth have often made dry land out of land that was once under water. One of the places where this happened is along the English Channel. The chalk layers at the bottom of the sea were pushed up. Later the soft parts were cut away by water, leaving huge cliffs of chalk. The two most famous ones are the chalk cliffs at Dover on the English side and at Dieppe on the French side of the Channel.

In other parts of the world, chalk deposits appear far inland in areas that were once under water. We have examples of these in our own country in Kansas, Arkansas, and Texas. But the finest natural chalk comes from England which produces more than 4,500,000 tonnes of it every year!

Chalk in one form or another has been used by man for hundreds of years. The blackboard chalk with which we are all familiar is mixed with some binding substance to prevent it from crumbling. The best blackboard chalk is about 95 per cent chalk. By adding pigments to it, chalk can be made in any color.

When chalk is pulverized, washed, and filtered, it is called "whiting." It can then be used in the making of many useful products such as putty, paints, medicines, paper, and toothpastes and powders!

WHAT ARE FATS?

Animals and plants have fats in their bodies which may be either solid or liquid. Most, but not all, animal fats are solid. Liquid fats are usually called oils, or more exactly, fat oils. But not all oils are fats.

All fats, solid or liquid, have this in common: They do not dissolve (are not "soluble") in water. Water does not even wet a fat; water will not spread on a greasy surface but will gather in drops. Fats are lighter than water; that is why fats and oils float on water.

Chemical study of fats has shown that they are all composed of the three elements, carbon, hydrogen, and oxygen. There are, therefore, organic compounds. A fat can always be split by chemical action into two compounds. One of them is always the same; it is glycerin. The other compound is what we called "a fatty acid." What makes the various kinds of fats and oils different from each other is the kind of fatty acid in them.

While fats do not dissolve in water, they can be dissolved in certain kinds of liquids, such as benzene. Some of these liquids, which take out grease spots, are sold as "spot removers."

When a fat is boiled with an alkali, it is split into glycerin and a soap. A soap is nothing else than an alkali salt of a fatty acid. This process is called "saponification." When a fat is shaken or rubbed with water containing some soap, it falls apart into a mass of tiny droplets which make the soapy water appear milky. This is called "emulsification," and all fats can be emulsified.

Along with carbohydrates and proteins, fats are one of the three main classes of human foods. They are emulsified in the body and then burned and this provides energy. In energy value, 30 grams of fat are worth about 60 grams of carbohydrate or protein.

Both solid and liquid fats become spoiled when they are left for too long in the air. They become "rancid," that is, they get an unpleasant taste and odor. This is because some of the fat is split and the fatty acid is chemically changed.

Animal Cell

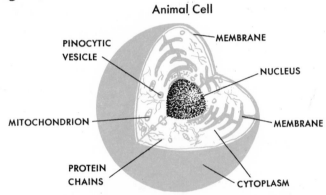

PINOCYTIC VESICLE
MEMBRANE
NUCLEUS
MITOCHONDRION
MEMBRANE
PROTEIN CHAINS
CYTOPLASM

WHAT IS PROTOPLASM?

Science has made many great advances. In its laboratories it can duplicate many of the wonders of nature. But there is one substance that no scientist has yet been able to make. That substance is protoplasm, which is the living part of all plants and animals.

All organisms, whether they are plant or animal, are composed of cells. There may be millions of cells, as in the human being, or there may be one, as in the Protozoa. But whether the organism is a whale, a man, or a rose, the walls of the cells enclose the same life substance—protoplasm.

In each cell the protoplasm consists chiefly of two parts. One is the more solid, central part called "the nucleus." The other is the softer, more liquid part called "the cytoplasm."

All protoplasm is not alike. In fact, each type of living thing has its own kind of protoplasm. And the different types of cells within an organism each have special forms of protoplasm.

Although protoplasm varies, 99 per cent of its bulk is made of carbon, hydrogen, oxygen, and nitrogen, with traces of many other elements. Just what makes protoplasm alive is still unknown. But we do know that everything that can be done only by living things is carried out by protoplasm.

When food is taken into the body, it is first digested, or made into liquid form. Then the digested food must be taken into and made a part of the protoplasm. This process is known as "assimilation." As a result of assimilation, worn-out protoplasm is made. This is an amazing process, because it means that protoplasm builds up dead matter into living material, and changes foreign material into substances like itself.

Protoplasm also stores and releases all the energy that plants and animals have. All protoplasm, and bodies built from protoplasm, have periods of action and of rest. Protoplasm is sensitive to stimuli or shocks from the outside. A strong light or heat will kill it. Chemicals attract or repel it. Electric currents cause it to behave in various ways. But much about protoplasm and how it behaves still remains a great challenge to science.

WHAT IS CELLULOSE?

The softer parts of the bodies of plants are made up mostly of cellulose. It is the cellulose which enables a plant to bend and have flexibility.

Nearly all green plants manufacture cellulose for their own use. It is made up of the same chemical elements as is sugar, namely, carbon, hydrogen, and oxygen. These materials are found in air and water. The sugar which is formed in the leaves is dissolved in the sap of the plant and soaks all through the body of the plant. Most of it goes to those places in the plant where growth or repair is taking place and part of this sugar is changed into cellulose. The plant uses it to make the walls of new cells.

Cellulose is one of those natural products that man cannot produce chemically in the laboratory. But, of course, he uses it in many ways. He can obtain cellulose from plants even after the plant is dead and all the moisture in the plant has evaporated. For instance, raw cotton is one of the purest forms of cellulose found in nature, and man uses the cotton fibers for cloth.

Cellulose makes up a large part of many foods, such as lettuce, celery, and bran. Man cannot digest cellulose, but it serves a useful purpose in his diet by providing bulk or roughage. Goats and camels, and other animals who have certain bacteria in their stomachs, are able to digest cellulose with the help of these bacteria.

Cellulose is a valuable raw material which man uses to make a great many interesting and useful products. Cotton, which is 99.8 per cent cellulose, is probably the outstanding example of what man can do with cellulose fibers. When the cotton is treated with a mixture of nitric acid and sulphuric acid, we have guncotton, which is an explosive.

By treating cellulose chemically in various ways, a number of other products may be derived from it. Some of these products are: the base for photographic films, substitutes for varnish, threads such as rayon for weaving, cellophane, and various other plastics. Cellulose can also be used in the making of paper.

WHAT IS CHLOROPHYLL?

If you had to pick the one chief thing that sets plants apart from animals, what would it be? The answer is that plants are green. Of course, there are some exceptions, but this is really the one basic law of plants—their greenness.

Now, this greenness of plants is one of the most important things in the entire world. Because the green coloring matter in plants—chlorophyll—enables them to take substances from the soil and the air and to manufacture living food. If plants couldn't do this, men and animals couldn't exist, for they would have no food! Even those creatures which live on meat depend on other creatures who live on plants. In fact, you can trace any food back to its original source and find it was made by a plant!

So you can see that chlorophyll, this miraculous green substance which enables plants to supply man and animals with food, is vital to our life, too! Chlorophyll is contained in the cells of leaves and often in the stem and flowers.

With the help of chlorophyll, the plant's living tissue is able to absorb the energy from sunlight and to use this energy to transform inorganic chemicals into organic or "life-giving" chemicals. This process is called "photosynthesis." The word comes from the Greek words which mean "light" and "put together."

There are some plants which have no green color, no chlorophyll. How do they live? Mushrooms, and a whole group of fungi, which have no chlorophyll, can't make their own food. So they have to get it in some way from something else. If they get their food from other plants or animals, they are called "parasites." If they get it from the decaying remains of plants and animals, they are called "saprophytes."

Chlorophyll can be extracted from plants and used in various ways by man. In such cases, it may help destroy certain bacteria.

WHAT IS OSMOSIS?

How do plants take water from the soil into their roots? How do animals absorb digested food from the intestines into the blood vessels? After all, no holes can be seen in the roots of a plant or in the walls of animal intestines. The process by which this is done is called "osmosis."

When you place any two gases side by side with nothing to separate them, they will mix quickly. The same is true of most liquids. For instance, a drop of ink will gradually give a faint and uniform color to a whole pint of water.

In osmosis, this mixing goes on through a membrane, such as the thin walls of the tiny root hairs of a plant or the lining of the intestines. The membrane slows down the mixing process, but does not stop it. During osmosis in living things, the membranes allow certain substances to pass through while others are stopped. This is decided partly by the structure of a membrane and partly by the structure of the substance in contact with it. Scientists think that in osmosis dissolved substances pass through the spaces between the molecules making up the membrane.

The substances in solution in contact· with a membrane push against it and exert what is called "osmotic pressure." The side with more particles of dissolved substance has the greater osmotic pressure, and therefore the direction in which most of the traffic goes is from the region of greater to lesser pressure.

But the traffic moves in both directions, for anything that can go through an osmotic membrane can also come out. In our body, the membranes of the blood vessels, for example, are letting substances pass through in both directions constantly. In this way, digested food goes into the blood stream, and waste carbon dioxide comes out from the blood through the lungs.

106

WHAT IS A SEED?

One of the ways in which a plant produces another plant of its own kind is the seed. Just as birds lay eggs to reproduce their kind, the plant grows a seed that makes another plant.

The flower or blossom of a plant must be fertilized or the seed it produces will not grow. After the seed is fully grown, or mature, it must rest. The rest period varies among different kinds of seeds. Many of them will not grow until they have rested through the winter.

Seed growth requires moisture, oxygen, and warmth. Light helps some plants start seed growth. If seed growth doesn't start within a certain time, the seed will die. When seeds are stored by man for future use, they must be kept dry and within a certain temperature range.

Seeds vary greatly in size, shape, pattern, and color. The seeds of different plants are made in different ways. There is one kind of seed, for example, that has the tiny new plant in the center. Around this is stored food which will tide the young plant over until it has developed roots and leaves and can make its own food.

If a seed is fertile, has rested, and has received the proper amounts of moisture, oxygen, and warmth, it begins to grow. This is called "sprouting" or "germination." Growth often starts when moisture reaches the seed. As the seed absorbs water, it swells. As chemical changes take place, the cells of the seeds begin to show life again and the tiny young plant within the seed begins to grow. Most parts of the seed go into the growing plant. The seed cover drops off and the new plant grows larger until it matures and makes seeds of its own.

Seeds may be small or large. Begonia seeds are so small they look like dust. Coconuts are seeds which may weigh as much as 18 kilograms. Some plants have only about twenty seeds, while others, such as the maple, have thousands.

There are special ways seeds are made so that they will be spread. Burr-type seeds hitch a ride on the fur of animals. Seeds that stick in mud cling to animals' feet. Seeds contained in fruit are carried by man and animals. Some seeds have "wings" and are blown by the wind, other seeds float on water, and some are even "exploded" away from the parent plant!

HOW DO TREES GROW?

Like all living things, trees need nourishment in order to be able to grow. Where does the tree obtain this?

From the soil, the tree obtains water and minerals. From the air, it takes in carbon dioxide. And the green of the leaves of trees harnesses the energy of the sun's rays to make starches, sugars, and cellulose. So the tree carries on a chemical process of its own in order to be able to live and grow.

Between the wood of a tree and its bark, there is a thin band of living, dividing cells called "the cambium." As new cells are formed here, those that are formed on the wood side of the cambium mature as wood. The cells formed toward the outside mature as bark. In this way, as the tree grows older it increases in diameter.

The diameter of the woody part of the tree continues to grow greater and greater. But this doesn't always happen with the bark. Often the outer bark becomes broken, dies, and falls off.

Trees grow in height as well as in diameter. At the end of each branch or twig there is a group of living cells. During periods of active growth, these cells keep dividing, producing many more cells. These new cells enlarge and form new leaves as well as additional portions of the stem or twig. In this way, the twig grows longer.

After a time, these cells at the tip of the twig become less active and the twig grows longer more slowly. Then the new cells are firm and scale-like and they form a bud. You can easily notice these buds on trees during the winter.

In the spring, the bud scales are spread apart or fall off and the twig starts growing longer again. So you see that by means of the cambium layer in the tree, and by means of the active cells at the tips of twigs, trees may grow both in thickness and in length, year after year.

A cross section of a tree shows alternating bands of light and dark wood. This difference in color is due to differences in size of the cells which make up the wood. The lighter bands have bigger cells which were formed in spring and early summer. The narrow dark bands are made up of smaller cells packed tightly together which were formed in late summer. Together, they show the amount of wood formed during a year, and by counting them, we can tell the age of a tree.

WHAT GIVES FLOWERS THEIR SCENT AND COLOR?

Curiously enough, we often look at a plant and admire its "flowers" when we are actually not looking at the flowers at all! If we think of a flower as something brightly colored which grows on a plant, we may be quite mistaken.

For instance, the "petals of the dogwood "blossoms" that bloom in the spring are not petals at all. Nor is the white sheath on a callas plant a flower. Poinsettia blossoms are another example of colored leaves rather than true flowers.

On the other hand, the bearded tufts at the tips of grasses are really flowers! An unripe ear of corn is actually a flower. According to the botanist, a flower is a group of parts whose function is to produce pollen or seeds or both. Only seed-bearing plants have flowers. And only those parts of a plant which are closely concerned with the formation and production of the seed can be considered as parts of the flower.

What gives flowers their scent? A flower has a fragrance when certain essential oils are found in the petals. These oils are produced by the plant as part of its growing process. These essential oils are very complex substances. Under certain conditions, this complex substance is broken down or decomposed and is formed into a volatile oil, which means it evaporates readily. When this happens, we can smell the fragrance it gives off.

The specific type of fragrance a flower gives off depends on the chemicals in that volatile oil, and various combinations produce different scents. By the way, these same oils are found not only in the flowers of plants but often in leaves, barks, roots, fruit, and seeds. For instance, oranges and lemons have them in the fruit, almonds have them in the seeds, cinnamon has them in the bark, and so on.

What gives flowers their color? "Anthocyanin" is the name for the pigments which give flowers the red, mauve, blue, purple, and violet colors. These pigments are dissolved in the sap of the cells of the flower. Other colors, such as yellow, orange, and green, are due to other pigments. These substances include chlorophyll, carotene, etc. There is no chemical link between them.

So we can attribute the colors in flowers to pigments called "anthocyanins" and to other pigments called "plastids." One group supplies a certain range of colors and the other group supplies the rest of the colors.

WHY DO LEAVES HAVE DIFFERENT COLORS IN THE AUTUMN?

When you look at a group of trees in the summertime, you see only one color: green. Of course, there are various shades of green, but it's as if it were all painted by one brush. Yet in autumn, these same leaves take on a whole variety of colors. Where do all these colors come from?

Well, to begin with, as most of us know, the green color of leaves is due to chlorophyll. Chlorophyll is the complete food factory that is found in each leaf. Two-thirds of the color of the leaves (their pigmentation) are due to this chlorophyll. There are other colors present in the leaf, too, but there is so much chlorophyll that we usually can't see them.

What are some of these other colors? A substance called "xanthophyll," which consists of carbon, hydrogen and oxygen, is yellow. It makes up about 23 per cent of the pigmentation of the leaf. Carotin, the substance which makes carrots the color they are, is also present in the leaf and makes up about 10 per cent of the pigment. Another pigment present is anthocyanin, which gives the sugar maple and the scarlet oak their bright red colors.

During the summer, we see none of these other pigments; we only see the green chlorophyll. When it becomes cold, the food that has been stored away in the leaf by the trees begins to flow out to the branches and trunks. Since no more food will be produced in the winter, the chlorophyll food factory closes down and the chlorophyll disintegrates. And as the chlorophyll disappears, the other pigments that have been present all the time become visible. The leaves take on all those beautiful colors which we enjoy seeing!

Before the leaves fall, a compact layer of cells is formed at the base of each leaf; then when the wind blows, the leaves are dislodged. On the twig there is a scar that marks the former position of each leaf.

Most evergreen trees do not shed all their leaves at the approach of winter, but lose them gradually through the year; thus they are always green.

HOW CAN CACTI LIVE WITHOUT WATER?

Every living thing that has its home in the desert must face the problem of getting along with very little water. In fact, if it can't find an answer to this question it can't survive.

The cactus does not live without water, but it does manage to survive long periods of no rain in a remarkable manner. Plants which grow under ordinary conditions waste a great deal of water. Water is taken up from the sap by the leaves and then the water is given out to the air.

The cactus gets around this by having no leaves. Its stems are formed in such a way that as little surface as possible is exposed to the direct rays of the sun. Thus almost no moisture is given up. In addition, the stems are thick so that water can be stored away inside them, and there's a thick covering on the stem to keep the water even more safely protected. The spines or scales on the cactus plant also discourage any thirsty animals around who might want to take a drink from its reservoir. In this way, some of the larger cacti plants can live for two years or more without water.

Cacti (which is the plural of "cactus") are actually regular flowering plants with blossoms that develop into seed-bearing fruits. The flowers of most cacti are beautiful, and a desert in full bloom will have bright yellow, red, and purple blooms springing from the polished cacti stems.

There are more than 1,000 species of cacti. They are natives of South and Central America, Mexico, and the Southwestern part of the United States. The varieties differ greatly, ranging from the tiny pincushions, which grow close to the ground, to the giant saguaro cactus, which is the state flower of Arizona. This cactus grows from 10 to 20 metres high.

The juice found in cactus stems is made into medicines and fermented drinks by many people. Delicious candies and preserves can also be made from the stems and fruits of this tough plant. In fact, some of the smaller cacti can be grown around the house. When they are planted in pots, good drainage is essential. The cactus should be watered every four days in summer and every two weeks in winter.

WHAT IS MOSS?

In almost any moist, shaded wood, small plants can be found forming a green carpet on the surface of the ground. Most of these are mosses.

Unlike such plants as the pea or bean, mosses have no roots or flowers. Instead, they have little threads which grow over the surface of the soil or into it. These absorb water and minerals from the soil. They also lack a system for carrying water inside the plant such as larger plants have. So they are found most often growing only in the presence of moisture. That's why moss on trees usually grows on the side that gets little or no sunshine. Some mosses grow on a rock when it is moist. When the rock dries, the mosses also dry up, but they do not die. When moisture comes again, they revive and grow.

There are several hundred different kinds of moss. One of the easiest forms to recognize is the white moss. It forms light green clumps like pincushions on moist ground. One of the largest species, the hairy-cap moss, gets its name from the fact that the capsule is covered by a little downy cap.

Peat moss is very light grey-green in color and grows in swampy soil. It is also found at the margins of lakes, in pools, and small lakes where it may be so abundant as to form a bog. Its leaves have large, barrel-shaped cells which aid in absorbing and storing water. For this reason, it is used by florists for keeping plants moist.

Peat moss, because of its capacity for absorbing liquids, was used as a wound dressing during the early part of World War I. It forms an excellent carpet for an aquarium containing salamanders or frogs. Peat is made up of partially decomposed moss and other vegetation. When dried, it is used in many countries as fuel.

The word "moss" is often applied incorrectly. "Irish moss" is really a seaweed; "Spanish moss" is a plant that bears flowers and is not really a moss.

HOW DO ALGAE GROW?

If you've ever tried to have an aquarium at home, you've probably noticed the green scum that seems to gather from nowhere. These are algae. And when you go swimming in certain ponds and lakes, there are slippery weeds that tangle around your feet. These are algae, too.

There are thousands of kinds of algae and they grow all over the world, in swamps, ponds, lakes, rivers, and even oceans. They range from fine, spongy scum to tough, leathery seaweeds which may be more than 30 metres long.

Algae are among the most primitive forms of plant life. Some of them always remain single, independent cells. Others bud out, one cell from another, forming long, beadlike strings, while others bud and mass about one another in graceful patterns, forming an intricate network of cells. Still others break away in groups and start new colonies.

All algae contain a green substance called "chlorophyll," which enables them to absorb the sun's rays and to manufacture their own food. In this way, algae differ from fungi, which are a related group of plants.

The most common of the green algae form the green scum on quiet pools. In addition to chlorophyll, some of the larger ocean seaweeds and kelps contain a yellowish-brown pigment. Some of these brown algae have stems so thick and tough that they can be used for ropes; others supply us with iodine.

The red algae are fascinating sea plants, very delicate in form and of various shades of red. They are sometimes so numerous that they color the water in which they live, as they do in the Red Sea.

Diatoms are algae that have tiny shells. As these algae die, the shells fall to the bottom and form deposits several metres thick.

WHAT IS MILDEW?

Sometimes it seems as if nature is constantly battling against man, making it hard for him just to stay alive. It's as if the insect world and the plant world were trying to overcome the human world.

For example, if we were just to sit back and do nothing, all kinds of things would "attack" us or our property. And one of these enemies, lurking and waiting for us to give it a chance to go to work, is mildew.

Just leave some leather things around, or cooked food or fruit preserves instead of putting them in cold, dry places and presto! Mildew appears.

You've probably noticed this most often with a piece of bread. If it's left in a warm, moist place for several days, it becomes covered with a mesh of white, cobweblike threads which seem powdered with black dust.

If you looked at this under a microscope, you'd see that the web is made up of many long, colorless threads with two kinds of branches. One is topped by little black balls which contain spores. The other kind, which is shorter and penetrates into the bread, serves as roots and absorbers of nourishment. What you would be looking at are molds or mildews.

Molds and mildews each grow in moist, hot air, especially where their food is plentiful. As a rule, molds feed on dead vegetable and animal matter, while mildews are parasites, which means they feed on living things. Often, however, the words "mold" and "mildew" are used interchangeably.

Mildews are usually divided into two groups. Powdery mildews grow on the surfaces of leaves, twigs, flowers, and fruits of plants and trees. Downy, or flaser, mildews grow on the inside of the plants. These downy mildews cause great damage to potatoes and grapevines and are hard to destroy.

WHAT ARE FUNGI?

Fungi are very important to man for two opposite reasons: They do a great deal of good and they do a great deal of damage.

Fungi helps man by causing decay so that rubbish doesn't accumulate endlessly. This also returns mineral salts to the earth which plants need. Other fungi even create drugs which man uses to fight disease.

There are other fungi which cause diseases of plants and animals, and man is waging a constant battle against them.

What are fungi? They are simple, dependent plants. We call them "simple" plants because they don't have roots, stems, and leaves as complex plants have. We call them "dependent" because they have no chlorophyll, which means they can't manufacture sugar from carbon dioxide and water, as green plants do. So they depend on food that has been made by green plants.

There are a great many different kinds of fungi, and they differ considerably in their structure. Some fungi consist of a single cell. For example, bacteria and yeasts are examples of one-celled fungi. The average length of bacteria is about 0.005 millimetres.

Slime mold is another type of fungus. It differs from all other plants in that it consists of a mass of naked protoplasm that looks like a film of jelly on the surface of a rotting log or other moist object.

All other fungi except these three, bacteria, yeast, and slime mold, consist of a mass of colorless threads. This is called "a mycelium." The mycelium shoots out branches which grow into the material on which the fungus is growing and absorb food from it. Fungi need water for the digestion of their food and for growth, so they cannot grow on anything that is really dry.

The big group of fungi called "molds" range from those that live on bread to those that attack damp fabrics. Certain molds give flavor to cheese and others are used to prepare drugs.

Did you know the mushrooms and toadstools are fungi? The main part of this fungus is the mycelium that branches underground. The mushroom itself is only the spore-producing part, and is almost completely formed before it pushes out of the ground.

GREEN GILL FUNGUS

JACK-O-LANTERN

DEATH CUP

HOW CAN YOU TELL POISONOUS MUSHROOMS?

The best rule to follow about telling safe mushrooms from poisonous mushrooms is not to try! Despite what anyone may tell you, despite any "methods" you may know for telling them apart, you should never eat or even taste any mushroom that you find growing anywhere. The only safe mushrooms are those you buy in a food store!

There are a great many false ideas that people have about mushrooms. For example, some think that when poisonous mushrooms are cooked they will blacken a silver spoon if they are stirred with it. This "test" is wrong!

117

It is also untrue that certain mushrooms can harm you if you simply touch them. And there is no difference between a mushroom and a toadstool. They are simply two names for one thing!

Another false idea about mushrooms is that those with pink gills are safe to eat. This is based on the fact that the two best-known kinds which are safe to eat happen to have pink gills, and that the *Amanitas*, which are poisonous, have white gills. But the truth is that this difference between the two kinds can't always be detected. Besides, many safe mushrooms have gills that are not pink at all. Only one British species, called the Death Cap is deadly. It looks at first like a half-buried egg: later the cap appears as olive or greenish-yellow with a dark centre and white stem.

WHAT IS A GERM?

For thousands of years of his existence, man lived in ignorance of what caused disease. Primitive people had "explanations" and beliefs about the subject, the most common of which was that sickness was caused by evil spirits inside the body of the victim.

It wasn't until 1865 that science was able to prove that germs were the cause of disease, and it was Louis Pasteur who first stated the germ theory of disease as we know it. Today we recognize that the most dangerous enemies of mankind are germs. These are tiny one-celled organisms, so small that we can't see them without a microscope, and in fact, some are so small that they cannot be seen at all!

Germs, which are also called "microbes" and "micro-organisms," may be either plants or animals. The animal forms are called "Protozoa," and the plant forms are called "bacteria." A third group of germs is called "filterable viruses," which means they are so small that they pass through even the finest filters which hold back larger bodies.

Every germ disease is caused by some particular kind of germ and by no other kind. For example, the germ of microbe that causes scarlet fever cannot cause malaria or any other sickness. Nor can scarlet fever be caused by anything except this specific germ! Many of the germs, however, which cause terrible diseases have near-relatives which are not harmful but may be helpful to man.

In most germ diseases, if the germs don't kill the patient, the body sooner or later destroys them and they disappear. In certain diseases, such as scarlet fever, measles, or mumps, one attack protects the patient from a second attack by the same germ. This protection against two attacks of the same germ is called "active immunity." Some animals possess a "natural immunity," which means they don't get diseases which attack other animals. Vaccination and antitoxins can give people immunity against attack by specific germs.

Among the diseases caused by the smallest germs, the filterable viruses, are: measles, rabies, chicken pox, infantile paralysis, the common cold, and influenza. Science still has a great deal to learn about these tiny, often-invisible organisms.

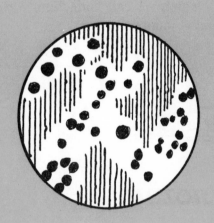 

WHERE DO BACTERIA COME FROM?

Bacteria are living beings (organisms) so small that they can be seen only with a microscope which enlarges several hundred times. Therefore, they are called "micro-organisms."

Long before people were able to see bacteria, they knew about the results of bacteria at work. For example, people knew that wine ferments, milk turns sour, and dead plants and animals decay. But people had superstitious or religious beliefs as to why this happened. Today, we know that bacteria are all about us—in the air, in water, in food, on the skin, and even inside the body. Bacteria multiply by splitting in half. There are no males or females among bacteria. If they have the right conditions and food for living, they will simply multiply and keep on multiplying.

Bacteria have only one cell which is more like that of a plant than an animal. The outside is a skinlike cover, or "membrane," which is not water-proof. The inside is filled with a material called "protoplasm" and usually does not have a single center, or nucleus.

The outside cover is important because any chemical used to destroy the bacteria must be able to pass through the membrane. Around the whole is a slimy material which can change shape and often forms tiny threadlike tails, called "flagella." Bacteria can move, although they have no feet. Some move by waving the flagella, and others seem to move by shortening and lengthening the cell, the way worms move.

Bacteria, as we know, cause diseases which we call "infections." But bacteria can also be very helpful and useful to human beings.

Trypanosoma, Protozoa which live
off the blood of vertebrates.

WHAT ARE PROTOZOA?

If you were to scoop up a teaspoonful of water from a pond and could examine it under a microscope, you would see more than a million tiny animals swarming about in the water! These animals are the "Protozoa," and they are the simplest animals known to exist, since they consist of a single cell.

All Protozoa live in water or in moist places. Scientists have been very interested in studying them, because even though they are made up of only one cell, that cell can carry on all the tasks necessary to keep an animal alive! It can hunt and eat food, digest it and make it into living matter. It can breathe and burn the food it eats and throw off waste. It can also reproduce itself.

Protozoa reproduce themselves either by dividing themselves into halves, each of which becomes a complete, separate animal, or by growing little swellings, called "buds," which break off and form separate, new animals.

There are more than 15,000 different types of Protozoa, so scientists have divided them into subgroups or classes. The two chief classes are called the "Rhizopoda" and the "Infusoria."

The Rhizopoda have "false feet" which flow out in various directions and can be pulled back into the body. One of the more interesting orders belonging to this class is called the "Foraminifera," or hole-borers. They have tiny shells of chalk with little holes. They live in warm and temperate seas. When they die their shells fall to the bottom, and in the course of centuries their skeletons create chalk deposits.

The Infusoria are a group of more complicated Protozoa. They have little hairs extending from their cells which they use like oars in pushing their way through the water. The most advanced forms of Protozoa have these hairlike threads, which are called "cilia."

Some Protozoa live as parasites in man and other animals. In certain stages of their life cycles they form spores. Some of these Protozoa cause diseases such as malaria and sleeping sickness in man.

WHAT IS CHLORINE?

Pure chlorine is a gas. It is one of the most deadly poisonous gases—and also one of the most useful! In nature, chlorine is a part of compounds such as common salt (sodium chloride).

Pure chlorine was first prepared by a Swedish chemist called Karl Scheele in 1774. It is now made cheaply by passing a current of electricity through a solution of common salt.

The first poison gas used during World War I was almost pure chlorine. The Germans used it on April 22, 1915. After that, both the Germans and the Allied forces used a variety of gases, all manufactured from chlorine compounds. During World War II, the Allies and the enemy had large stores of chlorine gases and others, but did not use them.

Yet despite the fact that chlorine can be so poisonous and dangerous, it is one of man's most useful weapons for health. Chlorine destroys germs as part of many germicides and disinfectants. Most city water-purification systems use chlorine to kill any bacteria that live through the treatment process. Only about four or five parts of the liquid chlorine per 1,000,000 parts of water are used. This amount is not harmful to human beings, although the water may sometimes have a chlorinated taste.

Chlorine may be changed to a liquid by refrigeration or by compressing it. In liquid form, it is shipped in iron cylinders or even in specially designed tank cars.

Chlorine is used for bleaching and in preparing bleaching powder. In normal times, the largest single use is in bleaching in the process of making paper. It is also used in making dyes, and a compound of it with oxygen and potassium is used in fireworks and certain kinds of safety matches.

A nonexplosive dry cleaner, known as carbon tetrachloride, is another compound of chlorine. It is used in certain types of fire extinguishers. And chlorine itself is an important part of modern antiseptics.

WHAT IS AN ACID?

Now and then, we read a newspaper story about someone being terribly burned by an acid. In fact, most of us think of acids as dangerous liquids which can burn the skin and eat holes in clothing.

This is only true of a very small number of acids. There are many acids in foods, and they are necessary for good health. Other acids are used to make drugs, paints, cosmetics, and industrial products.

There are many kinds of acids but they all may be divided into two classes, inorganic acids and organic acids. Here is a brief description of some of the more important acids in each group.

Sulphuric acid is an important industrial acid. It can cause severe damage to the eyes and serious burns on the skin. Hydrochloric acid is another very strong acid. It can be made from sulphuric acid and common table salt. It is used to make other chemicals and is very good for cleaning metals. The human body makes a small amount of weak hydrochloric acid, which helps in digestion.

Nitric acid is another powerful acid which can harm the skin and eyes. Boric acid, on the other hand, is a very weak acid. It occurs naturally in Italy. It is used to make ceramics, cements, pigments, and cosmetics. It is sometimes used as a germ-killer, but is not very good for this purpose. Carbonic acid comes from carbon dioxide gas, and there is some of it in the soda pop we drink. Arsenic acid is used to make insect-killing products.

Organic acids are not as strong as inorganic acids. Acetic acid is found in vinegar, and can be made by fermenting apple cider. When sugar ferments in milk, lactic acid is formed. It turns the milk sour, but it is also used in making cheese.

Amino acids are needed to keep the body in good health, and they come from protein foods. Oranges, lemons, and grapefruit contain ascorbic acid, which is the chemical name for Vitamin C. Liver, poultry, and beef contain nicotinic acid, which helps prevent skin diseases.

So you see that the story of acids is a long and complicated one. Some are dangerous to human beings, but useful in industry. Some are necessary for human life and are supplied by various foods. Some are made by the body itself to keep it functioning.

WHAT IS ASBESTOS?

Many people think asbestos is a modern invention, but it has actually been known and used for thousands of years! In ancient temples, it was used for torch wicks and to protect fires lit on the altars. The Romans used asbestos 2,000 years ago for winding sheets to preserve the ashes of the dead when bodies were cremated. There is even a legend that Charlemagne had an asbestos tablecloth. He laundered it by putting it in the fire to burn off stains.

Asbestos is a Greek word that means "inextinguishable" or "unquench-able." Today we apply it to a group of fibrous minerals which have the property of resisting fire. The minerals that make up asbestos differ widely in composition, and each has a different strength, flexibility, and usefulness. From the chemical point of view, asbestos usually consists of silicates of lime and magnesia and sometimes contains iron.

Because it is made up of fibers, asbestos is similar to cotton and wool, but asbestos has the added advantage of being heat- and fire-resistant. This makes it very valuable for many uses in industry, and science has not yet been able to find a substitute for it.

No other mineral we know can be spun into yarn or thread, woven into cloth, or made into sheets. Workers in plants who are exposed to risks of fire sometimes wear complete outfits made of asbestos, including helmets, gloves, suits, and boots. Asbestos can withstand temperatures of 1,090 to 1,650 degrees centigrade, and there are some kinds of asbestos that can even resist temperatures as high as 2,760 degrees!

The United States manufactures almost half of all the asbestos products made in the world, but less than five per cent of the raw material is found in this country. The Province of Quebec, Canada, supplies about 75 per cent of the world's asbestos.

Asbestos is found in veins in certain types of rocks, and sometimes it's necessary to mine and treat as much as 45 tonnes of rock to get one tonne of asbestos fiber!

WHAT IS CHAMOIS?

In your hardware store you will see for sale a cloth called "chamois." People buy it because it is very soft and doesn't scratch a surface when you use it for cleaning. Many people use it for cleaning their automobiles and on furniture.

Chamois cloth is skin of the chamois, made into a soft leather. Actually, however, this animal is quite scarce, so that most of the "chamois" sold in the United States is really a fine grade of sheepskin instead!

A long time ago, the chamois lived in the plains of Europe. In time, as it was hunted for its soft skin and delicately flavored meat, it retreated to the safety of the mountains. It is now found mostly in the Alps and the Pyrenees, ranging as far up as the snow line in summer.

Like the Rocky Mountain goat, the chamois is one of the goatlike antelopes. It is one of the shyest animals known, and it has highly developed sight and smell to warn it of danger. When a chamois wants to escape over rocks and cliffs, it is nimbler than even an antelope and it is more sure-footed than the mountain goat!

Some people who have observed chamois grazing claim that the herd keeps guards on watch while the rest graze. When a chamois is frightened, it sets up a shrill whistle that will send the whole herd racing off. They escape by jumping a big ravine or bounding up or down the face of a precipice where no man could pass.

The chamois is about the size of a domestic goat and usually weighs about 30 kilograms. Its gray or brown coat changes colour seasonally, but this follows a peculiar pattern. Unlike other animals, it is lightest in summer and darkest, almost black, in winter. Occasionally a white chamois, an albino, is seen. There is a superstition among the people in the Alps that whoever kills a white chamois will be killed by gnomes and fairies within a year.

The small herds are always led by an old female and through the summer are made up of females and young, while the males live scattered higher on the mountainsides. The horns of chamois are black and smooth with tips that hook backward and downward.

WHAT IS AMMONIA?

Ammonia is a colorless gas with a very strong odor. In fact, breathing in too much ammonia may cause death. Ammonia gets its name from the discovery of a certain compound, ammonium chloride, near the Temple of Jupiter Ammon in Egypt. The first man to make pure ammonium gas was Joseph Priestley, an English chemist, who produced it in 1774 and called it "alkaline air."

Traces of ammonia are found in the air, having come from the decay of animal and vegetable matter. Sometimes it is found in minute quantities in rain water. But most of the ammonia used in commerce is artificially made.

Ammonia is composed of the elements nitrogen and hydrogen. By combining these two gases, ammonia is obtained. The nitrogen is obtained from the air and the hydrogen from water. The two gases are dried, compressed, heated to a temperature of about 530 degrees centigrade, and passed over a mixture of various salts, whereupon they combine to form ammonia.

Ammonia is about three-fifths as heavy as air. When compressed and cooled, it becomes a colorless liquid which looks much like water, but which boils at the low temperature of minus 34 degrees centigrade. When the pressure is released, the liquid vaporizes again. As it does this, it absorbs much heat. This is why ammonia is used in making ice and in refrigeration.

The ammonia that you may have at home, "household ammonia," is a dilute solution of ammonia in water. It is used to soften water for cleaning and washing.

When ammonia comes in contact with acids, it forms ammonium salts.

Many ammonium salts are very useful. Ammonium chloride is used in soldering, in dry cells, and in medicine. Ammonium sulphate is a valuable fertilizer. Ammonium nitrate is also used in fertilizers, as well as in explosives. Smelling salts contain ammonium carbonate.

All of these salts are formed by treating ammonia with the proper acid, though some ammonium salts are formed in nature.

WHAT IS TAPIOCA?

Do you like tapioca pudding? You would never believe, by looking at it, what that food was originally and everything it went through before it became the pudding in your plate!

Tapioca is made from the roots of a large shrub which grows in the warm countries of the world. The shrub is called "manioc" or "cassava" in English, and is also known as "yuca" or "mandioca."

The roots of the manioc plant are about one-third starch and two-thirds water, and a great deal of time is needed to get these roots ready for eating. They are first washed and peeled. They may then be put into water in a pot or a stream and left to soak for three or four days. Or they may be grated or pounded into a paste without soaking. The paste can be cooked and eaten, or it can be dried and made into flour.

To make tapioca, the grated root is mixed well with very clean water, and then left to stand. The pure starch grains slowly settle to the bottom, and any dirt can be poured off with the water.

The starch is then taken out and mixed with clean water again and the process repeated, sometimes four or five times. When the starch is perfectly clean, it is spread on a metal plate over a low fire and cooked. It is stirred all the time it is over the fire. As the starch grains cook, they stick together to form irregular little balls.

After the pure starch is cooked, it is called "tapioca." So you can see it's quite a long way from the roots of the shrub to the tapioca you eat! Most of the tapioca used in the United States and Europe comes from Java, Brazil, and Madagascar.

Pure manioc starch that has not been cooked is known in the United States as "tapioca flour." It is used to give a good finish to cotton cloth, to make fine adhesives such as are used on postage stamps, and it has many other uses, as well.

WHAT ARE ANTIBIOTICS?

Antibiotics are drugs which are useful in the prevention and treatment of infections. "Anti" means "against," and "biotic" means "life." Antibiotics work only against certain forms of life: the bacteria which cause disease. Antibiotics are themselves substances made from living matter—from bacteria, molds, or larger plants.

The development of antibiotics began with the discovery of penicillin by Sir Alexander Fleming in 1928. His discovery was studied and developed further by other scientists, and eventually the search was on for other "antibiotics."

Soil samples from all over the world were examined to see if they contained molds which could produce substances useful against infective bacteria. As a result, there are many antibiotics in use today. Among these are penicillin, streptomycin, aureomycin chloramphenicol, and terramycin. Some antibiotics have a toxic (poisonous) effect on the body's tissues as well as on the disease-causing bacteria.

Just how antibiotics stop the growth of bacteria is not completely clear. It is believed that antibiotics stop bacteria from using the normal food substances they need for growth.

Each kind of bacterial infection is best treated by a specific antibiotic. Certain patients have sensitivity (allergy) to one or another antibiotic. These people may develop hives, asthma, or more serious illnesses.

Sometimes, antibiotics are given for long periods of time. And sometimes, antibiotics are given not for treatment, but for prevention of disease. Since the use of antibiotics, deaths due to infections alone are rare. The infectious diseases are no longer such a menace to man's health.

Penicillin mold.

DO THE SEVEN WONDERS OF THE WORLD STILL EXIST?

It was probably hard for the people of ancient times to imagine that the great monuments which they called "the Seven Wonders of the World" would ever vanish. But except for one, they have all disappeared!

That single remaining one is the pyramid of Cheops at Gizeh, Egypt. It was built about 5,000 years ago to serve as a tomb for a pharaoh and his queen.

The second wonder was the great Walls of Babylon, in what is now Iraq. They were built about 600 B.C. by the famous King Nebuchadnezzar. Made of brick and 100 metres high, today they are just a mass of ruins.

The third wonder of the world was the statue of the God Zeus, at Olympia, Greece, fashioned by the Greek sculptor Phidias. The figure was about 12 metres high, with gold robes, ivory flesh, and eyes of precious gems. No trace of it exists.

The fourth wonder was the Temple of the goddess Diana at Ephesus, in what is now Turkey. The roof was supported by great stone columns 18 metres high, and the temple contained some of the best works of Grecian art. It was burned by the invading Goths in A.D. 262.

The fifth wonder was the tomb in the city of Halicarnassus in what is now Turkey. It was built for King Mausolus, who died in 353 B.C. This was such a splendid structure and cost so much money, that we now call any elaborately decorated tomb "a mausoleum."

The sixth wonder was the Colossus of Rhodes, a bronze statue of Helios, the sun god. It was about 32 metres high, and stood on the island of Rhodes. It was destroyed in an earthquake in 224 B.C.

The seventh and last wonder was the lighthouse of Pharos, begun about 283 B.C. on the island of Pharos off the coast of Egypt. It is believed it was almost 180 metres high above its base, with a light burning at the top which guided ships to port. The beacon served for more than 1,500 years before it was finally destroyed by an earthquake.

WHAT IS THE MYSTERY OF THE SPHINX?

The Great Sphinx sits in the desert of Egypt, about eight miles from Cairo, guarding the three large pyramids of Giza. It is a monster made of rock, with the head of a man and the body of a crouching lion with forepaws extended in front.

While the body is roughly sculptured, the head is carved with care. The eyes are mysterious and have a look which nobody has quite been able to explain. They gaze out over the desert with a kind of mystical superiority.

The figure is over 18 metres high and 57 metres long. It is believed that the sphinx is at least 5,000 years old! Why was it built? One piece of evidence we have comes from a little chapel that is found between the paws of the monster. This chapel has inscriptions put there by two

ancient Egyptian kings. They explain that the sphinx represents one of the forms of the sun god Harmachis. And they say that the purpose of the sphinx is to keep away all evil from the cemetery around the pyramids.

There are many sphinxes in Egypt besides the Great Sphinx of Giza. Their heads represent kings. In the sacred writing of the Egyptians, "sphinx" means "lord." In primitive religions, the king was believed to have the strength and cunning of various beasts. He acquired these powers by putting on their heads or their skins. So the Egyptians sculptured their gods and kings as half-human and half-beast.

The idea of the sphinx spread from Egypt to other civilizations, such as Assyria and Greece. In these regions, sphinxes were usually represented with wings. In Assyria they were usually male, but in Greece they had the head of a woman. Our word "sphinx," by the way, comes from the Greek.

The Greeks probably thought of the sphinx much the way we think of dragons. We may use the figure of a dragon as a sign of destructive power, but we don't really believe in dragons.

The Greeks had a legend about the sphinx. She lived on a rock and killed every traveler who couldn't answer this riddle: "What walks on four legs in the morning, on two legs at noon, on three legs at night?" Oedipus answered that it was a man, who crawled on all fours as a baby, walked erect on two legs as a man, and walked with a cane when he was old. This was the right answer, so the sphinx threw herself from the rock in rage and died.

WHAT CAUSED THE TOWER OF PISA TO LEAN?

When something captures the imagination of the world, it is remembered by people far more than things that may be more important. Everybody knows that in the city of Pisa in Italy, there is a tower that "leans." Very few people know that this town has a great and glorious history.

Of course, the tower itself is quite a marvel, too. It is built entirely of white marble. The walls are 4 metres thick at its base. It has eight storeys and is 54.5 metres high, which in our country would be about the height of a 15-storey building.

There is a stairway built into the walls consisting of 300 steps, which leads to the top. And by the way, those people who climb these stairs to the top get a magnificent view of the city and of the sea, which is six miles away.

At the top, the tower is 5 metres out of the perpendicular. In other words, it "leans" over by 5 metres. If you were to stand at the top and drop a stone to the ground, it would hit 5 metres away from the wall at the bottom of the tower!

What makes it lean? Nobody really knows the answer. Of course, it wasn't supposed to lean when it was built; it was supposed to stand straight. It was intended as a bell-tower for the cathedral which is nearby and was begun in 1174 and finished in 1350.

The foundations of the tower were laid in sand, and this may explain why it leans. But it didn't suddenly begin to lean—this began to happen when only three of its storeys, or "galleries," had been built. So the plans were changed slightly and construction went right on! In the last hundred years, the tower has leaned nearly 0.3 metres more. Some engineers say it should be called "the falling tower," because they believe that it will eventually topple over.

Did you know that Galileo, who was born in Pisa, is said to have performed some of his experiments concerning the speed of falling bodies at this tower?

WHY WAS THE GREAT WALL OF CHINA BUILT?

If you owned a certain piece of territory and wanted to prevent outsiders from entering, wouldn't you think of building a wall around it? In ancient times in China, such walls were built around entire cities to protect them from invasion!

About the year 221 B.C., a great Emperor united different parts of China into an empire. His name was Shih Huang Ti. But north of his empire there lived barbaric wanderers of the desert lands and he felt they were a danger to his new empire. So he ordered that a wall be built so long and so high that all the northern provinces of China would be protected.

This Great Wall, which was truly a tremendous project, was completed in only 15 years. Since that time it has been extended, rebuilt many times, and destroyed in part. But despite that, much of it still stands.

Did the Emperor accomplish his goal with the Great Wall? Unfortunately, no. It simply wasn't too good a way of preventing the barbarians from invading China. Besides, there were always some parts of the Wall that were in need of repair. So the barbarians, who were called Mongols, wandered back and forth across these broken-down parts. Not only that, but the Chinese themselves didn't even stay within the Wall. Sometimes Chinese farmers would plant crops beyond the Wall.

Despite this, the Great Wall did serve (and still serves today) as a kind of boundary between Chinese and Mongol culture, and between a way of life based on agriculture and one of nomadic (wandering) herding.

The Great Wall is the longest wall in the world. With all its windings, it is more than 1,500 miles long. Because it was built as a defense system, it follows mountain crests and takes advantage of narrow gorges.

The Wall is built of earth, stone, and brick. Its height ranges from 4 to 9 metres, with watchtowers rising at regular intervals above it. Along the top runs a 4-metre wide roadway.

DO THE NORTHERN LIGHTS APPEAR IN THE SOUTH?

The Northern Lights, or the Aurora Borealis, is one of nature's most dazzling spectacles.

When it appears, there is often a crackling sound coming from the sky. A huge, luminous arc lights up the night, and this arc is constantly in motion. Sometimes, the brilliant rays of light spread upward in the shape of a fan. At other times, they flash here and there like giant searchlights, or move up and down so suddenly that they have been called "the merry dancers."

Farther north, the Aurora frequently looks like vast, fiery draperies which hang from the sky and sway to and fro while flames of red, orange, green, and blue play up and down the moving folds.

According to scientific measurements, this discharge of light takes place from 50 to 100 miles above the earth. But it doesn't reach its greatest brilliance at the North Pole. It is seen at its best around the Hudson Bay region in Canada, in northern Scotland, and in southern Norway and Sweden. It may sometimes be seen even in the United States as it flashes across the northern sky.

We call this "the Northern Lights," or "Aurora Borealis." But such lights occur in the Southern Hemisphere, too! They are known as "the Aurora Australis." In fact, sometimes both lights are called "Aurora Polaris."

Science is still not certain regarding exactly what these lights are and what causes them. But it is believed that the rays are due to discharges of electricity in the rare upper atmosphere.

The displays seem to center about the earth's magnetic poles, and electrical and magnetic disturbances often occur when the lights are especially brilliant. They also seem to be related to sun spots in some unknown way.

If nearly all the air is pumped out of a glass tube, and a current of electricity is then passed through the rarefied gases, there will be a display of lights inside the tube. The Aurora displays seen high above the earth may be caused by the same phenomenon, electrical discharges from the sun passing through rarefied gases.

HOW BIG IS THE LARGEST PEARL?

Pearls are things of such beauty that they have been treasured by man for thousands of years. As far as we know, the first people to discover pearls were the Chinese. They found them in mussels taken from shallow rivers about 4,000 years ago. By the sixth or seventh century B.C., pearls had been discovered along the coasts of India, Persia, and Ceylon.

The biggest one found is 50 millimetres long by 100 millimetres round. Another way of measuring it is by weight, and this pearl, known as "the Hope Pearl," weighed 1,800 grains. One pearl "grain" is 50 milligrams. Other large pearls that are known are: Shah Sofi's pearl, about 513 grains; La Regente, 346 grains; La Pellegrina 111½ grains.

Of course, weight and size aren't the only ways the value of a pearl is determined. Some pearls have an irregular shape (baroque pearls), and some pearls have an imperfect outer covering. In fact, a jeweler may "skin" a pearl that has an imperfect covering by removing the outer layers until he finds a better coat beneath.

This tells you that a pearl is made up of layers. Layers of what, and how are they made? Pearls are made of the same material as the mother-of-pearl lining that is in the shells of certain varieties of oysters. This lining is secreted by the oysters to provide a smooth surface against their tender bodies.

When an irritating object gets inside the oyster's shell, the oyster coats it over with layer after layer of nacre, which is the material of a pearl. You can see how people got the idea for making "cultured" pearls. If the oyster is going to cover an irritating object with nacre—well, let's put an irritating object into the oyster and get it started. So a tiny bit of sand, or mother-of-pearl is inserted either between the shell and the oyster's body, even within the body of the animal. A cultured pearl is therefore a real pearl, but it was started because man made the oyster create it.

WHAT MAKES A JUMPING BEAN JUMP?

The bean itself doesn't "jump." But there is something inside the bean that moves, and this gives us the impression that it's jumping. What is that thing inside the bean?

In Chihuahua, in Mexico, a three-celled bean pod grows which is used as a home by the bean moth. The moth lays its eggs early in the flower of the plant. After a time, the meat of the bean pod grows around the egg.

The larva of the moth eats away the meat and lines the pod with silk from a spinneret in its head. Nobody knows why, but every now and then the larva contracts its body suddenly, or wriggles, and the bean "jumps"! After several months, the insect pierces the side of wall of the bean and an adult moth comes out.

The Mexican jumping bean is only one of many curious things about beans. Did you know that in Greek times, beans were used in voting? A white bean meant yes, and a black one, no.

In early Roman times, the father of a family, after washing his hands, would throw black beans over his head nine times to purify himself and his family. Beans have been known and used for so long in so many ways that when a person doesn't have much sense we say of him, "He doesn't know beans!"

There's a very good reason why beans have been so popular the world over. First of all, they grow in almost every country. Secondly, they are very nourishing. They are so rich in protein that they are often used as an inexpensive substitute for meat.

The bean is a legume, which means it bears its seeds in pods. All beans are annuals and are grown from seeds. In some varieties of beans, such as the string bean, we can eat the unripe pod, but in most varieties, only the seeds are eaten.

One of America's favorite beans, the Lima bean, originally came from Peru. The navy bean, which we use in baked beans, probably also came from South America. One of the most useful beans in the world is the soybean.

The soybean has been known for generations in China, Japan, and Korea. But oddly enough, it is seldom eaten as a vegetable. It is made into a sauce, into cakes, it is used in making bread, and recently it has become the basis for many manufactured products.

HOW DOES VENTRILOQUISM WORK?

The fun of watching a ventriloquist work is that the "dummy" he works with seems to have a life and personality of his own. Sometimes it's hard to believe the dummy isn't a real person.

But, of course, the voice of the dummy comes from the ventriloquist. By the way, isn't that a strange word? Do you know what it really means? It comes from the Latin *venter,* which means "belly," and *loqui,* "to speak." So a ventriloquist really means "a belly-speaker"!

This name came about because at one time it was believed that ventriloquism was the result of using the stomach in a special way while breathing in. But this is not the way it works.

A ventriloquist forms the words in a normal manner. What he does is allow the breath to escape slowly, the tones are muffled, and the mouth is opened as little as possible. The tongue is pulled back and only the tip is moved. The pressure on the vocal cords to muffle the tones spreads the sound, and the greater the pressure, the greater is the illusion that the sound is coming from a distance.

The reason a dummy is sometimes used by a ventriloquist is to get your attention away from his own mouth. By moving the mouth of the dummy as he keeps his own lips still, the ventriloquist is able to fool you even more.

Did you know that ventriloquism is a very old art? Archeologists who have studied ancient Egyptian and Hebrew ruins believe that ventriloquism was practiced in those times. In ancient Greece, in Athens, there was a very famous ventriloquist called Eurycles, and he had many students and followers who used his methods.

It is also probable that priests in ancient times knew how to use ventriloquism. In Egypt, for example, there were supposed to be statues that "spoke," but this was probably the result of ventriloquism.

Many primitive people of modern times, such as the Zulus, the Maoris, and the Eskimos are quite good at ventriloquism!

Chapter 2

HOW IT BEGAN

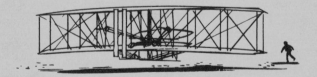

WHAT IS MYTHOLOGY?

Man has always wondered why the world is the way it is. He has tried to explain to himself why things happen as they do. Today, we have scientific explanations for things that happen in the universe. But in earlier times, man had to make up his "explanations."

Just consider all the strange things he couldn't understand. Why did the sun rise and set so regularly? Why were there different seasons? What were the stars, and why did they move as they did?

Then there were all the events in man's personal life to consider. Why did unpredictable events happen? Why did men dream? Why did people get sick? Where did people come from and where did they go after death? How was the world and everything in it created?

All primitive people have asked these questions and tried to answer them. Different tribes of people in various parts of the world have had different explanations. But their "explanations" somehow accounted for the events of their world. The fanciful stories which contain these explanations are called "myths." All the myths of a people taken together form a mythology.

By their myths, early men tried to "humanize," or "personalize," their world. That is, they imagined the objects around them to be persons like themselves, thoughtful beings, some with great power. All these objects, animals, plants, stars, rivers, the sun and moon, came to be gods with magic powers. Some of these gods were thought to be good and kind, some were evil and brought pain, hunger, and death.

Because they thought all these objects, or gods, were intelligent beings, they felt they could appeal to them. Since the sun had a mind, they could beg him to send his rays so that plants would grow. They could pray to the rain god for rain and the rain god could understand them.

This led to all kinds of rituals, or ceremonies. There was a certain way to appeal to a god, and if you did it the wrong way the god would be angry. The purpose of these ceremonies and rituals was to keep men on good terms with their gods. In that way, men believed they were able to direct and control events and live happier lives.

WAS AMERICA DISCOVERED BEFORE COLUMBUS?

When we say "discovered," we usually have a very special meaning in mind. We mean that people from one civilization came to a region where no one from their place had been before. As you know, an explorer often finds a people and a civilization already living in the place he "discovers." Why not say these people discovered it before him?

From our Western-civilization point of view, we say that Columbus discovered America. This is because after his discovery the New World he found began to be visited and finally populated from the Old World. But 500 years before Columbus was born, the Norsemen did a bit of "discovering," too. They sailed west to discover Iceland, then Greenland, and later the American mainland.

Did you know that the Chinese tell of an even earlier voyage by Chinese sailors to discover what has become California? And people of the South Sea Islands still sing of the great men of their distant past who sailed to South America long before the white man reached either South America or the South Sea Islands.

For all we know, there may have been many ages of exploration thousands of years ago. There were certainly ages of exploration before the time of Columbus. Perhaps we might say that neither Columbus, nor the Norsemen before him, "discovered" America. Weren't the Indians already living here for many centuries before the white man arrived?

And who can say that they didn't set out on a voyage of discovery? It is believed that they came from Asia, though we don't know when or how they made the trip. Probably they reached America over a period of centuries and by different routes. They also probably sent their scouts ahead to seek out routes by land or sea. These scouts were their explorers, and perhaps it was really they who discovered America!

WHICH NATION HAD THE FIRST FLAG?

The idea of a nation having a flag is fairly new, but flags have existed from earliest times. They were used in war to mark the positions of leaders.

In very ancient times, most of the flags were carved poles. The ancient Greeks' flag was merely a piece of armor or single letters held aloft upon poles. The first cloth flag was the invention of the Romans and consisted of a square banner attached to a crossbar at the end of a spear.

When the United States adopted a national flag, the idea was still very new. Most European nations were then fighting under the flags of their kings. The French used the white flag of the Bourbon family. The original national flag of England was the banner of St. George. The present form of union flag was proclaimed January 1, 1801. Probably the two oldest national flags are those of Denmark, adopted in 1219, and of Switzerland, used as early as 1339.

After the United States had chosen a national flag, many other nations followed that example. After the French Revolution, the Tricolor was chosen to represent France. The green, white, and red flag of the Italians was first established in 1805. In the 19th century, many South American republics designed flags for themselves and the idea of a national flag became universally accepted.

Did you know that in the early stages of the American Revolutionary War the Colonies had flags of their own? Massachusetts had a flag with a pine tree; South Carolina had a rattlesnake; New York had a white flag with a black beaver on it.

In designing America's flag it was first proposed that the English Union Jack be part of it. But this was rejected and it was decided to substitute 13 stars for the Union Jack.

WHO MADE THE FIRST MAP?

Imagine how hard it would be to tell in words the exact location of all the streets and buildings in your town. It would be simpler to make a picture or diagram of the location of such objects. The result would be a map!

The first map we have any record of was modeled in clay and then

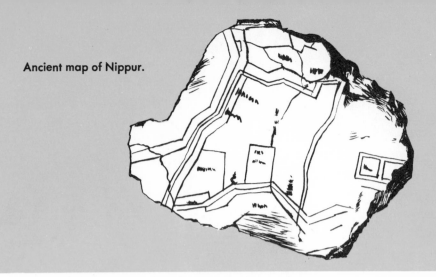

Ancient map of Nippur.

baked more than 4,000 years ago, in Egypt. In ancient times, landowners marked the outlines of their land, and kings, the boundaries of their kingdom on maps. But when people tried to show on maps the location of faraway places, they ran into problems.

This was because the earth is round and it was difficult to measure large distances accurately. Astronomers were a great help to early mapmakers, because their studies had to do with the size and shape of the earth.

A Greek called Eratosthenes, who was born in 276 B.C., figured the distance around the earth and came very close to the truth. His methods made it possible for the first time to calculate north-south distances correctly.

About the same time, Hipparchus suggested that a map of the world be divided evenly by imaginary lines of latitude, or parallels, and of longitude, or meridians. The proper positions of these lines, he said, should be based on knowledge gained from study of the heavens.

Ptolemy, in the 2nd century A.D., used this same idea and made an improved map with evenly spaced lines of latitude and longitude. His book on geography was the standard text until after the discovery of America.

The discoveries of Columbus and others greatly increased interest in maps and charts. The first large collection of maps was published by Abraham Ortelius of Antwerp in 1570. Geradus Mercator became the father of modern map-making. He made a map on which all the curved lines on a globe were straight ones on a map. This enabled the map to show a straight line between two places which would give a true course by the compass. This kind of map is known as "a projection"; it "projects" or transfers the earth's surface onto that of a map.

On the title page of his book there was a drawing of the giant Atlas, and this is why a collection of maps has come to be known as an "atlas"!

WHAT IS EVOLUTION?

In trying to explain the existence of the complicated body structures we see in living things around us, a theory of evolution has been developed. While most scientists accept this theory, many people do not. They feel it goes against what is written in the Bible.

This theory is that all the plants and animals in the world today have developed in a natural way from earlier forms that were simpler. These earlier forms developed from still simpler ancestors, and so on back through millions of years to the very beginning when life was in its simplest form, merely a tiny mass of jellylike protoplasm.

According to this theory, man, too, developed from some simpler form, just as the modern one-hoofed horse is the descendant of a small five-toed ancestor.

In trying to prove that evolution did take place, scientists depend on three chief "signs." One of these is the study of fossil remains of animals and plants of past ages. Some of these fossils seem to trace the steps of evolution at work. Fossil remains of primitive men have been found that go back to a time 1,000,000 years ago. Fossils of certain crablike animals go back nearly 500,000,000 years. These fossils show that fish developed in the waters of the earth before amphibians, amphibians before reptiles, reptiles before birds, and so on. Scientists believe this proves life has progressed from one form to another.

Another "sign" of evolution comes from the study of embryology, the growth of a new living thing from an egg. In studying the development of the chick from the hen's egg, there is a time when this embryo is like a fish, later it's like an amphibian, then it passes through the reptile stage, and finally develops into its bird form. The unborn young of all animals go through the same kind of process, repeating their history of development.

The third "sign" is the bodies of living animals. For example, the bone and muscle structure in the paddles of a turtle, the wings of a bird, the flippers of a whale, the front legs of a horse, and the arms of a man are similar in structure. And man has many organs in his body which seem of no use. They are thought to be relics handed down from his earlier ancestors. These are some of the "signs" that led to a theory of evolution.

HOW DID THE RACES OF MANKIND ORIGINATE?

Scientific authorities believe, based on evidence they have found, that man originated in one place and that all races of mankind have a common ancestor. Man's common ancestor, according to some of these scientists, looked very much like modern man and probably first appeared in Asia. Other scientists believe man first appeared in several places, at different times, and later met and mingled to form the present races of man.

About 500,000 years ago, in western Asia, man's ancestors lived in small groups. In these small, isolated groups, the first signs of differences appeared—differences in head shape, or eye sockets, or body build. Later, they began to look for new places to live, and about 300,000 years ago,

groups of men began to move southeast toward Indonesia and north toward China. Still later, other migrations took man to other parts of the world, where some developed in separate ways while others met and mingled.

Modern students say that there are three major divisions or "stocks" of mankind. These are: the Caucasoids, similar to the people who lived in the Caucasus Mountains and who were thought by early scholars to be typical of the "white" race; the Mongoloids, similar to the Mongols who lived in Mongolia in Asia; and the Negroids, like the Negroes who lived in the forest regions of Africa.

Early scholars divided man into five groups based on skin color. This classification is no longer accepted, because the color of the skin doesn't tell to which main stock a group of people belongs. Nor can any other single trait, such as head shape, blood type, or nose shape, tell the stock to which a man belongs. Many physical traits must be considered.

A race, therefore, is simply a group of people who have in common certain physical traits which they inherited from their ancestors and which set them apart from other groups.

WHO WERE THE FIRST PEOPLE TO BELIEVE IN ONE GOD?

The belief in one God is called "monotheism." The belief in many gods is called "polytheism."

Most of the "dead" religions—religions which no longer have any followers—were religions having many gods. Among these are the Egyptian, Babylonian, Assyrian, Greek, Roman, Celtic, and Norse. In very primitive times and among primitive peoples everywhere, there were only religions having many gods.

The idea of monotheism—one God—developed quite late in the history of religion. And according to most people and students of the subject, it is the fullest and best expression of the spirit and meaning of religion. It is built on the conviction that the ethical and religious values we hold must have a basis, and this is the one God on whom all existence and value depend.

But the idea of monotheism took a long time to develop. It first started with what is called "monarchianism." Just as a monarch is set above his people, so the idea arose that one god should be exalted above the rest and should be the king of the gods. Among the ancient Greeks, for example, Zeus stood supreme over all the gods.

The same idea existed among the Babylonians and the Egyptians. The Babylonians had a god called Marduk who was supreme over all the other gods, and the Egyptians had Ra, who was ruler over all the other gods.

The next step was the idea of "monolatry." According to this concept, other gods do exist, but only one is worshipped. About the 14th century B.C., an attempt was made in Egypt to introduce the idea of monotheism, with the sun as the one god. But it failed. And about 800 years before Christ, a Zoroastrian religion in Persia held that there was the great one god. But true monotheism, the belief that Christians, Jews, and Mohammedans hold in one God, comes from the Hebrew religion as expressed in the Old Testament.

HOW LONG HAVE PEOPLE BEEN USING LAST NAMES?

"Hey, Shorty!" "Hi, Skinny." "Here comes Blondie." Sound familiar to you? It's a perfectly natural way to call people—give them a name that describes them in some way.

And you know, that's exactly the way first names were given originally! A girl born during a famine might be called Una (Celtic for "famine"), a golden haired blonde might be called Blanche (French for "white"). A boy might be called David because it means "beloved."

A first name was all anybody had for thousands of years. Then, about the time the Normans conquered England in 1066, last names, or surnames, were added to identify people better. The first name wasn't enough to set one person apart from another. For example, there might be two Davids in town, and one of them was quite lazy. So people began to call this one "David, who is also lazy," or "David do little." And this became David Doolittle.

The last names were originally called "ekenames." The word "eke" meant "also." And by the way, we get our word "nickname" from this word!

Once people got into the habit of giving a person two names, they thought of many ways of creating this second name. For example, one way was to mention the father's name. If John had a father called William, he might be called John Williamson, or John Williams, or John Wilson (Will's son), or John Wills.

Another good way to identify people with second names was to mention the place where they lived or came from. A person who lived near the woods might be called Wood, or if he lived near the village green he might be called John Green.

And then, of course, the work that a person did was a good way to identify him. So we have last names like Smith, Taylor, and Wright. ("Wright" means someone who does mechanical work.)

The nearest thing to last names in ancient times existed among the Romans. A second name was sometimes added to indicate the family or clan to which a child belonged. Later, they even added a third name, which was a kind of descriptive nickname.

HOW DID THE CUSTOM OF KISSING START?

We know the kiss as a form of expressing affection. But long before it became this, it was the custom in many parts of the world to use the kiss as an expression of homage.

In many African tribes the natives kiss the ground over which a chief has walked. Kissing the hand and foot has been a mark of respect and homage from the earliest times. The early Romans kissed the mouth or eyes as a form of dignified greeting. One Roman emperor allowed his important nobles to kiss his lips, but the less important ones had to his kiss his hands, and the least important ones were only allowed to kiss his feet!

It is quite probable that the kiss as a form of affection can be traced back to primitive times when a mother would fondle her child, just as a mother does today. It only remained for society to accept this as a custom for expressing affection between adults.

We have evidence that this was already the case by the time of the sixth century, but we can only assume it was practiced long before that. The first country where the kiss became accepted in courtship and love was in France. When dancing became popular, almost every dance figure ended with a kiss.

From France the kiss spread rapidly all over Europe. Russia, which loved to copy the customs of France, adopted the kiss and it spread there through all the upper classes. A kiss from the Tsar became one of the highest form of recognition from the Crown.

In time, the kiss became a part of courtship. As marriage customs developed, the kiss became a part of the wedding ceremony. Today, of course, we regard the kiss as an expression of love and tenderness. But there are still many places in the world where the kiss is part of formal ceremonies and is intended to convey respect and homage.

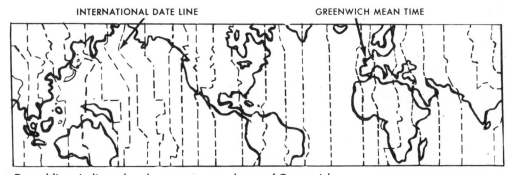

INTERNATIONAL DATE LINE   GREENWICH MEAN TIME

Dotted lines indicate hourly zones east and west of Greenwich.

DOES THE WHOLE WORLD HAVE TIME ZONES?

Now that we can travel so fast by jet plane over big distances, the differences in time have become even more startling. We can leave New York at a certain hour, for example, and arrive in Los Angeles just a little while later—on the clock.

The reason for this is that the U.S.A. is divided into time zones. This division was adopted in 1833, when the United States was divided into four time belts or zones—Eastern, central, mountain, and Pacific.

The division was based on meridians, the imaginary lines that run around the earth through the North and South Poles. The time kept in each belt varies exactly an hour from the belt next to it. And the time kept everywhere within each belt is exactly the same.

As you move from one belt to another, going east, the time advances an hour. If you go west, it goes back an hour. But the time belts do not follow perfectly straight lines. The reason for this is that some community may be closely linked with an area very near it and wish to keep the same time. For example, Georgia, most of Florida, and the lower peninsula of Michigan could all be in the central time zone, but they include themselves in the Eastern zone.

The whole world is divided into time zones exactly as the United States is. Every 15 degrees as one goes around the world, in terms of meridians, there is a new time zone. Where does the measuring start?

It starts in Greenwich, England, which has 0-degree meredian running through it. As you move east from Greenwich, you add an hour to Greenwich time every 15 degrees. As you move west from Greenwich, you subtract an hour from Greenwich time in the same way.

So when it is 12:00 noon in Greenwich, it is 4:00 in the morning in California, because you have moved west nine 15-degree intervals, and it is 2:00 in the afternoon in Egypt, because you have moved east two 15-degree intervals.

Exactly on the opposite side of the world from Greenwich is an imaginary line called "the International Date Line." If you cross this line moving west, you "lose" a whole day, and if you cross it moving east, you "gain" a whole day.

WHY IS THERE DAYLIGHT SAVING TIME?

Let's say a person gets up at 7:00 in the morning and goes to bed at 11:00 at night. He comes home from work about 6:30, and by the time he's finished with dinner it's after 8:00. He steps outside in the summer to relax—but it's already getting dark! Not much time to enjoy the summer day.

Now suppose you set the clock ahead one hour. This person still does everything at the same hour—but this time, when he steps out at 8:00 o'clock there's still plenty of light to enjoy. An hour of daylight has been "saved" for him!

Daylight saving time doesn't, of course, add any hours to a day. That's impossible. All it does is increase the number of useful hours of daylight during the seasons when the sun rises early.

Daylight saving is most popular in cities. It permits the closing of offices, shops, and factories at the end of the working day while the sun is still high. Farmers, who do their work by sun time, usually do not observe daylight saving time. They cannot work in the field before the morning dew has dried or after it appears in the evening.

Did you know who first thought of daylight saving time? It was Benjamin Franklin! When he was living in France in the 18th century, he suggested the idea to the people in Paris. But it was not adopted then.

Daylight saving laws were first passed during World War I. At this time, fuel for generating electricity was scarce, and so it was necessary to save on artificial light. With daylight saving, the bedtime of many people comes soon after it gets dark, while without it, if they stay up until the same hour they may have to use artificial light.

The first country to adopt daylight saving time was Germany in 1915. Then England used it in 1916, and the United States adopted it in 1918.

HOW DID THE CALENDAR BEGIN?

When men first began to plant seeds and harvest crops, they noticed that the time for planting came at a regular time each year. Then they tried to count how many days came between one planting time and the next. This was man's first attempt to find out how long a year was!

The ancient Egyptians were the first to measure a year with any exactness. They knew that the best time to plant was right after the Nile River overflowed each year. Their priests noticed that between each overflowing the moon rose 12 times. So they counted 12 *moonths* or months, and figured out when the Nile would rise again.

But it still wasn't exact enough. At last the Egyptian priests noticed that each year, about the time of the flood, a certain bright star would rise just before the sun rose. They counted the days that passed before this happened again and found that it added up to 365 days. This was 6000 years ago, and before that no one had ever known that there were 365 days in a year! The Egyptians divided this year into 12 months of 30 days each, with 5 extra days at the end of the year. Thus they invented the first calendar.

Eventually, the calendar was based not on the moon (lunar calendar) but on the number of days (365¼) it takes the earth to go around the sun (solar calendar). The extra quarter of day began to cause more and more confusion. Finally, Julius Caesar decided to straighten it all out. He ordered that the year 46 B.C. should have 445 days to "catch up," and that every year from then on was to have 365 days, except every fourth year. This fourth year would have a leap year of 366 days to use up the fraction left over in each ordinary year.

But as time went on it was discovered that Easter and other holy days were not coming where they belonged in the seasons. Too many "extra" days had piled up. In the year 1582, Pope Gregory XIII decided to do something about it. He ordered that ten days should be dropped from the year 1582. And to keep the calendar accurate for all future time, he ordered that leap year should be skipped in the last year of every century unless that year could be divided by 400. Thus 1700, 1800, and 1900 were not leap years, but the year 2000 will be a leap year!

This system is called the Gregorian calendar and is now used all over the world for everyday purposes, though various religions still use their own calendar for religious purposes!

HOW DID THE DAYS OF THE WEEK GET THEIR NAMES?

There was a time in the early history of man when the days had no names! The reason was quite simple. Men had not invented the week.

In those days, the only division of times was the month, and there were too many days in the month for each of them to have a separate name. But when men began to build cities, they wanted to have a special day on which to trade, a market day. Sometimes these market days were fixed at every tenth day, sometimes every seventh or every fifth day. The Babylonians decided that it should be every seventh day. On this day they didn't work, but met for trade and religious festivals.

The Jews followed their example, but kept every seventh day for religious purposes. In this way the week came into existence. It was the space between market days. The Jews gave each of the seven days a name, but it was really a number after the Sabbath day (which was Saturday). For example, Wednesday was called the fourth day (four days after Saturday).

When the Egyptians adopted the seven-day week, they named the days after five planets, the sun, and the moon. The Romans used the Egyptian names for their days of the week: the day of the sun, of the moon, of the planet Mars, of Mercury, of Jupiter, of Venus, and of Saturn.

We get our names for the days not from the Romans but from the Anglo-Saxons, who called most of the days after their own gods, which were roughly the same as the gods of the Romans. The day of the sun became *Sunnandaeg,* or Sunday. The day of the moon was called *Monandaeg,* or Monday. The day of Mars became the day of Tiw, who was their god of war. This became *Tiwesdaeg,* or Tuesday. Instead of Mercury's name, that of the god Woden was given to Wednesday. The Roman day of Jupiter, the thunderer, became the day of the thunder god Thor, and this became Thursday. The next day was named for Frigg, the wife of their god Odin, and so we have Friday. The day of Saturn became *Saeternsdaeg,* a translation from the Roman, and then Saturday.

A day, by the way, used to be counted as the space between sunrise and sunset. The Romans counted it as from midnight to midnight, and most modern nations use this method.

WHY ARE EGGS AND RABBITS ASSOCIATED WITH EASTER?

Easter is the most joyous of Christian holidays. It is celebrated in commemoration of the Resurrection of Jesus Christ.

The exact day on which Easter falls may vary from year to year, but it always comes, of course, in the spring of the year. Thus, as Christianity spread, the celebration of Easter included many customs that were linked with the celebration of spring's arrival. This explains why many Easter customs go back to traditions that existed before Christianity itself.

Both Easter and the coming of spring are symbols of new life. The ancient Egyptians and Persians celebrated their spring festivals by coloring and eating eggs. This is because they considered the egg a symbol of fertility and new life. The Christians adopted the egg as symbolic of new life, the symbol of the Resurrection.

There is another reason why we observe the practice of eating eggs on Easter Sunday and of giving them as gifts to friends or children. In the early days of the Church, eggs were forbidden food during Lent. With the ending of Lent, people were so glad to see and eat eggs again that they made it a tradition to eat them on Easter Sunday.

The Easter hare also was part of the spring celebrations long before Christianity. In the legends of ancient Egypt, the hare is associated with the moon. The hare is linked with the night because it comes out only then to feed. By being associated with the moon, the hare became a symbol of a new period of life. Thus the hare stood for the renewal of life and for fertility. The early Christians therefore took it over and linked it with Easter, the holiday that symbolizes new life!

By the way, the tradition of wearing new clothes on Easter Sunday is also symbolic of casting off the old and the beginning of the new!

HOW DID HALLOWEEN ORIGINATE?

The name Halloween means "hallowed, or holy, evening." Yet, for some reason this holiday has become one of the most popular and best liked holidays of the entire year and is celebrated with great enthusiasm in many countries.

Halloween, which takes place on October 31st, is really a festival to celebrate autumn, just as May Day is a festival to celebrate spring. The ancient Druids (the Druids were the religious priests in ancient Gaul, Britain, and Ireland) had a great festival to celebrate autumn which began at midnight on October 31st and lasted through the next day, November 1st.

They believed that on this night their great god of death, called Saman, called together all the wicked souls who had died during the year and whose punishment had been to take up life in the bodies of animals. Of course, the very idea of such a gathering was enough to frighten the simple-minded people of that time. So they lit huge bonfires and kept a sharp watch for these evil spirits. This is actually where the idea that witches and ghosts are about on Halloween began. And there are still people in certain isolated parts of Europe who believe this to be true!

The Romans also had a holiday about the 1st of November which was in honour of their goddess Pomona. Nuts and apples were roasted before great bonfires. Our own Halloween seems to be a combination of the Roman and Druid festivals.

Originally, the Halloween festival was quite simple and was celebrated mostly in church. But all over Europe, people looked upon this occasion as an opportunity to have fun and excitement, to tell spooky tales, and to scare each other. So instead of being devoted to the celebration of autumn, it became a holiday devoted to the supernatural, to witches, and to ghosts.

Here are some of the curious customs which sprang up in connection with Halloween: Young girls who "ducked" for apples on this night could see their future husbands if they slept with the apple under their pillow. Stealing gates, furniture, signs, and so on, is done to make people think they were stolen by the evil spirits. And, of course, no one goes near a cemetery on Halloween because spirits rise up on that night! Today we use these superstitions as a way of having fun on Halloween.

WHO FIRST THOUGHT OF THE ALPHABET?

The letters of an alphabet are really sound signs. Those of the English alphabet are based on the Roman alphabet, which is about 2,500 years old. The capital letters are almost exactly like those used in Roman inscriptions of the third century B.C.

Before alphabets were invented men used pictures to record events or communicate ideas. A picture of several antelopes might mean "Here are good hunting grounds," so this was really a form of writing. Such "picture writing" was highly developed by the ancient Babylonians, Egyptians, and Chinese.

In time, picture writing underwent a change. The picture, instead of just standing for the object that was drawn, came to represent an idea connected with the object drawn. For example, the picture of a foot might indicate the verb "to walk." This stage of writing is called "ideographic," or "idea writing."

The trouble with this kind of writing was that the messages might be interpreted by different people in different ways. So little by little this method was changed. The symbols came to represent combinations of sounds. For example, if the word for "arm" were "id," the picture of an arm would stand for the sound of "id." So the picture of an arm was used every time they wanted to convey the sound "id." This stage of writing might be called "syllabic writing."

The Babylonians and Chinese and the Egyptians never passed beyond this stage of writing. The Egyptians did make up a kind of alphabet by including among their pictures 24 signs which stood for separate letters or words of one consonant each. But they didn't realize the value of their invention.

About 3,500 years ago, people living near the eastern shore of the Mediterranean made the great step leading to our alphabet. They realized that the same sign could be used for the same sound in all cases, so they used a limited number of signs in this manner and these signs made up an alphabet.

A development of their alphabet was used by the Hebrews and later the Phoenicians. The Phoenicians carried their alphabet to the Greeks. The Romans adopted the Greek alphabet with certain changes and additions and handed it down to the people of Western Europe in the Latin alphabet. From this came the alphabet we use today.

WHY DON'T WE ALL SPEAK THE SAME LANGUAGE?

At one time, at the beginning of history, what there was of mankind then probably spoke one language. As time went on, this parent language, or perhaps there were several parent languages, spread and changed.

At first, the parent languages were spoken by small numbers of persons or by scattered small groups. Gradually, some groups increased in numbers and there wasn't enough food for all of them. So some people would form a band to move to a new location.

When these people arrived at a new location and settled down, they would speak almost the same as the people from whom they had parted. Gradually, though, new pronunciations would creep in. The people would begin to say things a little differently and there would be changes in the sounds of words.

Some words that were needed in the old home were no longer needed in the new place and would be dropped. New experiences would require new words to describe them. Ways of making sentences would change. And suppose the people had settled in a place where others were already living? The two languages would blend, and thus both of the old languages would change.

At first, when the speech of the new people had changed only slightly from the original language, it would be called "a dialect." After a longer time, when there were many changes in words, sounds, and grammar, it would be considered a new language.

In just these ways, Spanish, French, and Portuguese developed from Latin; and English, Norwegian, Swedish, Danish, and Dutch grew from an early form of the German language.

The ancestor language, together with all the languages which developed from it, is called "a family" of languages.

HOW DID THE ENGLISH LANGUAGE BEGIN?

Practically all languages spoken on earth today can be traced by scholars back to some common source, that is, an ancestor language which has many descendants. The ancestor language—together with all the languages which have developed from it—is called a "family" of languages.

English is considered a member of the Indo-European family of languages. Other languages belonging to the same family are French, Italian, German, Norwegian, and Greek.

In this Indo-European family of languages there are various branches and English is a member of the "West Teutonic" branch. Actually, English dates from about the middle of the fifth century, when invaders from across the North Sea conquered the native Celts and settled on the island now known as Great Britain.

For the sake of convenience, the history of the English language is divided into three great periods: the old English (or Anglo-Saxon), from about 400 to 1100; Middle English, from 1100 to 1500; and Modern English, from 1500 to the present day.

So the original language spoken in English was Celtic. But the Anglo-Saxons (the Angles, the Jutes, and the Saxons) conquered the island so thoroughly that very few Celtic words were kept in the new language.

The Anglo-Saxons themselves spoke several dialects. Later on, the Norsemen invaded England and they introduced a Scandinavian element into the language. This influence, which was a Germanic language, became a part of the language.

In 1066, William the Conqueror brought over still another influence to the language. He made Norman French the language of his Court. At first, this "Norman" language was spoken only by the upper classes. But gradually its influence spread and a language quite different from the Anglo-Saxon developed. This language became the chief source of modern English.

HOW DID SLANG BEGIN?

Slang is a variation of or addition to standard speech. If you stop to think of it, you'll realize how many forms of slang there are.

For example, slang may be formed by compounding words ("low-down") or by clipping words ("pro," "mike," "pix") or abbreviation ("O.K.," "snafu," "q.t."), or onomatopoeia ("boom," "whiz," "bang"), or borrowing from foreign languages ("pronto," "savvy"), or by analogy ("Park your hat," "He got pickled").

These various forms of slang arise for many reasons and under many different conditions. One of the most common ways is among people who belong to the same group. It might be the same trade, profession, hobby, age, or social position. For example, students have their "lab" and their "gym." Second-hand car dealers have their "creampuffs" (good cars) and their "dogs" (bad cars.) A waitress will say, "Drop two on," when she orders poached eggs on toast.

But the same slang word in one group may mean something else to another group. In the underworld, "cat" doesn't mean the same thing it does in the jazz world. Some social conditions tend to produce slang more easily. If there is excitement, crowding, or people have been suddenly assembled for a particular purpose (as in time of war), then a large number of slang words are formed. "Blitz," "doodlebug," and "walkie-talkie" were slang expressions created in the last world war.

Sometimes one clever person may launch a new slang expression and it is picked up by a lot of people. In many cases, new expressions that were once considered slang have been accepted into the dictionary in time. Among these are "bet," "shabby," "chap," "cab," and "kidnap." Some words have lasted as slang for hundreds of years, as, for example, the word "booze."

WHO INVENTED THE PEN?

The art of writing is one of the most important contributions to the development of civilization. It enables man to record his thoughts and deeds. But there were a great many writing tools before a real pen was first made.

For instance, early man used pointed flints to scratch records and pictures on cave walls. He even dipped his finger in plant juices or the blood of an animal and used it as a pen. Later on, he tried lumps of earth and pieces of chalk. The Chinese painted their letters with a fine camel's hair brush.

Probably the first real pens were made by the Egyptians. They fastened a piece of copper, similar to a modern steel pen point, to the end of a hollow stem. The first letter handwriting was done by the Greeks almost 4,000 years ago. They used a "pen" made of metal, bone, or ivory, and wrote on wax-coated tablets. Later still, a split pen was made from hollow, tubelike grasses which was dipped into a form of ink and used to write on papyrus.

When paper was introduced in the Middle Ages, man learned that the tail or wing feathers of a goose, crow, or swan could be made into a pen. The tip was pointed and split so that the ink could flow down the channel to the paper. It may interest you to know that the word "pen" itself comes from the Latin *penna,* which means "feather"! Even though a feather pen didn't last long, this was man's writing instrument for a thousand years.

Steel pens began to be made in England as early as 1780, but they didn't become popular for another 40 years. The first fountain pens, our modern writing instruments, were made in the United States during the 1880's. The point, or nib, of a fountain pen is usually made of 14-carat gold, and is tipped with osmiridium or iridium. These are smooth, hard metals which enable the pen to write without scratching. Inside, the barrel holds a supply of ink and usually is made of hard rubber or plastic.

The ball-point pen is a 20th century invention. The writing point is a tiny ball of chrome steel which is about one millimetre in diameter. The ball sits in a socket and revolves as it is dragged across the writing surface. It picks up the ink from a reservoir inside.

WHO INVENTED THE PENCIL?

There is a Latin word, *penicillus,* which means "little tail." This word was used to indicate a fine brush, and the word "pencil" originally meant a small, fine pointed brush.

Today, of course, a pencil means something altogether different. Pencils as we know them are less than 200 years old. About 500 years ago, graphite was discovered in a mine in Cumberland, England, and it is believed that some sort of crude pencils may have been made then.

In Nuremberg, Germany, the famous Faber family established its business in 1760 and used pulverized graphite to make a kind of pencil, but they were not very successful. Finally in 1795, a man called N. J. Conte produced pencils made of graphite which had been ground with certain clays, pressed into sticks, and fired in a kiln. This method is the basis for the manufacture of all modern pencils.

As you might have guessed by now, a "lead" pencil doesn't contain lead but a mineral substance called graphite. Graphite, like lead, leaves a mark when drawn across paper. Because of this it is called "black lead," and that's where we get the name "lead pencil."

In manufacturing pencils, dried ground graphite is mixed with clay and water. The more clay, the harder the pencil will be; the more graphite, the softer the pencil. After the mixture reaches a doughy consistency, it passes through a forming press and comes out as a thin, sleek rope. This is straightened out, cut into lengths, dried, and put into huge ovens to bake.

Meanwhile, the pencil case has been prepared. The wood, either red cedar or pine, is shaped in halves and grooved to hold the lead. After the finished leads are inserted in the grooves, the halves of the pencil are glued together. A saw cuts the slats into individual pencils, and a shaping machine gives the surface a smooth finish.

Today, more than 350 different kinds of pencils are made, each for a special use. You can buy black lead pencils in 19 degrees of hardness and intensity, or get them in 72 different colors! There are pencils that write on glass, cloth, cellophane, plastics, and movie film. There are even pencils, used by engineers and in outdoor construction work, that leave a mark that won't fade after years of exposure to any weather!

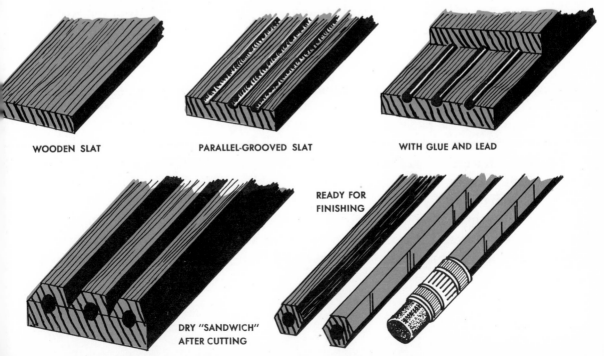

WOODEN SLAT   PARALLEL-GROOVED SLAT   WITH GLUE AND LEAD

READY FOR FINISHING

DRY "SANDWICH" AFTER CUTTING

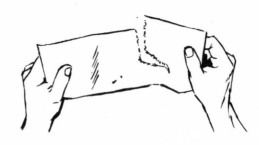

WHO DISCOVERED HOW TO MAKE PAPER?

Take a piece of paper and tear it in both directions. You will notice two things. It tore more easily in one direction than in the other, and hairlike fibers stick out from the edges of the tear.

The first shows that the paper was made by machine; otherwise it would tear the same way in all directions. The second shows that paper is a mat of tiny fibers, felted together. These fibers are the small particles of cellulose that help form the framework of plants.

Man had created a writing material before he invented paper. The ancient Egyptians, about 4000 years ago, took the stems of the papyrus plant and peeled them apart and flattened them. Then they laid them cross-wise and pressed them down to stick them together. When dry, this made a sheet of papyrus and could be written on.

But it wasn't paper. This was invented in China about the year 105, by a man called Ts'ai Lun. He found a way to make paper from the stringy inner bark of the mulberry tree.

The Chinese pounded the bark in water to separate the fibers, then poured the soup mixture onto a tray with a bottom of thin bamboo strips. The water drained away and the soft mat was laid on a smooth surface to dry. Bamboo and old rags were also used. Later on, somebody thought how to improve the paper by brushing starch on it.

Chinese traders traveled far to the west and came to the city of Samarkand in Russia. There they met Arabs who learned their secret and took it to Spain. From there the art of papermaking spread over Europe and to England.

In time, all kinds of improved methods and machines for making paper were discovered. One of the most important, for example, was a machine developed in France in 1798 that could make a continuous sheet or web of paper.

162

WHERE WAS THE FIRST NEWSPAPER PRINTED?

You probably have a bulletin board in your school. When you read what's posted on it, what do you get? You get news! At one time, this was the only form of "newspaper" that existed. News would be gathered from travelers or from government sources, and posted on a bulletin board for everyone to read.

Of course, this isn't really a newspaper, because you can take a newspaper with you to read whenever you like. So for the first newspaper ever printed we must go to China about 1300 years ago. At that time the government printed a paper called *Tching pao,* which meant "News of the Capital." In this way the government was able to keep its people informed of important developments.

There was also a government newspaper in ancient Rome which was distributed among the people. This was called *Acta Diurna,* which meant "Daily Happenings." These two are the first newspapers of which we have any records.

By the 16th century, people were already paying to buy a newspaper! In Venice the government put out a paper called *Notizie Scritte* ("Written News") and people paid one *gazetta* for a copy.

By the 18th century, newspapers were coming out more or less regularly which not only contained news but also opinion. One such paper was started in London as early as 1663 and was called *The Intelligencer.* Most early papers, however, came out only once a week because both communication and production were slow.

The first American newspaper was called *Publick Occurrences,* and was started in Boston, Massachusetts, in 1690. It was quickly stopped by the Governor of the colony. Benjamin Franklin conducted a newspaper, *The Pennsylvania Gazette,* from 1729 to 1765. In 1752, the Colonies had only two newspapers, but at the time of the American Revolution there were 37!

Probably the most influential newspaper ever published, *The London Times,* began in 1785 and is still published today.

WHEN WERE BOOKS FIRST MADE?

Books as we know them didn't appear until the Middle Ages. The nearest thing to them were rolls of papyrus. Sheets of papyrus were glued together to form long rolls. The Romans called them *volumen,* from which we get our word "volume."

About the middle of the fifth century, parchment and vellum had replaced papyrus. Parchment is made from the skins of sheep and goats and vellum is made from calfskin. Sheets of this material, with writing on one side, were cut to uniform size and bound together at one side with leather tongs. So they were "books" in a way.

But it was in the Middle Ages that books were first made that resemble our printed books of today. Four pieces of vellum were folded in such a way so that each piece formed two leaves. These pieces were then placed inside one another so that there was a group of eight leaves, which is called "a section."

These sections were sent to a scribe to write the book. He took them apart and wrote a single page at a time. Vellum was thick enough so there could be writing on both sides.

The next step was to send the finished sections that made up the book to the binder. He sewed the sections through the back fold with cords.

Wooden covers were made and the ends were laced through holes in the boards to bind together the sections and the covers. Then a large piece of leather was glued over the back of the sections and the wooden sides. Other steps were taken to decorate and preserve these books, but these were the first books that resemble those we have today.

Most of the medieval books were Bibles, sermons, and other religious books. Next came books of law, medicine, natural history, and later came a few chronicles and romances. Most books of the Middle Ages are in Latin.

From the Gutenberg Bible.

WHO INVENTED CARTOONS?

You know that between the way something started years ago, and the way it is today, there may be quite a difference! There is no better example of this than the cartoon.

The word "cartoon" was originally used by painters during the period of the Italian Renaissance. And in fact, it is still used today by artists. What they are referring to, however, is the first sketch in actual size of any work of art which covers a large area, such as a mural, a tapestry, or a stained-glass window.

When newspapers and magazines began to use drawings to illustrate news and editorial opinion and to provide amusement, these drawings also came to be called "cartoons"!

In the days before newspapers, famous caricaturists like Hogarth, Goya, Daumier, and Rowlandson made series of drawings on a single theme. These drawings often pictured the adventures of one character. They were the ancestors of present-day cartoons and comic strips.

In the 19th and early 20th century there were a number of magazines which specialized in cartoons—*Charivari* in Paris, *Punch* in London, and

Life and *Judge* in the United States. When most newspapers and magazines in the United States began to include cartoons as regular features, the humorous magazines lost their appeal and many of them stopped appearing.

The first comic strips appeared in the early 1900's. Richard Outcault, the artist who created *Buster Brown,* published this comic strip in 1902. It was so popular that children all over the country wanted to dress in "Buster Brown" clothes.

Another of the early comic strips was *Bringing Up Father.* This came out in 1912. It has since been translated into 27 different languages, and published in 71 countries!

WHO WROTE THE FIRST ENGLISH DICTIONARY?

Do you know what the word "dictionary" means? It comes from the Latin *dictionarius,* meaning "a collection of words." This word was first used in this way about the year 1225 by an English scholar called John Garland, as the title for a manuscript of Latin words to be learned by heart.

In fact, it wasn't for another 300 years that any English words appeared in any dictionary. Most of the "dictionaries" that had been written were really to help people study Latin. They had all sorts of colorful names, such as *Storehouse for the Little Ones* and *Garden of Words.*

Finally in 1552, the first real English dictionary appeared. It was compiled by a man called Richard Huloet and had this very long title: *Abcedarium Anglico-Latinum pro Tyrunculis.* As you can see, the name of this book was still in Latin. But what made this book unusual was that each word was first given in English, then defined in English, and then came the Latin translation. Because it listed English words first and gave the English definitions, it can be regarded as an English dictionary, the first ever printed.

The *Abcedarium* contained 26,000 words and was very popular, but it was quite expensive. As a result, many other works soon came out that were smaller in scope and intended for poorer people.

In those days, the compilers of the dictionaries made no attempt to include all the words; they were satisfied to define just the hard words. The first book with the title *The English Dictionairie* appeared in 1623, and was compiled by Henry Cockeram.

166

In the United States, Noah Webster began his great dictionary in 1807 and it was finally published in 1828. It contained 12,000 words and 40,000 definitions that had never appeared in any similar list before. Webster favored simpler spelling, and because of this Americans write "color," "labor," and "honor" instead of "colour," "labour," and "honour."

WHO WROTE THE FIRST ENCYCLOPAEDIA?

You go to an encyclopaedia to get information. That means you expect it to contain the facts on all important subjects. The word "encyclopaedia" began as a Greek word and means "instruction in the whole circle." It was first used in English by Sir Thomas Elyot in 1538 who said it was "the ernynge whiche comprehendth all lyberall science and studies."

Today, encyclopaedias are generally arranged alphabetically, so that it's easy to look something up. But in early times they were arranged in any way the author liked. For example, one author of an encyclopaedia in the Middle Ages began with a discussion of God and angels, and ended with descriptions of scents, colors, and a list of 36 kinds of eggs!

The oldest encyclopaedia in existence that covers many subjects was written by a Roman called Pliny. It was called *Natural History* and it was written in the 1st century A.D. It had 37 volumes and contained more than 20,000 items. Pliny quoted from more than 450 authors. This book was considered so valuable that there were 43 editions of it up to 1536!

The largest encyclopaedia ever written was the third Chinese encyclopaedia, which was ordered put together by a Chinese emperor who died in 1721. The set contained 5,020 volumes! The first encyclopaedia which had the subjects arranged in alphabetical order was written by an English Clergyman, John Harris, and was published in 1704. It was called *Universal English Dictionary of Arts and Sciences.*

One of the greatest efforts to put together an encyclopaedia was made by the French in the 18th century. It was called the *Encyclopedie* and was begun in 1743. What made it unusual was that many of the most famous Frenchmen of the time wrote articles for it, including Voltaire, Rousseau, and Diderot.

The *Encyclopaedia Britannica or Dictionary of Arts and Sciences* was started in Scotland in 1768. It has been published in the United States since 1911.

HOW DID OUR SYSTEM OF COUNTING BEGIN?

It seems very natural to you that if you have two pennies and you add two pennies to them, you have four pennies. But did you know it may have taken man millions of years to be able to think this way? In fact, one of the most difficult things to teach children is the concept of numbers.

In ancient times, when a man wanted to tell how many animals he owned, he had no system of numbers to use. What he did was put a stone or pebble into a bag for each animal. The more animals, the more stones he had. Which may explain why our word "calculate" comes from the Latin word *calculus* which means "stone"!

Later on, man used tally marks to count. He would just scratch a line or tally mark for each object he wanted to count, but he had no word to tell the number.

The next step in the development of the number system was probably the use of fingers. And again we have a word that goes back to this. The word "digit" comes from the Latin word *digitus,* which means "finger"! And since we have 10 fingers, this led to the general use of "10" in systems of numbers.

But in ancient times there was no single number system used all over the world. Some number systems were based on 12, others were based on 60, others on 20, and still others on 2, 5, and 8. The system invented by the Romans about 2,000 years ago was widely used by the people of Europe until about the 16th century. In fact, we still use it on clocks and to show chapters in books. But it was a very complicated system.

The number system we use today was invented by the Hindus in India thousands of years ago and was brought to Europe about the year 900 by Arab traders. In this system all numbers are written with the nine digits 1, 2, 3, 4, 5, 6, 7, 8, 9 to show how many, and the zero. It is a decimal system, that is, it is built on the base 10.

WHERE WAS GOLD FIRST MINED?

Gold is so rare and precious that you would imagine man didn't discover it until quite recently in his history. But the opposite is true! Gold was one of the first metals known to man.

We will never know when man first found it and began to desire it, since it was long before history was written down. But since gold is found in the free state, that is, it is not always combined with other metals or rocks, it was the first metal that man knew.

The first evidence we have of mining work to obtain gold comes from the Egyptians. They were mining gold more than 5,000 years ago! We also have records to show that the ancient Assyrians were conquering their neighbors to obtain gold about 4,500 years ago!

The Greek and Roman kings also loved gold. They obtained as much gold as possible by stealing from countries which they had conquered and by using slaves to dig in the mines. So you see, the mining of gold goes back to the very beginnings of man.

In the New World, gold must have been mined from very ancient times, too, because when the Spaniards came to Mexico, they found that the Aztecs had huge quantities of gold in their cities. In Peru, South America, the ancient Incas also had collected gold for hundreds of years before the white man came.

The discovery of gold anywhere in the world has always caused a rush of adventurous people to the spot in search of the yellow metal. In the year 1848, a man named John Sutter was building a sawmill in California. James Marshall, who was helping him, noticed some flakes of yellow metal mixed with the gravel from the stream. Tests showed these flakes to be gold.

The news of this discovery spread rapidly over the whole world and the "Gold Rush of '49" was on. It was the large number of settlers who came to California in 1849 that started the development of the Pacific Coast region of the United States.

ALASKAN FISH HOOK MONEY

CHINESE SPEAR MONEY

AFRICAN THROW-ING KNIFE MONEY

ZULU RING

YAP STONE MONEY

WHAT MAKES MONEY VALUABLE?

The idea of having such a thing as money is one of the most fascinating ever developed by man. But many people don't know where this idea came from, or why money is valuable.

Thousands of years ago, money was not used. Instead, man had the "barter" system. This meant that if a man wanted something he didn't happen to make or raise himself, he had to find someone who had this article. Then he had to offer him something in exchange. And if the man didn't like what he offered in exchange, he couldn't get his article!

In time, certain things came to be used as money because practically everyone would take these things in exchange. For example, cows, tobacco, grains, skins, salt, and beads were all used as money among people who were always ready to accept them.

Eventually, all these varieties of money were replaced by pieces of metal, especially gold and silver. Later on, coins were made of a certain purity and weight, and these represented certain amounts of various objects. So many coins represented a cow, or 20 kilograms of tobacco, and so on.

Today, of course, we have bills and coins issued by the Government, and everybody accepts and uses this money. What makes the money valuable, what use does it have for us? There are four chief things that money does for you.

First, it makes possible exchange and trade. Suppose you want a bicycle. You're willing to work for it by mowing lawns. But the person for whom you mow the lawn has no bicycles. He pays you with money and you take this to the bicycle shop and buy your bicycle. Money made it possible to exchange your work for something you wanted.

Second, money is a "yardstick of value." This means money may be used to measure and compare the values of various things. You're willing to mow the lawn for an hour for £1.50. A bicycle costs £50. You now have an idea of the value of a bicycle in terms of your work.

Third, money is a "storehouse of value." You can't store up your crop of tomatoes, because they're perishable. But if you sell them you can store up the money for future use.

Fourth, money serves as a "standard for future payments." You pay £10 down on the bicyle and promise to pay more later. You will not pay in eggs or tomatoes or cricket balls. You and the bicycle shop owner have agreed on exactly what you will pay later. You use money as a form in which later payments can be made.

 ROMAN SILVER
DENARIUS
200 B.C.—A.D. 250

 ROMAN GOLD
AUREUS
100 B.C.—A.D. 300

 ROMAN GOLD
SOLIDUS
A.D. 300—1200

HOW DID COINS GET THEIR NAMES?

In the world of coins and money there are many fascinating stories of how things came to get their names. Let's consider just a few of them in this column.

We'll start with the word "money" itself. In ancient Roman times, Juno was the goddess of warning. The Romans were so grateful to her for warning them of important dangers, that they put their mint in her temple and made her guardian of the finances. They called her Juno Moneta. "Moneta" came from the Latin word *moneo,* meaning "to warn." Our word "money" is derived from this.

The word "coin" comes from the Latin *cuneus,* which means "wedge." This is because the dies that made pieces of money looked like wedges.

The "dollar" goes back to the days when money was being coined in

Bohemia, where there were silver mines. The mint was located in a place called Joachimsthal, so the coins were called *Joachimsthaler*. In time this became *thaler* and finally "dollar."

The "dime" comes originally from the Latin word *decimus*, which means "tenth."

The "cent" comes directly from the French word *cent*, which means "one hundred," and the Latin *centum*. The idea was that one hundred cents make a dollar.

The English "pound" comes from the Latin *pondo*, which means "pound" as a weight. Originally the full expression was *libra pondo*, or "a pound by weight." By the way, that's where we get our abbreviation for a pound—lb.

The Spanish *peso* and Italian *lira* also refer to certain weights.

The French *franc* came from the Latin words *Francorum Rex*, for "King of the Franks," which appeared on their first coins. Peru has a coin called the *sol*. This is the Spanish name for the sun. As you know, the Incas of Peru worshipped the sun long ago!

The words crown, sovereign, *krone, kroon, krona,* and *corona,* all used as names of coins in different countries, show that some crown authority first gave permission to make them. In Panama, the *balboa* is named in honor of the great explorer, and Venezuela has the *bolivar* after its national hero.

HOW DID WE GET OUR SYSTEM OF MEASUREMENT?

Every country in the world has some way of measuring weight, volume, and quantity. This is necessary in order to carry on trade or any form of exchange. But the system of weight and measurement in one country is not always the same as that in another

Most of the measures used in the United States came from England and are called "the English system of measures". However, the United States is now practically the only country that uses this system today.

The units of measurement in this system have come down to us from ancient times. Most of them grew out of simple, practical ways of measuring. For instance, when people in ancient Rome wanted to measure length, they used the length of a man's foot as a standard. The width of a finger, or the length of the index finger to the first joint, was the origin of the inch!

To measure a yard, people used to take the length of a man's arm. In Rome the length of a thousand paces (a pace was a double step) was used for long distances and became a mile. Of course, this was not a very exact way of measuring. In fact, at one time in the Roman Empire there were 200 different lengths for the foot! And in the American Colonies in Colonial times, the units of measurement were different from colony to colony.

In modern times, it is very important that units of measurement be the same everywhere. So Congress was given the right to fix the standards of weights and measures, and in Washington, D.C., the Bureau of Standards keeps the standard units of measure. For instance, there is a platinum bar, very carefully guarded, which is the standard for measuring length. The correctness of all other measuring units can be checked by comparing them with the standard units in Washington. In Britain similar standards are to be seen at Greenwich Observatory near London.

An international system of weights and measures is now being adopted, which is called the metric system. This was worked out in France in 1789, and is used by most countries today. The metric system is based on the meter, which is 39.37 inches. The metric system is based on 10, so each unit of length is 10 times as large as the next smaller unit.

WHO DISCOVERED HOW TO WEIGH THINGS?

If you tried to think of all the things that have to be weighed in the course of a day in your town alone, you'd probably never be able to list them all! In our modern life, weighing is not only important to business (as in stores and in factories), but it plays a vital part in scientific work, too.

Who were the first people to discover how to weigh things? We may never know the exact answer to this, but as far as history is concerned, it was the Egyptians. About 7,000 years ago the Egyptians had developed the simplest form of weighing scale. This is the balance. Weighing is done by balancing two loads from opposite ends of a horizontal bar.

This is probably what the first weighing machine looked like: There was an upright beam. A bar was balanced from this beam by a cord through the center. At either end of the bar were two pans hanging from cords. When empty, this balance hung straight horizontally. Then a certain object with a known weight, that is, a weight that everybody knew and agreed upon, was put in one pan, and the object to be weighed was put in the other pan.

This was the best weighing machine known to man for about 5,000 years! Then, about the time of Christ, the Romans made an improvement in it. They used a pin through the center of the beam to act as the central bearing for the horizontal bar. The Romans also created "the steelyard."

This was a beam usually hung from a hook, with two unequal arms or levers. The article to be weighed is hung from the short arm. Then a weight is moved along the longer arm until a balance is reached. The markings on the long arm show the weight. These two simple devices are the basis on which most modern scales are built.

Today, of course, we have scales that can weigh things never imagined possible before. For example, there are scales that can weigh a human hair, or the writing on a piece of paper! And there are scales that can weigh a whole loaded freight car!

In scientific work, where scales have to be very exact, they know that humidity, vibration, magnetic influences, all sorts of forces, can upset the scales. Yet they can weigh accurately to one part in 100,000,000!

WHERE WERE THE FIRST SCHOOLS?

A school is a place where people, usually children, are brought together to be taught. You'll notice that there are two important points in this definition: There is a definite place, and more than one child is taught at a time.

Our modern schools are derived from the ancient Greek and Roman schools. But even in Greece, there was a period where there were only professional teachers to whom boys were brought as single pupils, and there was no teaching in classes.

Then a little later, the Grecian orators and philosophers who had been teaching the single pupils brought to them, or who traveled about to do their teaching, settled down in fixed places and began to establish something more like schools. Plato, the great Greek philosopher, was the first to give a regular educational course extending over three or four years in a fixed place, which was called "the Academy."

This "school" was held in the gymnasium, which was originally a parade or practice ground for the militia. Later on, Aristotle set up a school of his own in the Lyceum, which was another public gymnasium. Now, here is a curious thing: The German term for a school is *gymnasium,* the French term is *lycée,* and the Scotch term is "academy"—all coming from Plato's and Aristotle's institutions!

Neither of these two "schools," however, were like our modern schools. They were chiefly places for discussions and sometimes courses of lectures. About the year 250, the Greeks realized that grammar was a subject that had to be taught to all young people, and "the grammar school" was established. And this is how we got our name "grammar school" for our secondary schools.

Later on, the Romans, who were influenced by the Greeks, set up schools that were very much like our modern schools. And believe it or not, it was just as miserable to go to a Roman school as it is to any school you know! Boys had to get up early, learn a great deal of grammar, a foreign language, and above all, behave properly. If they didn't, they were flogged!

HOW DID LIBRARIES BEGIN?

The first real libraries we know of existed about 8,000 years ago!

The Mesopotamians were a people who wrote on wet clay tablets with a wedge-shaped stick called "a cuneus." Hence their writing is known as "cuneiform." The tablets were baked and the rarest of them placed in clay envelopes for safekeeping. Thousands of these tablets, stored in palaces and temples and arranged in subject order, have been found. Such palace collections were the first real libraries.

The libraries in early Egypt were in the temples and were under the care of priests. The Egyptians wrote on sheets of papyrus, which were then wound in a long roll around a knobbed stick and placed in chests or on shelves.

The most famous library of ancient times was the library in Alexandria, established about 300 B.C. It had as many as 700,000 papyrus rolls and was completely catalogued and classified under 120 classes.

It was the Romans who first had the idea of establishing public libraries.

Julius Caesar had a plan for a system of public libraries, and after him the public library was a Roman institution. Wealthy citizens in Rome took an interest in founding libraries for the people and in making large collections for themselves. Twenty-eight public libraries existed in Rome in the fourth century!

When the Christian Era began, libraries became part of churches and monasteries. The monks read and copied books, and most of the libraries that existed were due to their efforts.

When the great cathedrals were built toward the end of the Dark Ages, small libraries were established in the cathedrals. Universities, too, began to collect books. The Universities of Paris, France, Heidelberg, and Florence had collections of "chained" books. Books were so difficult to make that to protect them they were chained.

By 1400, the University of Oxford began to organize its library. This library, which is called the Bodleian, is today the biggest university library in the world.

Public libraries as they are known today are not more than 100 years old. English leaders urged public support of libraries early in the 19th century. Finally, in 1850, the English Parliament passed an act permitting the establishment of public libraries and they have grown and developed everywhere since that time.

WHEN DID VOTING ORIGINATE?

The right to vote in political elections is called "suffrage." It includes voting on people for public office and on laws presented to the people for approval.

In the history of man, suffrage has usually been exercised by favored groups or individuals. The right of every individual to an equal vote in the government in which he lives, which would be complete democracy, hardly exists even today. At all times there have been certain restrictions on voting. Some have been wise, some wicked. But in different places and at different times these restrictions have included circumstances of birth, age, race, religion, sex, education, social or economic position, ownership of property, and payment of taxes.

With the beginnings of democracy in ancient Greece and Rome, there was a primitive form of suffrage. In the general assemblies of Athens, for example, voting was done by a show of hands when public matters were concerned. A secret ballot was held when individuals were involved, as when the citizens voted to send away some public man who had fallen into disfavor. But voting was limited to the free citizens. Slaves and foreigners were excluded, and there was no way a foreigner could become a citizen.

During the late Middle Ages, the burghers or freemen in the big cities could elect their own mayors. But very severe property qualifications limited the voting. During the Renaissance, the aristocracy ruled and the people had no suffrage.

It was when the business class arose in Europe, and trade and industry began to expand, that the suffrage was first extended considerably. Instead of qualifications of birth, property qualifications were set up for voting. Not even the American and French Revolutions could end the idea that only certain groups or classes should have the right to vote.

Every British subject, aged 18 or over, is entitled to vote, with the exception of peers, lunatics and criminals. Until 1832, few people in Britain had the right to vote. No women could vote until 1918, when those of 30 and over were given the vote. In 1928 universal suffrage was introduced.

The Reform Act of 1832 abolished the old freehold tenure vote and gave the right to vote to male holders of land (either landlords or tenants) of the value of £10.

In 1867 the second Reform Act gave the vote to most artisans and town workers. It was not until 1884 that the right to vote was extended to agricultural workers and every man (except those classes referred to above) was entitled to vote.

In the early 1800's there were many so-called "nomination boroughs" where the owner of the land had the right to nominate a member of parliament. In some cases, e.g. Old Sarum, in Wiltshire, there were no inhabitants at all; in others, such as Dunwich in Suffolk, the land has disappeared beneath the sea. Before 1832 only a small proportion of M.P.s were elected on the free vote of the electorate.

Today every candidate has to deposit £150 and forfeits this if he fails to poll one-eighth of the total votes cast. Until 1949 a man who lived in one parliamentary area and had business premises in another was entitled to vote in both constituencies. Graduates of certain universities could vote in their own constituencies and also for the candidate representing their university.

WHEN WERE THE FIRST POLICE ORGANIZED?

The old-fashioned policeman shown in the picture above belonged to one of the many independent police forces in America. In the U.S.A. there are over 40,000 separate units, most of whose authority is limited to a particular area or type of crime. In France, the Minister of the Interior directly controls a police force having authority throughout France, and indirectly controls municipal police.

Police date back to the very earliest history of man. The leader or ruler of a tribe or clan in primitive times depended upon his warriors to keep peace among the people and enforce rules of conduct. The pharaohs of ancient Egypt did the same thing—used their soldiers as police.

About the time of the birth of Christ, Caesar Augustus formed a special police force for the city of Rome, and this lasted for about 350 years. But the job of this police force was still to carry out the imperial orders.

Sometime between the years A.D. 700 and 800, a new idea arose regarding a police force. Instead of carrying out the king's orders against the people, it was felt a police force should enforce the law and protect the people! It was this idea which influenced the development of the police force in England, and later in the United States.

The English developed a system of "watch" and "ward." The watch was a night guard and the ward a day guard for the local area. The colonists brought this system to the United States. They had the night watch under constables, with all able-bodied men over 16 serving without pay. Most cities and towns used this system well into the 1800's.

In London the head of the Metropolitan Police Force is the Commissioner, who is responsible to the Home Secretary, i.e. the force is subject to direct government control. Outside London, nearly every county and county borough has its own police force, responsible to the local authority. But although in some ways independent, the provincial police forces are in other respects subject to central control.

WHAT IS THE F.B.I.?

The F.B.I. is one of the best-known and most "glamorous" departments of the Federal Government. Its full name is the Federal Bureau of Investigation, and it was founded in 1908 as a bureau within the United States Department of Justice.

The F.B.I. has authority to investigate violations of Federal laws and matters in which the United States is, or may be, a party in interest. In 1924, the Identification Division of the F.B.I. was created. It started with a library of 810,188 fingerprint records. Today, the F.B.I. has the fingerprint cards of more than 100,000,000 people!

The headquarters of the F.B.I. are in Washington, D. C., and it has 52 field offices throughout the United States and its possessions. Along with its own responsibilities, the F.B.I. is a service organization for local law enforcement agencies. Its facilities are available for the assistance of municipal, county, and state police departments.

The Identification Division serves as the central clearing house for fingerprints and criminal data. When a person is arrested and his fingerprints are sent to the F.B.I., it can be determined in less than five minutes whether he has a previous criminal record. A copy of this record is sent to the interested law enforcement agency within 36 hours after the card is received in Washington.

The facilities of the F.B.I. laboratory are likewise available to all law enforcement agencies. Provided with the most modern equipment, its scientists are daily making examinations of documents, blood, hair, soil, and

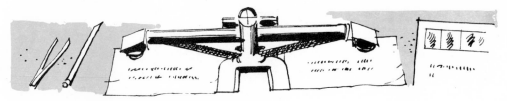

One of the special microscopes used by the F.B.I.
to examine and identify handwriting and fingerprints.

other types of matter. When evidence in a local case has been examined, F.B.I. experts will testify concerning their findings in the state court.

In June, 1939, the President of the United States selected the F.B.I. as the agency responsible for the investigation of espionage, sabotage, and other national defense matters. During the last war, the F.B.I. maintained the internal security of the nation and broke up various enemy spy rings.

WHAT IS SCOTLAND YARD?

Anyone who reads detective stories, goes to the cinema or watches television is sure to have heard of Scotland Yard. When you say the words "Scotland Yard" you somehow think of a very efficient, uniformed or plain-clothed policeman participating in the ceaseless war against crime.

Scotland Yard is the headquarters of the Metropolitan Police Force, the largest of its kind in Great Britain. The force consists of about 16,000 men who are responsible for an area of about 735 square miles and a population of about 8,500,000, living in an area of about 15 miles radius from Charing Cross.

Scotland Yard performs many services for the vast metropolitan area besides supplying it with policemen and detectives. It is in charge of London's traffic, it licences and controls taxis and their drivers and control all buses and their drivers. It also gets involved in civil defence, buildings, lost property and the registration of aliens. It maintains criminal records for the entire country, but does not intervene in criminal cases outside London unless expressly asked to do so by the provincial police forces.

The history of Scotland Yard is an interesting one. About a thousand years ago, King Edgar of England gave King Kenneth of Scotland a piece of ground near Westminster Palace in London. He required that King Kenneth build a residence there and visit it each year to pay homage for the kingdom of Scotland.

King Kenneth built a palace there, and lived in it whenever he came to England. It remained the property of the Scottish kings and came to be known to the people of London as "Scotland."

When Queen Elizabeth died in 1603 and James VI of Scotland became King of England and Scotland as James I, this palace no longer had a purpose. So it was divided into two yards, known as "Great Scotland Yard" and "Middle Scotland Yard," and was used for government buildings.

WHEN DID BANKS ORIGINATE?

Today your bank performs so many services that you might forget that it really has only two main purposes. The first is to accept deposits from people and hold that money until the person wants it; the second is to make loans to people who are willing to pay interest on them.

Because a bank charges interest on money, there was a time when banking was a business that people didn't approve of. The taking of interest was considered immoral, and some countries forbade their citizens from engaging in banking.

Nevertheless, banking is as old as history. In ancient Babylon, Egypt, and Greece, banking was carried on. In fact, the temples usually served as the places to deposit money. In Rome, in the year 210 B.C., an ordinance was issued that set aside a place in the Forum for money-changers.

The word "bank," by the way, comes to us from the Italian. In the Middle Ages the money-changers of Italy did their business in the street on a bench, and the Italian word for bench is *banco,* from which we get our word "bank."

Modern banking probably began in Venice in 1587 when the Banco di Rialto was established. It accepted deposits and permitted the depositors to write checks against their money. In 1619, the Banco del Giro took over this bank and gave receipts for gold or silver coins deposited. These receipts were used as money. The Bank of Amsterdam, organized in 1609, also gave receipts which were used as "bank money."

In England the goldsmiths were the bankers of the country until 1694 when the Bank of England was incorporated. It had a monopoly on public banking in England until 1825.

The first regular bank in the United States was the Bank of North America in Philadelphia, chartered by Congress in 1782.

HOW DID PRISONS ORIGINATE?

We usually think of a prison as a place where men and women are locked up for breaking the law. But this is a very recent development in the history of prisons.

Centuries ago, nobles and men of importance were often captured and imprisoned for revenge or until they were ransomed. It was not until the 19th century that prisons began to be used for the punishment or correction of law violators.

Prisons before that time were places where those accused of breaking the law were held until trial. After the prisoners were tried, the sentence of the court was immediately carried out. They were not sentenced to serve a term in prison. Those who had been declared guilty were put to death, whipped, or given other forms of bodily punishment, or fined.

Gradually men began to see that this cruel treatment did not prevent crime. The result was that imprisonment began to be used as a substitute for the death penalty and bodily punishment.

In England and in some of the European countries, places called "workhouses" or "houses of correction" were established after about 1550. Those places were used to imprison beggars, vagabonds, family deserters, debtors, and those guilty of minor offenses.

The workhouses were then right at hand for use as prisons for keeping more serious offenders. These workhouses were not safe enough for keeping long-term prisoners, and thus prisons began to be built which furnished greater security.

Most of these prisons were unfit places to keep human beings. They were dirty, badly lighted, and cold. Food was bad and the treatment was harsh. Prisoners were thrown together, whether they were young or old, first offenders or hardened criminals. There was no work or training program. The inmates sat idle.

In the late 18th century, men began to urge that the prisons be improved and better methods of caring for prisoners be developed. Prisons changed considerably with time, and today more and more people are coming to believe that a prison should help bring about the reformation of the inmate. There are all kinds of extensive programs to train them, as well as medical and psychological help, recreational activity, and schooling.

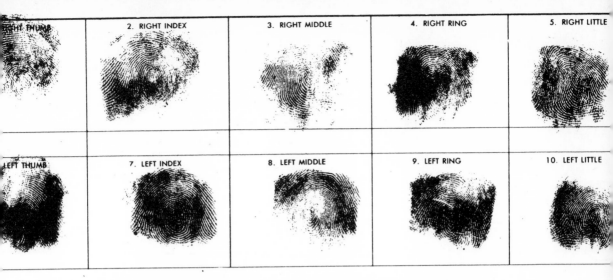

| 2. RIGHT INDEX | 3. RIGHT MIDDLE | 4. RIGHT RING | 5. RIGHT LITTLE |
| 7. LEFT INDEX | 8. LEFT MIDDLE | 9. LEFT RING | 10. LEFT LITTLE |

HOW DID FINGERPRINTING START?

Man has known for a long time that the ridges of his fingertips formed certain patterns. In fact, the Chinese have used fingerprints for hundreds of years in various forms and for various purposes.

But the value of fingerprints in detecting criminals was realized by science only in quite recent years. The first man to suggest that fingerprints be used to identify criminals was Dr. Henry Faulds of England in 1880. In 1892, Sir Francis Galton, a noted English scientist, scientifically established the fact that no two fingerprints were alike. He was the first one to set up a collection of fingerprint records.

The British Government became interested in his theories and ordered a commission to study the idea of using a fingerprint system in the identification of criminals. One of the members of this commission, Sir Edward Henry, later became head of Scotland Yard.

Sir Henry devised a system of classifying and filing fingerprints. You can understand that without such a system it would take very long to match up two sets of fingerprints, and in crime detection, speed is often very important.

According to Sir Henry's system, all finger impressions are divided into the following types of patterns: loops, central pocket loops, double loops, arches, tented arches, whorls, and accidentals. By counting the ridges between the fixed points in the pattern, it is possible to classify each of the 10 fingers into a definite group. The 10 fingers are then considered as a unit to obtain the complete classification. With this system, fingerprints are filed in a sequence, without reference to name, description, or crime speciality of the individual. An office can contain millions of prints, and yet identification can be established in a few minutes!

The FBI file of more than 100,000,000 fingerprint cards include fingerprints from many persons who want some means of identification in case of sickness. It also includes fingerprints of those in the Armed Services and Government employees.

Today, all aliens have to be fingerprinted, and many industries vital to the national defense require fingerprinting of their employees.

HOW DID MEDICINE BEGIN?

Medicine is the treating of disease. Now, you yourself know that there are many ways to treat disease. If someone in your family gets sick, you could call a doctor and he would apply all his knowledge and skill. He would treat the disease scientifically. But you might instead depend on some "remedy" your grandmother knew, or try to cure the person by saying some "magic" words. You would then be treating the disease unscientifically.

The history of medicine includes the prescientific stage, before it was a science, and the time when it became a science. The medicine of primitive peoples had all kinds of strange explanations of disease. And in treating disease, primitive medicine depended on magic or on anything that seemed to work. But surprisingly enough, medicine among primitive people included application of heat and cold, bloodletting, massage, the use of herbs.

Ancient Egyptian medicine, which was the best-known medicine before the scientific, depended chiefly on magic. It used all kinds of ointments and potions. Among the "drugs" it used were honey, salt, cedar oil, the brain, liver, heart, and blood of various animals. Sometimes this prescientific medicine seemed to work, sometimes it didn't.

But it wasn't until the time of the Greeks that scientific medicine began. More than two thousand years ago, a man called Hippocrates put together a collection of medical books, "The Hippocratic Collection." It was the beginning of scientific medicine because it depended on close observation of patients for learning about diseases.

In these books there were records of actual cases and what had happened to the patients. For the first time, instead of depending on some magic formula, treatment was given as the result of studying the patient and the disease and applying past experience. In this way modern medicine was born.

WHEN DID PEOPLE START CUTTING THEIR HAIR?

The hair is actually a development of the horn layer of the skin. Like our nails, it doesn't hurt us to cut it because these horn cells contain no nerves. Because the hair is such an important part of our appearance and because it is so easy to cut and arrange in almost any fashion, men and women have been "doing things" with their hair since the beginning of time.

No one can say who first thought of cutting the hair or arranging it in a special way. We know that women have had combs from the very earliest times, thousands of years ago! Men and women have also curled their hair since ancient times.

But the custom of long hair for women and short hair for men is more modern. During the Middle Ages men wore their hair long, curled it, even wore it with ribbons! If the hair wasn't long enough, they wore false hair bought from country people.

Henry VIII of England began the style of short hair for men. He ordered all men to wear their hair short but allowed them to grow beards and curl their moustaches. When James I became King, long hair for men reappeared, including wigs.

About the middle of the 17th century, there were two camps in England when it came to hair: those who believed in short hair and long beards for men, and those who believed in short beards and long hair. For the next hundred years the custom changed back and forth. Finally, about 1800, the custom became definitely established for men to wear their hair short.

Women have always tended to wear long hair, but bobbing the hair was a fad at the Court of Louis XIV! Today, of course, women wear their hair short not only because it is fashionable, but because it is simpler than having to bother with pins and combs and elaborate coifs.

Barbers and barber shops are a fairly recent development, too. In England, barbers were first incorporated as a craft in 1461, and in France, during the reign of Louis XIV.

WHY DO BARBER SHOPS HAVE BARBER POLES?

Have you ever wondered why barbers use a red-and-white pole as a sign of their profession? What has a barber pole to do with cutting hair?

The truth is it has nothing to do with a barber's work today. But a long time ago barbers used to perform certain minor operations on people. One of the most common of these operations was known as "bleeding." This meant that the patient would allow some blood to be taken out of his arm, and it was believed that when this "bad blood" left the body the patient would become well.

In order to perform the operation, the barber would ask the patient to hold on to a pole tightly. Every barber always had a pole and bandages ready in his shop. When the pole was not being used, the bandages were fastened to it and it was placed in the doorway of the shop as a sign to people that the barber was a good "bleeder."

As time went on, people considered it unsanitary to use the pole and bandages that stood in the doorway, so the barber painted stripes around a special pole for his advertising sign. The red stripes were meant to remind them of the blood-soaked bandages.

These poles became so identified with barbers that the custom of having one outside a barber shop has lasted right down to this day!

The beginning of tipping for work done goes back to barbers, too. A patient would pay the barber whatever he could afford, or whatever he thought the operation was worth. This method of paying spread throughout England, and soon little boxes appeared in places like inns and taverns into which people would drop money as payment for services. To make people drop in as much money as possible, these boxes had the words "To Insure Promptness" above them. Our word "tip" comes from the initials of these three words!

WHEN WERE MIRRORS FIRST USED?

Have you ever looked into a quiet pool of water and seen the reflection of the sky and trees in it? You were actually looking into a mirror! A mirror is only a smooth surface that reflects light and forms an image.

It's very important that the surface be smooth. The smoother it is, the better the reflection. For example, if a breeze springs up and ruffles the surface of that pond, it will still reflect light, but no image can be seen.

In ancient times, mirrors were made of polished metal. A modern mirror is usually a polished sheet of glass with silver on the back. But the glass is not the mirror. The surface that reflects the light and the image is the silver. All the glass does is protect the soft silver from scratches and tarnish.

We will never know when ancient man first discovered the idea of the mirror. He, too, must have looked into ponds of still water and seen his image. And perhaps quite by accident he noticed that polished bits of metal reflected his image, too. At one point or another (for all we know, inspired by women!) he deliberately took pieces of metal and shaped and polished them to make mirrors.

By the time we reached the civilization of ancient Greece, Egypt, and Rome, mirrors were accepted by the people as very useful articles. In fact, people then already had small mirrors they could carry about with them. They were made of round pieces of metal—brass, bronze, silver, or gold.

But just as a mirror mystifies a baby, so ancient people were mystified by mirrors. They didn't understand how they worked, so they thought mirrors had magic powers. In fact, they thought that the image they saw in a mirror was their spirit. That's why the superstition about breaking a mirror arose. It was bad luck because it was supposed to harm your spirit.

The first people to learn how to make mirrors of glass backed with mercury and tin were the Venetians. About the year 1300 they began to produce such mirrors and in a very short time they replaced the metal ones that had been used for thousands of years.

WHEN WAS SOAP FIRST MADE?

You might think that something as useful and necessary as soap had been one of the first inventions of man. But soap is quite a modern thing in man's history. It only goes back about 2,000 years.

What ancient peoples used to do was to anoint their bodies with olive oil. They also used the juices and ashes of various plants to clean themselves. But by the time of Pliny (a Roman writer of the first century A.D.) we already have a reference to two kinds of soap, soft and hard. He describes it as an invention for brightening up the hair and gives the Gauls credit for inventing it.

By the way, in the ruins of Pompeii, there was found buried an establishment for turning out soap that very much resembles the soap of today! And yet, just one hundred years ago, nearly all the soap used was made at home!

Soap is made by boiling fats and oils with an alkali. In the great soap factories, the fats and alkalis are first boiled in huge kettles. This process is called "saponification." When it is nearly completed, salt is added. This causes the soap to rise to the top of the kettle. The brine or salt solution containing glycerine, dirt, and some excess alkali sinks to the bottom and is drawn off. This process may be repeated as many as five or six times. More water and alkali are added each time until the last bit of fat is saponified, or converted from a fat into soap.

The next step is to churn the soap into a smooth mass while adding various ingredients, such as perfumes, coloring matter, water softeners, and preservatives. After this, the hot melted soap is ready to be fashioned into bars or cakes, or granules, flakes, or globules. Toilet soaps go through a process called "milling," which shreds and dries them, then rolls them into sheets.

WHO INVENTED PERFUME?

The use of perfume in one form or another is probably as old as the human race. Actually the word "perfume" comes from the Latin word *fumus,* meaning "smoke." So it's likely that in the early days people made a pleasant odor by burning certain nice-smelling woods, gums, and leaves.

We know that the Egyptians used perfume more than 5,000 years ago. But the first people to use rose petals to make rose water were the Arabians, about 1,300 years ago. They not only used it as a perfume, but as a medicine. One of the earliest true perfumes made was attar of rose, which means "essential oil of rose". Half a hectare of roses will yield 1 tonne of rose petals. And from these petals half a kilogram of attar is produced. No wonder this essence is very expensive.

Flowers such as roses, violets, jasmine, orange blossoms, and jonquils are the source of some of our greatest perfumes. But perfume essences are obtained from other materials as well. Did you know that perfume also comes from woods such as cedarwood and sandalwood, from leaves such as lavender, peppermint, and geranium, and even from certain roots such as orris and ginger?

The earliest way to make perfume from flowers was to distill the petals with water. The French use a process called *enfleurage*, which means "en-flowering." Sheets of glass in wooden frames and coated with purified lard are covered with flower petals and stacked one above another. The flower petals are replaced at intervals until the *pomode*, as the purified lard is called, has absorbed the desired amount of perfume.

A more modern method uses a very pure solvent obtained from petroleum. This solvent is circulated through fresh petals until it is saturated with perfume. The solvent is then removed by distillation and the perfume purified with alcohol.

Nowadays, chemistry competes with nature in producing perfume essence. The chemist makes synthetic perfume fragrances from coal tar and turpentine and from hundreds of other substances, and you can't tell them from the natural essence! In fact, a perfume chemist can actually produce certain "flower perfumes" which would be impossible to extract from the real flowers themselves.

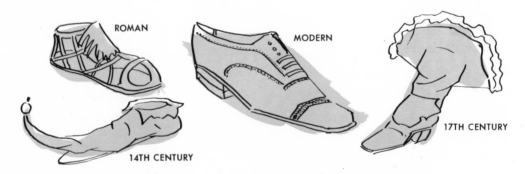

ROMAN

MODERN

17TH CENTURY

14TH CENTURY

WHO INVENTED SHOES?

When primitive man had to make his way over rocks, he discovered the need for covering his feet to protect them. So the first shoes, which were probably sandals, were mats of grass, strips of hide, or even flat pieces of wood.

These were fastened to the soles of the feet by thongs that were then bound around the ankles. Of course, in colder regions, these sandals didn't protect the feet sufficiently, so more material was added and gradually the sandals developed into shoes.

Among the first civilized people to make shoes were the Egyptians. They used pads of leather or papyrus, which were bound to the foot by two straps. In order to protect the toes, the front of the sandal was sometimes turned up.

The Romans went a step further and developed a kind of shoe called the *calceus*. This had slits at the side and straps knotted in front. There were different forms of the *calceus*, to be worn by the different classes of society.

In some of the cold regions of the earth, people developed a kind of shoe independently. For example, they sometimes wore bags padded with grass and tied around the feet. In time, these first foot coverings developed into the moccasins of the Eskimo and the Indian.

As far as our modern shoes are concerned, their beginnings can be traced to the Crusades. The Crusaders went on long pilgrimages, and they needed protection for their feet, so it became necessary to create shoes that would last a long time. In time, leather shoes of great beauty began to appear in Italy, France, and England.

Shoes have always been subject to whims of fashion. For example, at the time of King James I of England, high heels and very soft leathers were fashionable in society. It made for difficult walking, but people insisted on wearing them. At one time, before the appearance of the high heel, long-toed shoes were considered fashionable. The shoes were very narrow, and the toes were 12 and 15 centimetres long, and pointed. Shoemaking was introduced into the United States in 1629, when Thomas Beard arrived under contract to make shoes for the Pilgrim colony.

WHAT IS THE ORIGIN OF THE HAT?

The word "hat" itself gives us a clue as to why hats first began to be worn. It comes from the old Anglo-Saxon word *haet*, which means "to cover." Incidentally, from this same word came the words "house" and "hut."

The hat therefore was worn by early man to protect his head from the rain and snow as well as the rays of the sun. In the northern regions, it was probably made of leather for warmth. In the south, reeds or straw were used to make the first crude "hats."

The next development of the hat was the war helmet. All races of people have used military headdress for one reason or another. In some cases it was for protection and was made of metal to guard against swords and arrows. Among primitive tribes, the headdress often had a hideous form in order to frighten the enemy.

In time, each country and people developed its own style of headdress for decorative and ceremonial reasons. For instance, the fez, which is a small brimless felt cap, usually red in color, was developed in certain countries of western Asia. The Arabs developed the turban, which is worn with certain ornaments to indicate rank. Crowns of kings and queens, as we know, also had symbols of their rank.

It wasn't until five or six hundred years ago that manufacturing of hats as an industry really began. At first, hats were made out of wool. Later on, the fur of the beaver was used to make felt hats. By this time hats were being worn by the average person, and the broad-rimmed hat was the mark of a gentleman.

A curious use of hats has been for religious and political purposes. Nuns and monks, of course, have their own style of headdress. But did you know that the Puritan followers of Oliver Cromwell wore a special kind of "witch hat" with a "steeple" crown? The Quakers, too, proclaimed their faith by wearing hats with very broad brims and very low crowns.

Hats have been named after the people who first wore them, or invented them (the bowler), or after the place where they were first worn (Homburg). The Panama originated in Panama 300 years ago.

WHO MADE THE FIRST FALSE TEETH?

Nobody looks good when he has some teeth missing. Besides, it sometimes interferes very seriously with eating and chewing. So man decided long ago that when he lost his natural teeth for one reason or another, they should be replaced. Substituting artificial replacements for natural parts in teeth is called "prosthetics."

When the natural teeth are gone, they are replaced either by bridgework or by dentures. In bridgework, the "load" of false teeth is borne by our natural teeth on either side of the gap. The bridge fits on these natural teeth. In a denture, the false teeth are held in place by resting on the gum and other parts of the mouth under the gum.

It may amaze you to learn that bridges with false teeth were made 3,000 years ago by the Etruscans, who worked with gold! Dentures, including "complete" dentures for people who had no teeth left, have been made for about 300 years.

The first problems to be solved in making both bridges and dentures was how to make them stay in the mouth in the right position, and how to make the "baseplate material," the material that held the false teeth. Modern dentistry has solved both these problems so well that people with false teeth can eat and chew as well as anyone, and the false teeth feel light and natural in the mouth.

But what about the teeth themselves? In early times, false teeth were made from bone, ivory, and hippopotamus tooth! Sometimes the entire bridge or denture was carved from the same material, and it was all one piece that fitted into the mouth. Later on, individual human teeth, or the teeth of various animals, especially the sheep, were used. These were mounted on a gold or ivory base.

At the end of the 18th century, teeth were made of porcelain, and soon individual porcelain teeth were mounted on gold or platinum bases. The materials in making teeth are the same as those used in making other fine porcelain. They have a fine texture, are somewhat translucent, and have great strength.

About 100 years ago false teeth began to be designed to harmonize with the shape of the face. Today, false teeth are matched to natural teeth so closely in color and shape that it is hard to tell them apart!

WHO MADE THE FIRST SPECTACLES?

Today, many of the world's leading statesmen and other famous people wear spectacles. It would be interesting to wonder if the course of history would be different if some of the statesmen of the past wore spectacles—that is, if they needed them. Perhaps emperors and kings would have behaved quite differently if they had been able to see the world more clearly!

Nobody knows who actually made the first pair of spectacles. In the year 1266, Roger Bacon magnified writing by placing part of a sphere of glass on a book. But who first thought of putting the glass near the eyes and keeping it there? In a picture painted in 1352, a portrait of Cardinal Ugone, he is shown wearing two framed lenses with their handles riveted

together and fixed over the eyes. So somebody must have invented spectacles between 1266 and 1352.

As printed books began to appear, the need for spectacles was created. Since the glassworkers at that time were concentrated in north Italy and south Germany, this is where most of the spectacles were made during the 16th century. By 1629, Charles I of England was able to grant a charter to the Spectacle Makers Guild. And in 1784, bifocals were invented by Benjamin Franklin.

Today, aside from aiding people to read and see better, spectacles of all types have many, many uses. We know that dark glasses cut down glare and sunlight. Colored lenses are used to detect camouflage. Red lenses are used by night aviators and photographers. Lenses that absorb ultraviolet light are made for skiers, aviators, polar explorers, and mountain climbers.

Furnace workers wear lenses that stop infrared light. Glassblowers wear special glasses to help them see better. And it goes on and on, spectacles made to do specific jobs for people who have special problems.

HOW DID FORKS ORIGINATE?

The first man to use a crude kind of fork for eating probably lived thousands of years ago. But the everyday use of forks in dining is a very recent development in the history of man.

The primitive savage used a small pronged twig as a kind of natural fork to pick up his meat. Some authorities believe that the fork really originated with the arrow, and that at first it was a kind of toothpick used to remove food from between the teeth.

Actual forks as we know them were first used only for cooking and for holding the meat while it was being carved. These first forks were long, and two-pronged, and were made of iron, bone, and hard wood.

It took a very long time for forks to be accepted in general use in dining. Only 300 years ago, forks were great curiosities in Europe. In fact, in France everyone ate with his fingers until the 17th century. We all know about the magnificent Court of Louis XIV and the great banquets at his palaces. Did you know that no one used a fork at this very elegant Court!

When people first began to use forks for eating, other people used to ridicule them as being too dainty. When a rich woman in Venice in the 11th century had a small golden fork made, it was written about her: "Instead of eating like other people, she had her food cut up into little pieces, and ate the pieces by means of a two-pronged fork."

Five hundred years later, in the 16th century, people who used forks in Venice were still being described as somewhat peculiar: "At Venice each person is served, besides his knife and spoon, with a fork to hold the meat while he cuts it, for they deem it ill manners that one should touch it with his hand."

From the 17th century on, table manners developed along modern lines. Silver forks began to appear all over Italy. And by the end of the 18th century, the fork was accepted as a necessity in the homes of most cultivated people.

WHEN WAS BREAD FIRST MADE?

Every country, every part of the world, has some food that is peculiar to it. But there is one food that is eaten wherever man lives—and that is some form of bread.

This is because man has realized the value of cereal grains in his diet from the earliest days. In fact, early man first chewed grain seeds in order to get energy from this food. Later, he crushed grain to a flour between stones, as the Egyptians did more than 3,000 years before Christ.

They added water to form a dough, shaped it into flat cakes, and baked

it either in an oven hollowed out of the ground and lined with clay, or on the outside of earthenware jars which were heated from the inside. Such bread was very coarse and heavy; it contained no leavening agent to make the dough rise and so produce light, tender bread.

The early Hebrews used sour dough as a leaven, but the Egyptians were the first to discover that sour dough contained yeast. They were able to segregate this plant and so became the first people to produce a "yeast-raised" bread. Samples of this bread have been found in early Egyptian tombs.

The Hebrews baked their bread in thin sheets and broke it instead of cutting it. That's how we get the expression "to break bread" as a figure of speech for eating a meal. The Jews, for thousands of years, have observed the time of Passover by eating an unleavened bread known as "matzoth," which is made by forming a mixture of flour and water into thin, crackerlike wafers. The wafers used in the Christian communion service are much the same as matzoth but much smaller.

In different parts of the world, bread is made from a variety of things, including beans, potatoes, grass, tree bark, rice, and peas. In parts of the Far East, acorns and beechnuts are used for bread flour.

HOW IS AN EGG FORMED?

An egg may seem like a very simple thing to you, but producing it is quite a complicated process. In a bird, the first thing that forms is the yellow, or yolk, of the egg. This is formed within the reproductive organ of the bird or ovary.

The yellow breaks out of the ovary and enters the upper end of the reproductive tract. Here, the white of the egg is added. It then travels down to the lower part of the tube where the membranes and the shell are applied around the yellow and the white. Now the egg is ready to be laid!

The shell of the egg is hard, but porous. As the liquid contents of the egg evaporate through the pores of the shell, the air enters to supply the growing germ with fresh oxygen.

The "germ" is the part from which the young will develop. Lining the inside of the shell are two membranes. They separate at the large end of the egg to form an air cell.

Inside the membranes is the white of the egg, or albumen. This is a tasteless, odorless sort of jelly, which is mostly water. In the white are thickened strings. The purpose of these strings is to hold the yolk in the center of the egg like a hammock, and protect it from shock.

The yolk is almost round and is food for the germ, which lies in a tiny hollow on its surface. The germ of a fresh hen's egg can be seen if you look closely at the yolk. The germ in the eggs of many other kinds of birds is so tiny it can be seen only under a microscope!

The size of a bird's egg doesn't always depend on the size of the bird. Size depends on the amount of food needed to nourish the growing germ up to the point of hatching. Birds that are born blind and helpless come from smaller eggs in which there wasn't enough food to develop them to the point where they can take care of themselves at birth.

WHEN DID MAN BEGIN TO DRINK MILK?

Today, when we say "milk" we usually mean cows' milk, since most milk consumed by human beings is from the cow. But milk from other animals is consumed by people all over the world. Half the milk consumed in India is from the buffalo. Goats' milk is widely used in countries along the Mediterranean, and the milk of reindeer is used as food in Northern Europe.

When did man first begin to drink the milk of animals, and use milk products such as butter and cheese? No one can ever know, since it was before recorded history. Soured milks, butterlike products, and cheese were probably common foods of the people roaming the grasslands of Asia with their sheep and cattle thousands of years ago.

The Bible has many references to milk. Abel, son of Adam, was a "keeper of sheep" and probably consumed milk. The earliest mention of milk in the Bible is Jacob's prediction in 1700 B.C. that Judah's teeth shall be "white with milk." Canaan was "a land of milk and honey" in 1500 B.C. Job also refers to cheese. But in all these cases the mention of milk implies that it was used much earlier.

We may think that the idea of making concentrated and dry milk is a modern one. Actually, the Tatars prepared concentrated milks in paste, and probably in dry form as early as the year 1200 and used them as food during the raids under Genghis Khan.

The original patent for evaporated milk was granted in 1856, and this type of milk was widely used by soldiers in the Civil War.

About 87 per cent of the milk from the cow is water, but the remainder supplies man with a high percentage of his daily requirements in calcium, protein, and vitamins A and B.

WHO DISCOVERED BUTTER?

Butter is one of the oldest articles of diet known to man, and one of the most universally used. Yet strangely enough, in ancient times butter was not used as a food in many parts of the world!

The Hindus offered butter as a sacrifice in their worship. The Greeks and Romans didn't eat butter, but used it as a remedy for injuries to the skin. They believed that the soot of burned butter was good for sore eyes! The Romans also used it as an ointment for the skin and hair.

In Spain, as late as 300 years ago, butter was found in medicine shops only. When butter was eaten in early times, it was only by a few people and it was never eaten when fresh. It was stored in a melted condition, and there were some people who specially valued butter that was held more than 100 years!

Probably the making of butter for food was introduced into all Europe from Scandinavia.

Today, of course, butter is a very important food.

Butter is a fine energy food, and is quickly and easily digested. It also has "staying" qualities, which means that it stays in the stomach long enough to provide energy that is needed during the work period between meals.

Buttermaking begins with the cow. Because the milk of Guernseys and Jerseys has a high percentage of milk fat in it, they are sometimes called "the butter breeds." After the milk is obtained, the cream is taken off or separated. The cream is then "soured" by letting it stand at room temperature. Souring gives it flavor and makes it easier to churn. The cream is pasteurized to kill practically all of the bacteria and enzymes, so the lasting quality of the butter is improved.

The churning of the butter is done to collect the milk-fat globules, so that the buttermilk can be drawn off. The buttermilk is the nonfatty part of the cream. Then water is mixed with the butter in the churn to wash out every trace of buttermilk. After the water is drained away, the butter is "worked." The butter is forced between rollers to make it smooth and uniform in taste and color. Now the butter is ready to be packed and sent off to market.

HOW WAS COFFEE DISCOVERED?

As is true of so many other things, the discovery of coffee is lost in legend. No one really knows who had the first thrill of drinking a cup of coffee.

But there is a legend that perhaps a thousand years ago an Abyssinian was attracted by the pleasant smell that came from a certain wild shrub that was burning. He chewed a few of its berries and liked the taste so much that he brewed a beverage from them—and thus discovered coffee!

We do know that the Abyssinians in eastern Africa were the first to enjoy coffee. Until the 15th century, this was the only place in the world where the coffee tree grew. Then it was taken into Arabia. From then on, for 200 years, the world's coffee came from Yemen, in southern Arabia.

In the 17th century, the Dutch began to grow coffee in Java and they distributed the coffee plant to several tropical countries. The English took it to the island of Jamaica, from which it was taken to Central and South America. Soon coffee became very popular in both Europe and the Americas.

The coffee plant thrives in almost any tropical climate, but it grows best on fairly high ground with good drainage. This kind of soil and climate is found in the foothills of Brazil. That's why today three-fourths of the world's coffee are produced in Brazil.

In Brazil are found the largest coffee plantations in the world, some of them containing millions of trees and extending for miles. Coffee is grown in large quantities also in Venezuela, Colombia, Guatemala, and Mexico, and in some of the West Indies and Java.

The terms "Mocha" and "Java" used to refer to the places from which the coffee came. But today this is no longer true. They merely designate particular kinds of coffee. For example, they are both now grown in Brazil, as well as the types known as Rio and Santos. The greatest coffee port in the world is Santos, in Brazil.

The underground coffee bean is the seed, or stone, of a fruit resembling a small cherry. The fruit grows on a tall bush with shiny leaves. This bean occurs either singly or as two halves with their flat sides facing each other.

While there are more than 25 species of coffee that grow wild in the tropics, only two produce fruit with that distinctive flavor which is brought out by roasting.

WHERE DID TEA ORIGINATE?

When you think of it, it is rather remarkable that we still drink today some beverages that man enjoyed thousands of years ago!

Tea is definitely one of these. The Chinese have enjoyed the mildly stimulating effects of tea for 4,000 years! And the Western world had to wait a long time before it could enjoy this drink, because tea was not introduced into Europe until a little over 300 years ago.

In the early 18th century, Europe and North America began to cultivate the custom of tea drinking. As a result, the tea trade with China flourished. Speedy sailboats called "tea clippers" were built to carry the delicately flavored leaves to North America and Europe.

The British found the tea bush, or tree, growing wild in Assam, India. Botanists now believe that the Chinese brought seeds and planted them in China, because the plant does not grow wild there. The British found that the Indian plant made just as good tea as the Chinese plant. Gradually large plantations were established, first in India and then in Ceylon. In Ceylon, tea growing became the chief industry, surpassing China by 1940 in the quantity of tea it exported. Tea is also grown in Java, Sumatra, and Formosa.

There are two main varieties of the tea plant. That in China usually grows only about 1 metre high. The Indian plant reaches a height of over 6 metres, if allowed to do so.

Did you know that the British are among the world's greatest tea drinkers? The average Englishman drinks about 4 kilograms of tea a year— while people in the United States use only about 0.5 kilograms a year.

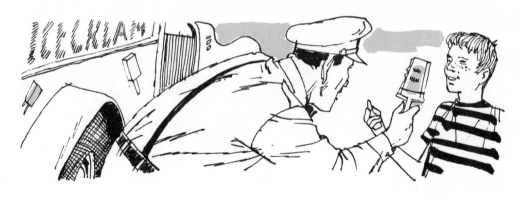

WHERE DID ICE CREAM ORIGINATE?

Fifty years ago people ate ice cream only in the summer. Now it is eaten all the year round. It originated in the Orient, centuries before English schoolboys first tasted ice cornets and wafers.

The explorer Marco Polo saw people eating it there and brought back the idea to Italy. From Italy the idea was carried to France. It became very popular in France with the nobility and an effort was made to keep the recipes for ice cream a secret from the common people. But, of course, they soon learned how delicious this new food was and ice cream became popular with everyone. Soon it spread all over the world, including the United States.

The first wholesale factory for the manufacture of ice cream was started in Baltimore, Maryland, in 1851. The real development of ice cream and the ice cream business didn't take place until after 1900 with new developments in refrigeration.

The basis of all ice cream is cream, milk or milk solids, sugar, and sometimes eggs. Vanilla, chocolate, berries, fruit ingredients, and nuts are added as flavors. This is the usual proportion of ingredients in ice cream: about 80 to 85 per cent cream and milk products, 15 per cent sugar, one-half to four and one-half per cent flavoring, and three-tenths of one per cent stabilizer.

The small amount of stabilizer is used in order to retain the smoothness of the ice cream by preventing the formation of coarse ice crystals. Pure food gelatine is usually used for this purpose.

When you eat one-third of a pint of vanilla ice cream you are getting about as much calcium, protein, and the B vitamins as are in one-half cup of whole milk, and as much vitamin A and calories as in one cup of milk.

HOW DID CANDY ORIGINATE?

In almost every country in ancient times people ate something that was like candy. In excavations in Egypt, pictures and written records have been found that showed sweets and how sweets in Egypt were made!

In those days, of course, the refining of sugar was unknown, so honey was used as a sweetener. The chief ingredient of the candy in Egypt was dates. (Americans give the name of candy to sugar confectionery.)

In parts of the East, each tribe had its official candy-maker and secret recipes. In these regions, almonds, honey, and figs have long been used in making candy. There is an ancient Roman recipe that directs nut meats and cooked poppy be boiled with honey, then peppered and sprinkled with ground sesame softened with honey. The result would probably be a sort of nougat.

In Europe, they had sweet sirup in early times, but it was used to hide the taste of medicines. No one thought of making candy for its own sake. But when large quantities of sugar from the Colonies began to appear in Europe in the 17th century, candy-making began to be a separate art.

The French candied fruits and developed other recipes. One of these, a nut- and sugar-sirup sweetmeat called "prawlings," may have been the ancestor of the famous New Orleans pralines.

In Colonial days and later, maple sugar, molasses, and honey were used in homemade sweetmeats. Our great-grandmothers candied iris root and ginger "varnished" apples, and made rock candy.

The main ingredients used for the manufacturing of candy are cane and beet sugars combined with corn sirup, corn sugar, corn starch, honey, molasses, and maple sugar. To this sweet base are added chocolate, fruits, nuts, eggs, milk, a variety of milk products, and, of course, flavors and colors. Some flavors are from natural sources, such as vanilla, peppermint, lemon, and so on, and others are imitations of true flavors.

There are more than 2,000 different kinds of candy being made today. In the United States more than 1,100,000,000 kilograms are made every year! In Britain, too, the sweet and chocolate making industries continue to flourish and expand. In 1965 over £100,000,000 was spent on sweets.

WHO WERE THE FIRST PEOPLE TO CHEW GUM?

Why do people chew? It's a form of relaxation. Chewing gum happens to be the form of this type of relaxation that we practice. But man has wanted to chew something to relax even when gum wasn't available. So in many parts of the world people have chewed various resins, or even leaves and grasses.

Gum is prepared from chicle and similar resilient substances. And chicle itself has been chewed for hundreds of years! The Mayans and other Central Americans chewed chicle for centuries before the white man came along.

As a matter of fact, the Indians of New England chewed resins from the spruce tree and the American colonists picked up the habit from them. In the early 1800's, the first commercial chewing gum marketed in the United States was spruce gum.

In the 1860's, the use of chicle as a chewing-gum base was developed.

It had a good chewy quality and it could hold flavors. As a result, it paved the way for the big rise in the popularity of chewing gum.

Modern chewing gum consists of about 20 per cent gum base, 19 per cent corn sirup, 60 per cent sugar, and 1 per cent flavoring. To get uniform chewing texture, the gum base may be blended of as many as 25 latex products and similar materials. The latex products are obtained from trees growing wild in tropical forests. The trees are tapped and the latex flows into containers. The latex is then collected, boiled down, and molded into blocks.

In making chewing gum, the gum-base ingredients are washed, ground, sterilized, and blended. In mixing kettles, the melted base is combined with corn sirup, sugar, and flavoring. The mixture is then rolled into sheets and divided into sticks or pellets. Peppermint and spearmint, which are essential oils from mint plants, are the two leading flavors. One stick of gum contains about nine calories.

HOW DID SMOKING TOBACCO BEGIN?

Tobacco is one of the most important gifts that the New World made to the Old. The people of Europe went along for thousands of years without smoking until America was discovered.

The Indians of North and South America were the first to cultivate tobacco. In North America, the Indians used tobacco in many of their ceremonials as, for example, in the smoking of the pipe of peace. Many of the Indians believed that tobacco had medicinal properties. In fact, the chief reason why tobacco was used after it was introduced into Europe was for medicinal purposes!

Once tobacco was introduced into Europe, the growing of tobacco was started in many parts of the world. Tobacco was first introduced into France in 1556; Portugal, in 1558; Spain, in 1559; and England, in 1565. Tobacco began to be grown in Cuba in 1580 and in Jamestown, Virginia, in 1612.

Curiously enough, not everybody approved the smoking of tobacco when it was first introduced. At one time the Turks actually imposed the death penalty for smoking, and the Emperor of Russia ordered that "tobacco drinkers" should have their noses slit after which they were to be whipped and then deported to Siberia!

Today, of course, tobacco is smoked in practically every corner of the world. The United States leads the world in tobacco production, and most of this is grown in the Eastern half of the country.

Different types of tobacco are used for different purposes, though the blending of various types is important in producing definite flavors. Cigarettes are made mostly from the lemon-yellow, flue-cured tobacco from Virginia and the Carolinas. It is blended with others, especially the Turkish types. Burley tobacco, common in Kentucky and Tennessee, is used for chewing tobacco and pipes. Cigars are made from still other types.

HOW WAS FIRE DISCOVERED?

Fire has been known to man since the very earliest times. In certain caves in Europe in which men lived hundreds of thousands of years ago, charcoal and charred bits of bone have been found among stones that were evidently used as fireplaces.

But how did men learn the trick of making a fire? We can only guess. Early man probably knew how to use fire before he knew how to start it. For example, lightning might strike a rotten tree and the trunk would smolder. From this he would light a fire and keep it going for years.

We can take a pretty good guess as to how the cave men learned to start a fire. In trampling among the loose stones in the dark, the first men must have noticed sparks when one stone struck another. But it may have taken many generations before anyone among these early men had the idea of purposely striking two stones together to produce a fire!

Another way we have of knowing how early men discovered fire is to observe the primitive people of today. Some of them are in a stage of development that our forefathers reached thousands of years ago.

Let's look at some of these primitive methods. In Alaska, Indians of certain tribes rub sulphur over two stones and strike them together. When the sulphur ignites, they drop the burning stone among some dried grass or other material.

In China and India, a piece of broken pottery is struck against a bamboo stick. The outer coating of the bamboo is very hard and seems to have the qualities of flint. The Eskimos strike a common piece of quartz against a piece of iron pyrites, which is very common where they live. Among the North American Indians, rubbing two sticks together to produce fire was a common method.

The ancient Greeks and Romans had still another method. They used a kind of lens, called "a burning glass," to focus the rays of the sun. When the heat rays were concentrated in this way, they were hot enough to set fire to dry wood.

An interesting thing about fire in early days, is that many ancient peoples kept "perpetual" fires going. The Mayas and Aztecs in Mexico kept a fire perpetually burning, and the Greeks, Egyptians, and Romans kept fires burning in their temples.

WHO INVENTED MATCHES?

Man's desire to be able to start a fire to warm himself and cook food has caused him to invent a variety of "matches." The cave man struck a spark from a flint and hoped it would ignite some dry leaves. The Romans, thousands of years later, were not much further advanced. They struck two flinty stones together and caught the spark on a split of wood covered with sulphur.

During the Middle Ages, sparks struck by flint and steel were caught on charred rags, dried moss, or fungus. Such material that catches fire easily is called "tinder."

Modern matches were made possible by the discovery of phosphorus, a substance which catches fire at a very low temperature. In 1681, an Englishman called Robert Boyle dipped a sliver of wood which had been treated with sulphur into a mixture of sulphur and phosphorus. But the matches took fire so easily that his invention wasn't practical.

The first practical matches were made in England by a druggist named John Walker. In order to light them, they were drawn between folds of paper covered with ground glass. By 1833, phosphorus-tipped matches that could be ignited by friction were being made in Austria and Germany. But there was one problem. White or yellow phosphorus was so dangerous to the match-workers that it had to be forbidden by an international treaty in 1906.

Finally, a non-poisonous red phosphorus was introduced, and this led to the invention of safety matches. The first safety matches, which light only on a prepared surface, were made in Sweden in 1844. Instead of putting all the necessary chemicals in the match-head, the red phosphorus was painted into the striking surface on the container. The match was thus "safe" unless it was rubbed on the striking area.

During World War II our troops were fighting in the Pacific tropics where long rainy periods made ordinary matches ineffective. A man called Raymond Cady invented a coating for matches which kept them efficient even after eight hours under water!

WHEN WERE CANDLES FIRST USED?

Man's first lighting device was a burning stick of wood he snatched from a fire. The first lamp used by man was a hollowed stone, shell, or skull filled with animal fat or fish oil as fuel, and the wick was a reed, rush, or twist of vegetable fiber.

Candles are very ancient. They were at first made of crude cylinders of wax or solid fatty matter rolled around a vegetable fiber or bit of twisted cloth for a wick. Beeswax candles have been used from the earliest times, and the ancient Roman writers mention them.

Candles didn't improve very much for a long time. In fact, as recently as the middle of the 19th century, candlemaking was considered an important duty of the housekeeper. They were made this way. Tallow, the fat of sheep or oxen, was heated in a pot. A loosely woven strand of cotton yarn, twice the length of the candle, was hung over a rod and the two ends twisted together. A number of these wicks, hanging from one rod, were then dipped several times in the tallow, being hung up to cool after each dip.

When the proper thickness of tallow covered the wick, the candles were ready for use. Sometimes the liquid was poured into tubelike molds in which the wick had been inserted, but usually the candles were dipped.

Modern candle factories have greatly improved on the homemade candle. The wick is still made of cotton yarn loosely twisted together, but beeswax, paraffin, and other fatty substances, as well as tallow, are now used.

The fats are so treated as to give the most light with the least amount of smoke. In the old days, the candle smoked continuously and gave off a disagreeable, oily odor, because of the glycerin in the fat. Modern candlemakers remove the glycerin.

WHO DISCOVERED ELECTRICITY?

The curious thing about electricity is that it has been studied for thousands of years—and we still don't know exactly what it is! Today, all matter is thought to consist of tiny charged particles. Electricity, according to this theory, is simply a moving stream of electrons or other charged particles.

The word "electricity" comes from the Greek word *electron*. And do you know what this word meant? It was the Greek word for "amber"! You see, as far back as 600 B.C. the Greeks knew that when amber was rubbed, it became capable of attracting to it light bits of cork or paper.

Not much progress was made in the study of electricity until 1672. In that year, a man called Otto von Guericke produced a more powerful charge of electricity by holding his hand against a ball of spinning sulphur. In 1729, Stephen Gray found that some substances, such as metals, carried electricity from one location to another. These came to be called "conductors." He found that others, such as glass, sulphur, amber, and wax, did not carry electricity. These were called "insulators."

The next important step took place in 1733 when a Frenchman called du Fay discovered positive and negative charges of electricity, although he thought these were two different kinds of electricity.

But it was Benjamin Franklin who tried to give an explanation of what electricity was. His idea was that all substances in nature contain "electrical fluid." Friction between certain substances removed some of this "fluid" from one and placed an extra amount in the other. Today, we would say that this "fluid" is composed of electrons which are negatively charged.

Probably the most important developments in the science of electricity started with the invention of the first battery in 1800 by Alessandro Volta. This battery gave the world its first continuous, reliable source of electric current, and led to all the important discoveries of the use of electricity.

BETTY LAMP

KEROSENE LAMP

WHEN WERE LAMPS INVENTED?

Before man discovered fire, the only heat and light he had was provided by the sun. Since he couldn't control this, he was quite helpless in dealing with cold and darkness.

Perhaps, after he discovered fire, he began to notice that some materials burned better than others. Perhaps, he observed that fat dripping into the fire from roasting meat burned brightly. As time passed, man began to select materials which, when burned, provided better light. Splinters of certain woods were stuck into the wall and they burned slowly. Pine knots were used as torches. Animal fats were placed in shallow stone dishes and moss and other materials were used as wicks. And thus oil lamps were born. Exactly when this happened we cannot know, since it was before recorded history.

Lard was used in lard-oil lamps in New England around 1820. From whale blubber, oil was extracted for whale-oil lamps. In fact, whatever kind of oil was easiest to obtain was used for lamps. Along the Mediterranean there are many olive trees. So olive oil was used for lamps there. The Japanese and Chinese obtained oil for their lamps from various nuts. Peanuts would probably be used for oil for lamps today—if mineral oil had not been discovered in the earth.

Petroleum was discovered in 1859. By heating this oil in a closed vessel, a thin, colorless product known as kerosene is obtained. This became the oil most commonly used for lamps. In fact, it was first called "coal oil," because people thought petroleum was associated with coal.

Do you have an oil lamp in your house today? Many homes keep one on hand to use in an emergency if the electricity should fail!

WHO BUILT THE FIRST LIGHTHOUSE?

Could you imagine a highway that had absolutely no signs at all to warn you of danger spots, crossings, turnoffs, and approaches to towns and cities? Well, the highways of the seas need such guides, too, and a lighthouse is one of them. Its lights flash to show sailors the way to port, to give them their position at sea, or to warn them of dangerous shoals.

The first lighthouses were low towers on which were placed metal baskets full of flaming wood or charcoal. They were probably put up as soon as men began to go out to sea in ships, thousands of years ago. Nobody knows when exactly this was done. But we know that in the 7th century B.C. there was a well known lighthouse already standing on Cape Sigeum at the Hellespont.

The most famous lighthouse of ancient times was the marble Pharos at Alexandria, Egypt, named for the island on which it stood. It cost the equivalent of $1,000,000 and was considered one of the seven wonders of the world. From the 3rd century B.C. on, the bright fire which blazed at its top guided ships into Alexandria.

The Romans built many famous lighthouses, such as the one at Boulogne, France, which was still in use in the 17th century. Their lighthouses would seem small and poorly constructed compared with those of today. Now almost every country with a seacoast has a government bureau which builds and maintains lighthouses.

When a lighthouse can be built on dry land, its construction is easy and it doesn't cost too much. But when it must be built on a wave-swept rock or on shifting shoals, difficult problems of engineering must be faced.

The tower of a lighthouse may be of hard stone, such as granite, or concrete faced with stone, or of cast-iron or steel.

WHERE DID THE STARS COME FROM?

From the point of view of science, we still don't have an answer to this question. How was the universe born? There are various scientific theories about this, but we still don't know. However, we might consider such a theory in trying to explain the life history of a star.

A star is a heavenly body which shines by its own light. Planets, as you know, shine only by light reflected from the sun. The planets shine with a steady light and the stars twinkle. This twinkling is caused by disturbances in the air between the star and the earth. The unsteady air bends the light from the star, which then appears to tremble.

Stars differ greatly in size, density, and temperature. At one end, there are stars called "red supergiants," which are many times larger than our sun (which is also a star). At the other end, there are stars called "white dwarfs," some of which are about the size of our earth.

The supergiants have a density that is only one-thousandth as great as the air we breathe. The white dwarfs are hundreds of thousands of times as dense.

One theory is that in the life history of a star it goes through both these phases. Stars start, according to this theory, as clouds of cosmic dust. This contracts, because the particles are attracted to each other. Eventually, this matter becomes gaseous and begins to glow and we have a red supergiant star.

Then there is more contraction and the star begins to resemble the size and temperature of our own sun. It remains this kind of "average" star for many billions of years, radiating energy all the time. This energy is obtained by changing hydrogen to heavier elements.

When the hydrogen supply is almost used up, the star collapses. Explosions take place and the star finally becomes a dense white dwarf. In time, as the sources of energy are used up, the star begins to lose its brightness and finally stops shining.

WHO DISCOVERED THE ATOM?

The ancient Greeks believed that all matter was composed of atoms. In fact, the word "atom" itself comes to us from a Greek word which means "indivisible." Because the Greeks believed that if something was divided and divided until it could be divided no more, the last bit was an atom.

Now even though the Greeks believed this, we cannot truly say they discovered the atom. First of all, their belief in the atom was not a scientific one; it didn't come from any scientific information and it wasn't supported by any. It was a sort of "philosophical" idea about matter and the world.

The atom as we know it is built on scientific investigations and theories. Until about the beginning of the 19th century the idea of how matter, or substance, is really put together was something only philosophers thought about! Then along came an English chemist and mathematician called John Dalton, and in 1803 he was the first man to develop a scientific atomic theory.

Dalton was a careful experimenter. He weighed samples of many gases and discovered differences in their weights. He found that gases, as well as solids and liquids, were made up of unbelievably tiny particles which he, too, called atoms. He figured out the relative weights for the atoms of those elements with which he was familiar. When Dalton stated that atoms of different elements have different properties and different weights, he really started the scientific knowledge of the atom.

Of course, exactly what an atom was and how it functioned still wasn't explained. Ernest Rutherford, another Englishman, almost a hundred years later developed a theory about the atom which was like a description of a solar system: a heavy nucleus in the center, with a positive charge of electricity, surrounded by negatively charged electrons.

Today, scientists believe the atom is made of electrons, protons, neutrons, positrons, neutrinos, mesons, and hyperons. In fact, they have found more than 20 different particles in the core of the atom. And strangely enough, there is still no single complete picture of the atom that can explain everything about it!

WHEN WERE ROCKETS FIRST USED?

Have you ever watched a lawn sprinkler work—the kind that spins around and around and sprays water in a circle? Well, you were actually watching the principle of the rocket at work!

The water in the sprinkler was escaping in one direction. This force pushed the sprinkler in the opposite direction. In a rocket, a fast-burning fuel or explosive exerts force in one direction, and this pushes the rocket forward in the opposite direction.

We think of ourselves as living in the age of rockets, and of rockets as being a rather modern invention. But rockets are a very old idea. The Chinese invented them and used them as fireworks more than 800 years ago! They then became known in Indian and Arabian countries. The first record of them in Western Europe was in A.D. 1256.

The first use of rockets in war was very similar to the way burning arrows had been used. They were aimed at homes to set them on fire. Soldiers and sailors continued to use rockets as signals, but they were no longer used for war for a long time.

In 1802, a British Army captain read how British troops in India had been attacked with rockets. This gave him the idea of trying them out with the British Army. The experiment was so successful that very soon most European armies as well as the Army of the United States began to use war rockets.

In Europe, rockets were used in the Battle of Leipzig, in which Napoleon was defeated. In the United States, the English used war rockets in the bombardment of Fort McHenry in Baltimore Harbor. This is why in the national anthem of the United States there is the phrase, "the rocket's red glare!"

During the 19th century, as artillery became more powerful and more accurate, it began to replace rockets, and they were not important in war again until World War II and the famous German V-2 rocket.

HOW WAS GLASS DISCOVERED?

For thousands of years glass was thought of as something to look at. It was valued for decoration and for making precious objects. Glass really became useful when it was thought of as something to look through.

No one really knows when or where the secret of making glass was first learned, though we know it has been used since very early days. The chief ingredients for making glass are sand, soda ash, or potash and lime, melted together at a high temperature. Since these materials are found in abundance in many parts of the world, the secret of glassmaking could have been discovered in many countries.

According to one story, the ancient Phoenicians deserve the credit for this discovery. A crew of a ship landed at the mouth of a river in Syria. When they were ready to cook their dinner, they could find no stones on which to support their kettle. So they used lumps of niter (a sodium compound) from the ship's cargo. The heat of the fire melted the niter, which mixed with the surrounding sand and flowed out as a stream of liquid glass!

This story may or may not be true, but Syria was one of the original homes of glassmaking. And ancient Phoenician traders sold glassware all through the Mediterranean countries.

Egypt was another country in which glassmaking was known at an early time. Glass beads and charms have been found in tombs which date back as far as 7000 B.C., but these glass objects may have come from Syria.

We know that about 1500 B.C. the Egyptians were making their own glass.

The Egyptians mixed crushed quartz pebbles with the sand to change the color of the glass. They learned, too, that by adding cobalt, copper, or manganese to the mixture, they could produce glass with rich blue, green, or purple color.

After 1200 B.C. the Egyptians learned to press glass into molds. But the blowpipe for blowing glass did not come into use until shortly before the beginning of the Christian Era. It was a Phoenician invention.

The Romans were great glassmakers, and even used glass in thin panes as a coating for walls. By the time of the Christian Era, glass was already being used for windowpanes!

WHO BUILT THE FIRST BRIDGE?

Since a bridge enables man to cross a body of water, we must go back to prehistoric times to answer this question. Wherever man lived and there were streams or rivers in his way, he must have searched for ways to be able to cross over.

Nature herself probably provided man with his first bridge when a tree fell across some stream. Man could easily copy this. Probably such tree-trunk bridges were made and used for a very long time before some prehistoric engineer thought of piling up stones in the middle of a stream and laying logs from the pile to the shores.

This made a simple beam, or girder, bridge, with one crude pier. It was but a step to building several of these piers in a broad, shallow stream and connecting them with logs or slabs of stone.

When two logs were laid side by side and crosspieces were laid over them as a flooring, the result was a wooden girder bridge, much like those that are still built across small streams in country districts. Stronger girder bridges now have iron or steel beams, and the strongest are built with steel trusses.

The spans of a girder bridge must not be too long, but where the required piers can be built, the total length of the bridge has no limit. Thus many long railroad viaducts are girder bridges.

Any bridge has two chief parts—the superstructure, or the span part of the bridge, and the substructure, or the piers and foundations it rests upon. Foundations must be solid, for if they settle or are washed away, the entire bridge may collapse. Today engineers usually go down to bedrock for the foundation, and this often means an enormous amount of digging. For example, in the case of the Eads Bridge over the Mississippi River at St. Louis, Missouri, they had to dig down 40 metres below high water. And for the Transbay Bridge between San Francisco and Oakland, they went down to 70 metres below water!

HOW WAS DYNAMITE DISCOVERED?

There are many things that have shaped man's history, but certainly one of the most important ones has been the development of explosives. According to tradition, the Chinese invented gunpowder before the Christian Era. But when European nations began to use it in the 14th century, they were able to spread their influence into the rest of the world.

Old-fashioned gunpowder is a mixture of potassium nitrate (saltpeter), charcoal, and sulphur. It was the prevailing explosive until near the end of the 19th century.

In 1845, a German chemist called Schoenbein treated cotton fibers with a mixture of concentrated nitric and sulphuric acids. This produced a white, fibrous product resembling cotton itself and known as nitro-cellulose, or guncotton. It was much more explosive than gunpowder.

At the same time, an Italian called Ascanio Sobrero, was experimenting with ordinary glycerin. He let it fall drop by drop into a mixture of strong nitric and sulphuric acids, which he kept cool. The result was a small quantity of nitroglycerin, which was an explosive even more powerful than guncotton.

About 20 years later, a Swedish chemist called Alfred Nobel discovered dynamite by chance. He had been working with nitroglycerin, which presented many problems. Although he had found a safe way to produce nitroglycerin, this material was still very dangerous to handle. It often exploded during transportation.

One day, Nobel was removing some cans of nitroglycerin from a box of kieselguhr (a light earth of volcanic origin) in which he had them packed. He found that one had sprung a leak and that the mixture of nitroglycerin and kieselguhr had formed a solid mass. This made an explosive much less sensitive to shock—and thus dynamite was discovered!

WHO INVENTED THE COMPASS?

The most common form of compass is a magnetic needle supported on a pivot so that it is free to swing in all directions. The needle of such a compass will point "north" to the earth's magnetic pole. Since the location of this north magnetic pole is known, all land and water areas are charted or mapped in relation to it. In this way, a compass can guide a traveler as far as direction is concerned anywhere in the world.

How and when it was first discovered that a magnetized iron needle, free to swing in a circle, would always point in a northerly direction, nobody knows! At one time it was believed that the Chinese had discovered it about 4500 years ago, but this is now disputed. In any case, the Chinese were among the very first people to know the principle of the compass.

Arab traders learned about the compass from them and introduced it into Europe. We do know that during the 12th century the compass was already quite well-known in Europe. The earliest type of compass probably consisted of a magnetized needle thrust through a crossbar of wood so that it would float in a bowl of water.

The next stop was to use a needle pivoted on a pin rising from the bottom of the bowl. At first, only the north-south direction was considered, and the bowl was kept turned so that the north end of the needle was over

the north end painted on the bowl. Finally, a card, marked with the points required, was attached to the needle itself.

As you know, the north magnetic pole and the North Pole are not located in the same place. The north magnetic pole is located at the northernmost point of the Arctic coast of North America at a place called Boothia Peninsula. All compass needles in the Northern Hemisphere point toward this spot.

To ancient peoples the difference between the north magnetic pole and the geographical North Pole was not known. They were far distant from both, and to them it seemed that the compass needle always pointed north. The sailors of later days, who ventured farther away from home, noticed the difference and were greatly puzzled. And you can imagine the bewilderment of the Norsemen who sailed the Arctic seas around Greenland when they found that in some parts of those regions the compass needle points almost west!

WHO INVENTED THE THERMOMETER?

Do you ever find yourself asking: I wonder how hot it is? Or: I wonder how cold this is? If you are interested in heat, just imagine all the questions about heat that scientists want to know! But the first step in developing the science of heat is to have some way of measuring it. And that's why the thermometer was invented. "Thermo" means "heat," and "meter" means "measure," so a thermometer measures heat.

The first condition about having a thermometer must be that it will always give the same indication at the same temperature. With this in mind, an Italian scientist called Galileo began certain experiments around 1592 (100 years after Columbus discovered America). He made a kind of thermometer which is really called "an air thermoscope." He had a glass tube with a hollow bulb at one end. In this tube there was air. The tube and bulb were heated to expand the air inside, and then the open end was placed in a fluid, such as water.

As the air in the tube cooled, its volume contracted or shrank, and the liquid rose in the tube to take its place. Changes in temperature could then be noted by the rising or falling level of the liquid in the tube. So here we have the first "thermometer" because it measures heat. But remember, it measures heat by measuring the expansion and contraction of air in a tube. So it was discovered that one of the problems with this thermometer was that it was affected by variations of atmospheric pressure, and therefore, wasn't completely accurate.

The type of thermometer we use today uses the expansion and contraction of a liquid to measure temperature. This liquid is hermetically sealed in a glass bulb with a fine tube attached. Higher temperature makes the liquid expand and go up the tube, lower temperature makes the liquid contract and drop in the tube. A scale on the tube tells us the temperature.

This kind of thermometer was first used about 1654 by the Grand Duke Ferdinand II of Tuscany.

WHO INVENTED THE MICROSCOPE?

The word microscope is a combination of two Greek words, *mikros,* or "small," and *skopos,* or "watcher." So a microscope is a "watcher of the small"! It is an instrument used to see tiny things which are invisible to the naked eye.

Normally an object appears larger the closer it is brought to the human eye. But when it is nearer than 25 centimetres, it is not clear. It is said to be out of focus. Now if a simple convex lens is placed between the eye and the object, the object can be brought nearer than 25 centimetres and still be in focus.

Today we describe this simply as "using a magnifying glass." But ordinary magnifying glasses are really "simple microscopes," and as such they have been known since remote times. So when we speak of the invention of

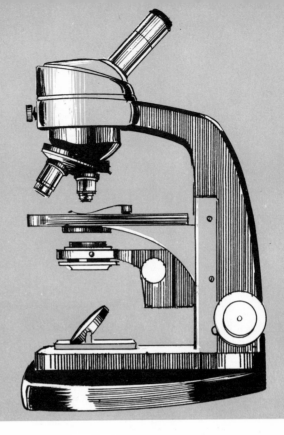

the microscope, we really mean "the compound microscope." In fact, today when we say "microscope," that's the only kind we mean.

What is a compound microscope? In this kind of microscope, magnification takes place in two stages. There is a lens called "the objective" which produces a primary magnified image. Then there is another lens called "the eyepiece" or "ocular," which magnifies that first image. In actual practice, there are several lenses used for both the objective and ocular, but the principle is that of two-stage magnification.

The compound microscope was invented some time between 1590 and 1610. While no one is quite sure who actually did it, the credit is usually given to Galileo. A Dutch scientist called Leeuwenhoek is sometimes called "the father of the microscope," but that's because of the many discoveries he made with the microscope.

Leeuwenhoek showed that weevils, fleas, and other minute creatures come from eggs and are not "spontaneously generated." He was the first to see such microscopic forms of life as the protozoa and bacteria. With his own microscope he was the first to see the whole circulation of the blood.

Today the microscope is important to man in almost every form of science and industry.

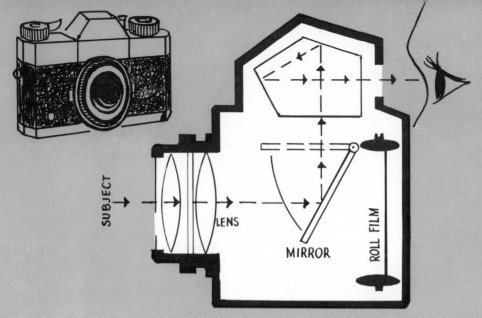

Simple single-lens reflex 35 MM. camera. Light reflects from subject through diaphragm and through lens to mirror; then to prism in reflex housing to viewer's eye. When shutter release is pressed, mirror first slips out of way and focal-plane shutter is activated.

WHO INVENTED THE CAMERA?

Today, when you snap a picture and have it developed so easily, it's hard to believe that hundreds of years of experimenting were needed before this became possible. Photography was not invented by any single person. Just to give you an idea of what went into bringing it to its present stage of perfection, here is a quick outline of the history of photography.

Between the 11th and 16th centuries, man had "the camera obscura." This enabled him to show on paper an image which could be traced by hand to give accurate drawings of natural scenes. It didn't really "take" a picture.

In 1568, Daniello Barbaro fitted the camera obscura with a lens and a changeable opening to sharpen the image. In 1802, Thomas Wedgwood and Sir Humphrey Davy recorded silhouettes and images of paintings on coated paper by contact printing, but they couldn't make the prints permanent.

In 1816, Joseph Niepce made a crude photographic camera from a jewel box and a lens taken from a microscope. He was able to make a negative image. In 1835, William Talbot was the first to make positives from negatives, the first to make permanent images.

In 1839, Louis Daguerre announced the daguerreotype process, which recorded the image on a silver plate. More and more developments were contributed by individuals all over the world as time went on. Many of them are too technical to discuss here, but as you can see, it was a long slow process of growth.

Finally, in 1888, a box camera was put on the market, developed by the Eastman Dry Plate and Film Company, using the Kodak system. The camera was sold already loaded with enough film for 100 exposures. The pictures were 6 centimetres wide. After exposure, camera and film were returned to Rochester, where the film was removed and processed and the camera reloaded and returned to the customer.

This box camera was probably the beginning of popular photography as we know it today when billions of pictures are taken every year by people all over the world.

WHO INVENTED THE BICYCLE?

If we try to trace the bicycle to its very first beginnings, we should probably go back thousands of years to Egyptian times! There is some evidence that the Egyptians had some sort of two-wheeled contrivance that was set in motion by the feet of the rider.

But for all practical purposes, the beginnings of the bicycle can be traced to 1817. In that year, a German called Baron von Drais introduced a machine which he named "the draisine," after himself. The two wheels of the draisine were connected by a wooden bar. The rider rested part of his weight on a wooden arm rest in front and propelled himself by kicking the ground, first with one foot and then with the other. He steered by turning a handle on the front wheel, which was pivoted. Because this machine was quite expensive, it was nicknamed "the dandy horse." King George IV of England loved to ride one!

About 1840, a Scotsman named Macmillan took an old dandy horse and put cranks on the axle of the rear wheel. These were connected by driving rods with pedals in front. He went so fast with it that he was actually arrested for "furious driving"!

The name "bicycle" was first used in 1865. A Frenchman called Lallement attached cranks and pedals to the front wheel of a velocipede much like the dandy horse. These "bicycles" were called "boneshakers," because they had heavy wooden frames and iron tires. In 1868, light metal wheels with wire spokes and solid rubber tires were introduced.

Soon afterward, "the Ordinary," a new type of bicycle, appeared. As this developed, the front wheel, which used to be the same size as the rear wheel, grew larger and larger. This meant that one circuit of the pedals attached to its axle would drive the bicycle farther. In some models, the front wheel was 1.5 metres high or even higher, while the rear wheel was only 30 centimetres across! The rider sat perched above the huge front wheel and unless he was very skillful, he was often tossed over the handlebars head first!

Finally, in about 1885, the modern "safety bicycle" was developed. In this type, the wheels were of equal size, and the rider's seat was slightly forward of the rear wheel. By making the sprocket on the pedals much larger than that on the rear wheel, the wheel could be made to cover as much ground at each turn of the pedals as the dangerous large front wheel.

In time, other improvements followed to produce the bicycle we have today.

WHO INVENTED THE AUTOMOBILE?

Unlike so many other great developments, no one man can claim credit for inventing the automobile. It has reached its present state of perfection as the result of a great many ideas contributed through the years.

For all practical purposes, the first land vehicle that was self-propelled with an engine was built in 1769 by a Frenchman named Nicholas Cugnot. It was a cumbersome three-wheeled cart with a steam engine and an enormous boiler. It could travel 3 miles an hour and had to be refueled every 15 miles!

In 1789, an American called Oliver Evans received the first United States patent for a self-propelled carriage. It was a four-wheeled wagon and had a paddle wheel at the rear so that it could operate either on land or in the water. It weighed 19 tonnes!

For nearly 80 years afterward, other men continued to experiment with powered carriages for use on roads. Most of them were steam, although a few were electrically driven and had to carry large batteries. Then, in the 1880's came two inventions that were to result in the automobile as we know it today. One was the development of the internal combustion engine. The other was the invention of the pneumatic, or air-filled, tyre.

The first petrol-powered car was put on the road in 1887 by Gottlieb Daimler, a German. In the United States, two brothers, Frank and Charles Duryea, built the first successful American petrol automobile in 1892 or 1893. Their machine was described as "a horseless buggy." As a matter of fact, all the early American automobiles that were to follow were much the same! Nobody attempted to design a completely different kind of vehicle. All they did was add a petrol engine to the vehicle and a connecting belt or chain to drive the rear wheels.

It was only after automobiles began to run successfully that attention was turned to making them comfortable and stronger. Car-makers soon found that the flimsy construction of buggies was not suitable for use in automobiles. Gradually, the familiar form of the automobile as we know it today began to emerge. Engines were removed from under the seats and placed in front. Stronger wheels replaced the spindly bicycle and carriage wheels. Steering wheels replaced "tillers." Finally, steel was used instead of wood to make stronger frames and our modern automobile became a reality.

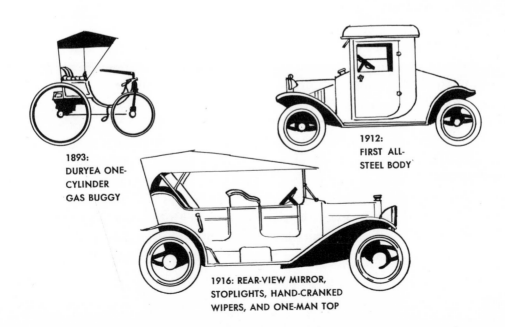

1893:
DURYEA ONE-
CYLINDER
GAS BUGGY

1912:
FIRST ALL-
STEEL BODY

1916: REAR-VIEW MIRROR,
STOPLIGHTS, HAND-CRANKED
WIPERS, AND ONE-MAN TOP

WHO INVENTED THE AIRPLANE?

Sometimes an invention starts with having the "idea." A man has the idea that people might want a certain kind of machine or product, and then he proceeds to "invent" it.

But when it comes to the airplane, the "idea" has been one of man's oldest dreams. The idea of flying has fascinated men since ancient days. In fact, one of our most famous legends tells of Icarus, who fastened wings to his body with wax and flew off! As he soared toward the sun, however, the wax melted and he fell to his death. Icarus is a symbol of man's striving to new heights.

Leonardo da Vinci, who was also quite an inventor, made sketches of a flying machine that used manpower, and other artists and "dreamers" had the idea of an airplane hundreds of years ago.

The earliest flying machines that were made had no power. They were actually huge kites or gliders, and during the 19th century many experiments with these were carried on.

But nobody had yet made a heavier-than-air machine that was equipped with its own power. In fact, there was some question that such a machine could actually be built. The first man to demonstrate that it could be done was Professor Samuel Langley, who was secretary of the Smithsonian Institution of Washington, D.C. He built two machines, each 3.5 metres wide and 4.5 metres long, driven by $1\frac{1}{2}$-horsepower steam engines. In 1896, these two models made successful flights. In 1903, when Langley's full-sized flying machine was tested, it was wrecked. This was on October 7, 1903.

On December 17, Orville and Wilbur Wright succeeded in making man's first flight in a heavier-than-air machine with its own power. At Kitty Hawk, North Carolina, they made one flight of 30 metres in 12 seconds, and a second flight of 260 metres in 59 seconds. The airplane was born!

WHO INVENTED THE PARACHUTE?

Imagine stepping off into space three miles in the air and then landing on the ground with no more shock than if you had jumped down from a 3-metre fence. You could do it—with a parachute! A parachute is simply a big umbrella that creates air resistance. With a parachute a man may drift down through the air slowly enough to avoid injury when striking the ground.

The parachute is probably the oldest idea for man-carrying aircraft. Leonardo da Vinci sketched one in his notebook in 1514. Fausto Veranzio published a description of a workable parachute in 1595. The first man to use a parachute is believed to be a Frenchmen called J. P. Blanchard. In 1785 he dropped a dog in a basket, to which a parachute was attached, from a balloon high in the air. Blanchard claimed that he himself descended from a balloon in a parachute in 1793, breaking his leg upon landing.

Another Frenchman, J. Garnerin, gets the credit for being the first man to use a parachute regularly. His first public exhibit of parachuting was made in Paris on October 22, 1797, when he jumped successfully from a height of more than 600 metres. His parachute was umbrella-shaped, made of white canvas, and was about 7 metres in diameter. In the center of the canopy was a disk-shaped piece of wood about 25 centimetres across, with a hole in the center which allowed air to escape from the canopy. The wooden piece was fastened to the canvas by many short pieces of tape.

The first successful use of a parachute in a descent from a moving airplane was made in 1912 by Captain Berry at St. Louis, Missouri. There was a great deal of discussion during 1913 and 1914 about whether it was practical to use parachutes to escape from airplanes. This question was still not decided by the time World War I started in 1914. The problem then was partly the size of the parachutes used and the fear that the pilot wouldn't be able to clear the plane and escape fouling of the parachute.

WHO INVENTED THE SUBMARINE?

Man's desire to be able to travel underwater goes back a long, long time. But the first craft actually designed to travel in this way of which we have a record goes back to 1578.

A British mathematician called William Bourne published a book in that year in which there was the design of a completely enclosed boat which could be submerged and rowed under the surface. It consisted of a wooden framework covered with waterproofed leather. It was to be submerged by reducing its volume by contracting the sides through the use of hand vises.

Bourne never built this boat, but a similar boat built by someone else was launched in 1605. The credit for building the first submarine is usually given to a Dutch inventor called Cornelius van Drebbel. He actually maneuvered his submarine in the river Thames many times at depths of 3 to 4 metres under the surface.

Van Drebbel's boat also had its outer hull made of greased leather over a wooden frame. It had oars which came out through the sides and were sealed with tight-fitting leather flaps. This boat was built in 1620.

The interest in building submarines was so great that by 1727 no fewer than 14 different types had been patented in England alone. The first time a submarine was used as an offensive weapon in naval warfare was during the American Revolution. A man called David Bushnell had invented a one-man submarine that was hand-operated by a screw propeller. It was called "the Turtle."

The Turtle tried to sink a British man-of-war in New York harbor by attaching a charge of gunpowder to the ship's bottom. It failed to do this, but after it released the charge, the British ship made certain to move farther out to sea!

Early submarine.

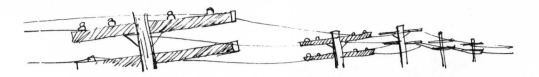

HOW WAS THE TELEPHONE INVENTED?

The story of the invention of the telephone is a very dramatic one. (No wonder they were able to make a movie about it!) But first let's make sure we understand the principle of how a telephone works.

When you speak, the air makes your vocal cords vibrate. These vibrations are passed on to the air molecules so that sound waves come out of your mouth, that is, vibrations in the air. These sound waves strike an aluminum disk or diaphragm in the transmitter of your telephone. And the disk vibrates back and forth in just the same way the molecules of air are vibrating.

These vibrations send a varying, or undulating, current over the telephone line. The weaker and stronger currents cause a disk in the receiver at the other end of the line to vibrate exactly as the diaphragm in the transmitter is vibrating. This sets up waves in the air exactly like those which you sent into the mouthpiece. When these sound waves reach the ear of the person at the other end, they have the same effect as they would have if they came directly from your mouth!

Now to the story of Alexander Graham Bell and how he invented the telephone. On June 2, 1875, he was experimenting in Boston with the idea of sending several telegraph messages over the same wire at the same time. He was using a set of spring-steel reeds. He was working with the receiving set in one room, while his assistant, Thomas Watson, operated the sending set in the other room.

Watson plucked a steel reed to make it vibrate, and it produced a twanging sound. Suddenly Bell came rushing in, crying to Watson: "Don't change anything. What did you do then? Let me see." He found that the steel rod, while vibrating over the magnet, had caused a current of varying strength to flow through the wire. This made the reed in Bell's room vibrate and produce a twanging sound.

The next day the first telephone was made and voice sounds could be recognized over the first telephone line, which was from the top of the building down two flights. Then, on March 10 of next year, the first sentence was heard: "Mr. Watson, come here, I want you."

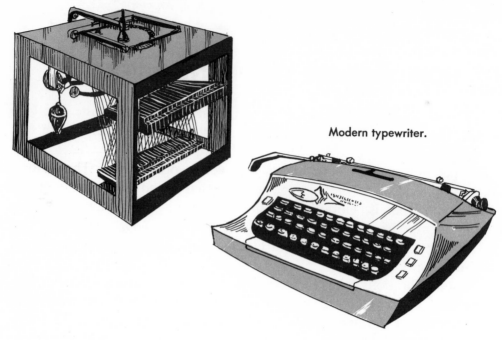

The typewriter in 1867.

Modern typewriter.

WHO INVENTED THE TYPEWRITER?

Typewriters are a very modern development and are still being constantly improved. But did you know that a patent for a typewriter was given to an Englishman called Henry Mill as long ago as 1714?

This typewriter, however, was never manufactured. At first, typewriters were patented as devices to aid the blind. In the United States the first typewriter was patented by William Burt in 1829. It was called "a typographer," and there is no example of this machine in existence today.

In 1833, a Frenchman, Xavier Progin, invented a machine which used type bars with a key lever for each letter. You can see that the development of the typewriter was the work of many men, each making some contribution.

In 1843, an American, Charles Thurber, patented a machine which made use of a set of type bars placed around a brass wheel. The wheel moved on a central pivot. It was brought around by hand to the letter desired, and the inked type struck directly upon the paper below. This operation, however, was too slow to make this machine practical.

Another step forward was made in 1856 with a machine that used the principle of a circle of type bars making an impression upon a common center, which is what we use today.

The first practical typewriter, and one that could be manufactured on a large scale, was the work of three United States inventors. They were Christopher Sholes, Samuel Soule, and Carlos Glidden. They perfected their machine in 1873 to the point where it could be sold.

This machine had paper inserted around a rubber cylinder, an inked ribbon, reversible spools for the ribbon, and a moving carriage. So it had many of the features of the modern typewriter.

In time other improvements were added, and today we have portable typewriters, noiseless typewriters, and electric typewriters. The latest development is an electric typewriter which allows the proper amount of space to each letter according to its width!

WHO MADE THE FIRST SEWING MACHINE?

There is a story about an explorer who found himself in one of the most remote regions of the world. When he met the natives, he expected to see no sign of civilization at all. Yet to his great surprise, he saw in the hut of the native chief a sewing machine! Somehow these people had obtained a sewing machine from the nearest civilized outpost.

Sewing is so important to man that a machine just had to be invented to uo it. The question was: Who would invent one first? And the history of the invention of the sewing machine is quite tragic. The first sewing machine was the invention of Thomas Saint, an Englishman. In 1790, he patented a machine that had many of the features of the modern chain-stitch one. It was largely intended for work on leather. But it was never used and the inventor made no profit by it.

In 1830, Barthelemy Thimmonier, a poor French tailor, invented a sewing machine which even more resembled the present model. This was actually used in France, but an angry mob of workers, fearing they would lose their jobs, wrecked the plant and the machines. Thimmonier died in poverty.

Meanwhile in New York, a man called Walter Hunt had invented, almost at the same time, a sewing machine which contained a curved needle, with the eye at the point. This needle passed a loop of thread through the cloth which was caught by a second thread, forming a lock stitch. But Hunt failed to obtain a patent!

So the honor of patenting the first sewing machine to be put into use fell to Elias Howe. In 1851, Isaac Singer obtained a United States patent on his sewing machine. There was a dispute between Singer and Howe over who had priority, and Howe won the case. So he was able to obtain royalties from practically every type of machine then in use.

Today, of course, there are thousands of kinds of sewing machines, including special machines for sewing leather, felt hats, quilts, and buttons, and for many other purposes.

HOW DID THE EGYPTIANS PRESERVE MUMMIES?

A mummy, as you know, is a dead body that has been preserved. The word "mummy" comes from the Arabic and means "a body preserved by wax or tar." Now, why should the Egyptians want to preserve the body of the dead?

The reason is that they believed in life after death, and so they wanted to prepare for it. They thought of the soul as a bird with a human face that could fly around by day but must return to the tomb at night for fear of evil spirits. The body was therefore preserved so that the soul could recognize it and know which tomb to enter.

Before about 3000 B.C., the Egyptians buried their dead in a curled-up position in the hot sand of the desert, and the sand preserved the bodies. Later, important persons were buried in tombs cut from the rock. But the pyramids and rock tombs were not so dry as the desert sand, so they had to develop some way of preserving the bodies in the tombs. This is why they developed the art of mummification.

When a person died, the brain, digestive organs, and lungs were removed. These were preserved separately and placed in four vases called "canopic jars." In later times, they were replaced in the body.

Then the body was treated with salts. The salts, put inside the body, together with the dryness of the desert air, took out the moisture. When the body had been dried out, it was bathed, rubbed with resin from pine trees, and wrapped in hundreds of yards of linen. All this took 70 days.

In the meantime, carpenters were making the mummy case. If the man had been rich and important, a number of mummy cases were made, each one fitting neatly inside the next. Artists decorated the cases with many bright colors. The walls of the tomb were decorated with texts and pictures which told the story of the man's life. Next, all the things that had made the man comfortable in his lifetime were collected. These were placed in his tomb. And in this way, the Egyptians believed they had prepared the man for his next life.

HOW DO SUPERSTITIONS BEGIN?

Superstition has existed from the beginning of civilization right down to this day. All over the world, millions of people still have faith in superstitions and refuse to give them up.

It is almost impossible to explain just how superstitions begin. There may be certain phenomena of nature which frighten or mystify people, or there may be certain events which they would like to control. Soon they begin to believe either in an explanation of why those things happen, or in an idea that by doing certain things, they can make them happen as they wish. A superstition is a belief, usually born of fear, which is contrary to reason and cannot be proved by experience.

For example, the heavenly bodies have mystified and frightened people for ages. So superstitions arose about them. A comet was a mysterious thing. People began to believe in the superstition that a comet was a sign that war or a plague was coming.

The moon has a mysterious quality about it. People began to believe that if you gazed at the moon for a long time you would be "moonstruck." In fact, our word "lunatic" comes from the Latin word *luna*, meaning "moon."

Because ancient peoples couldn't understand the behavior of animals, they built up superstitions around them. A black cat crossing your path was a sign of bad luck. The hoot of an owl is a sign of death approaching, and so on.

Sailors, who are constantly battling with the forces of nature, have always had many superstitions. For instance, winds and storms bring danger, so they have a superstition about them. Many sailors believe that whistling will raise a wind or storm.

Even today, the custom of christening a ship by breaking a bottle of wine over its prow is a throwback to an old superstition. The god of the sea was Neptune, and the wine was considered a sacrifice to Neptune!

Because people have to deal so much with numbers, they have developed superstitions about lucky and unlucky numbers. There may be different origins for these superstitions, but they all stem from the desire to control them or from ignorant fear.

WHAT IS THE ORIGIN OF MAGIC?

Originally, magic meant the use of mystic words or charms and the claiming of supernatural powers to do things which ordinarily could not be done. It was used by priests and medicine men of ancient Egypt, Greece, and Rome to convince the people that they had power.

But magic as we know it today is a form of entertainment. The magician uses the skill of his hands or certain mechanical aids to fool his spectators into thinking he has done something which cannot be done. We know there is some trick behind the "magic," but we enjoy being fooled.

In ancient times, every court in the world had magicians, or invited magicians to come to entertain them. The magicians who were not so clever performed in the market place for all who passed by. Their tricks were very simple, and they carried whatever they needed in their pockets. The first book on magic, by the way, was written in 1584, but, of course, magicians were practicing their tricks long before that.

In medieval times, magicians began to travel from city to city and even from country to country on regular trips, and the people would look forward to their visits. In time, they began to give bigger shows and use more equipment, so they traveled about in wagons and performed in stores or halls which they rented.

In the early part of the 19th century, the kind of magic we know today began to be performed. Instead of fancy costumes and heavy equipment, magicians started to dress in evening clothes and do tricks that depended on their personal skill.

A French magician called Robert-Houdin is considered the father of modern magic. He improved the magic equipment so that he could use common and familiar objects in his tricks, and he also brought together a great deal of knowledge on how to present tricks.

In time, another form of magic trick, called "an illusion," began to appear. In these tricks people seem to float in air, a woman is sawed in half, a person is made to disappear, and so on. One of the greatest magicians of all time, Cardini, created still another kind of magic. He started the kind of tricks in which lit pipes and cigarettes pop into his hands, cards appear from nowhere, all done without props and special equipment!

WHERE DID DOLLS ORIGINATE?

The answer to this is—everywhere. The doll is one of the oldest human institutions. It is found among both savage and civilized people, and we know that there were dolls in the ancient Egyptian, Greek, and Roman civilizations.

It is probable that the first dolls were invented by children themselves and were made from natural objects such as sticks and stones. But among most people dolls were more than just playthings.

For example, among the American Indians the child's doll was the image of a god, made of wood, and given to the child as part of religious instruction.

In Japan, a primitive type of child's doll was made of a shaved willow stick with shavings or strings for hair and paper clothes. There was also a "scapegoat" doll, which was fed and dressed and treated as though alive. This was given to mothers to ward off evil from their children. But apart from these "magical" dolls, Japanese girls also had ordinary dolls.

Among Mohammedans it is forbidden to represent the human figure. But despite this, elaborately dressed dolls are often given to a girl who is getting married, since the girl may be quite young. Mothers don't like to give dolls to their little girls, because they fear an evil spirit in the doll may harm the child. But many little girls make their own dolls of pieces of wood.

Dolls are common in Africa, but they are sometimes used for magical observances instead of as toys. In the same way, dolls in Europe were associated with religious observances in early times. Many dolls were connected with images of saints and were associated with the Christmas festival.

In the Protestant parts of Europe, dolls became purely toys long before they did in the Catholic countries.

236

WHO FIRST FLEW KITES?

The history of kites is such a long one that no one knows who first invented them. Some people say that it was a Greek called Archytas, who lived in the 4th century B.C. But kites were probably flown in Oriental countries long before that time.

In China, kites have always been an important part of many celebrations. On the ninth day of the ninth month there is a big celebration called the Feast of High Flight. The skies are dotted with kites of all shapes and sizes. Some of the kites are in the shapes of fishes, frogs, and birds. This is not just a festival for children, men join in the games. They even have "kite fights," in which kites with bits of glass on them are used to cut the strings of other kites!

In Western countries, kites have been used for more serious purposes. In 1752 Benjamin Franklin flew a silk kite in a thunderstorm and he used it to prove that lightning and electricity are the same thing. Even before Franklin, kites had been flown with thermometers attached to learn the temperature of the clouds.

By the end of the 19th century, kites were being used by most weather bureaus. They would be equipped with instruments to record the temperature, the speed of the wind, and the humidity of the air. Some of these kites were sent up to heights of over four miles! In order to reach such heights, more than one kite was used, several being attached together. The kite string was made of piano wire so light that a mile of it weighed only 7 kilograms, and strong enough to lift 110 kilograms without breaking.

Before the airplane was invented, kites were also used for military purposes. One kite, for example, was 11 metres long and lifted a man 30 metres in the air! Kites could be used in wartime during strong winds when balloons would be forced down.

While most kites are made in the familiar triangular shape, the most powerful kites are box kites. They are hollow boxes, open at both ends, and with the sides covered only at each end. Kites in the shape of butterflies, ships, and birds are made simply by using more sticks than in the ordinary kites and stretching the strings to get the outline you want.

WHEN WERE BELLS FIRST MADE?

Bells are a percussion instrument, which means we obtain a musical note by means of striking them. And since the earliest instruments in music were those of percussion, "bells" of one sort or another may be considered one of man's first musical instruments. They go back so far in history that it is impossible to trace them.

More than 4,000 years ago, for example, the Chinese had an instrument that consisted of 16 flat stones suspended in a frame, and this gave forth a scale of exotic notes when struck by a wooden mallet. Of course, we think of bells as being made of metal. Yet bells for horses are mentioned in the Bible (Zechariah XIV, 20). And King Solomon is supposed to have had large gold bells on the roof of his temple to keep the birds away.

The ancient Greeks and Romans had bells of all kinds, including hand bells. They were used in Athens by priests. When a king died in Sparta, women walked in the streets striking small bells.

Bronze bells have been found in excavations at Ninevah, which was destroyed about 612 B.C. And small bells, like our modern sleigh bells, have been found in ancient tombs in Peru about 1,500 years old.

As the bell developed from its most primitive form, it went in two directions. One was the Eastern and the other was Western. In the Orient, the bell developed into forms that are "pot" and "bowl." The bowl became the gong, which is a distinctively oriental instrument. The pot developed into the Chinese and Japanese "barrel-formed" bells.

In Western civilization the bell developed in a "cup" form, and later it had a clapper so it could be struck from the inside. The large copper or bronze kettle mounted upside down atop a church was developed about the year 400. The bronze bells used today have about 80 per cent copper and 20 per cent tin.

WHAT WAS THE FIRST MUSICAL INSTRUMENT?

There is a legend about this, but it is pure fancy. According to a Greek myth, Pan invented the first musical instrument—the shepherd's pipe. One day he sighed through the reeds on a river bank and heard his breath produce a mournful wail as it passed through them. He broke them off in unequal lengths, bound them together, and had the first musical instrument!

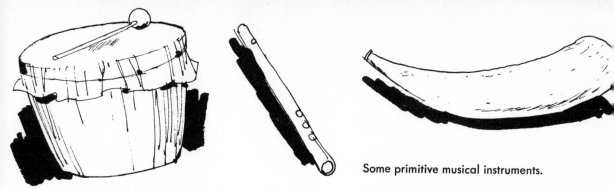

Some primitive musical instruments.

The fact is we can never trace the first musical instrument because all primitive people all over the world seem to have made music of some sort. It was usually music that had some religious significance and it was shared in by the spectators who would dance, drum, or clap hands and sing with the music. It was done more than for pleasure alone. This primitive music had a meaning as part of the lives of the people.

The legend of Pan and the reeds suggests, however, how man first had the idea for making various musical instruments. He may have imitated the sounds of nature, or used articles of nature all about him to create his music.

The first instruments were of the drum type. Later, man invented wind instruments, made from the horns of animals. From these crude wind instruments developed modern brass instruments. As man trained his musical sense, he began to use reeds and thus produced more natural tones of greater delicacy.

Last of all, man discovered the use of strings and invented the simple lyre and harp from which developed the instruments played with a bow.

In the Middle Ages, the Crusaders brought back many curious oriental instruments. These, combined with the folk instruments that already existed in Europe, developed into many of the instruments now in use.

WHO INVENTED THE PIANO?

Did you know that, with the exception of the organ, the piano is the most complex musical instrument? In fact, the proper name for the piano is "the pianoforte," which means "soft-strong," and which suggests the variety of tones of which the piano is capable.

Yet this very complicated instrument began with a most simple instrument called "the monochord." This was a box with a single string which had the intervals of the scale marked off on it. The dulcimer and psaltery of Old Testament times also had such soundboxes. The player plucked the strings with a pick.

About the year A.D. 1,000, Guido d'Arezzo invented a movable bridge for the monochord and added keys and more strings. This instrument was generally in use until the 16th century.

One of the most pleasing instruments that developed from this one was the clavichord. The sound in the clavichord is produced by the vibration of springs through the pressure of a brass pin flattened on top. This instrument had the power of increasing or diminishing tone at the command of the player.

A closely related instrument was the spinet. It was an oblong instrument with a compass of four octaves. Its strings were set in motion by picking or twanging.

In the middle of the 17th century, an instrument that become popular was the harpsichord. It is a larger instrument than either the clavichord or spinet and generally has two keyboards. In shape, it is like a grand piano. Its strings are twanged by tiny quills.

Finally, in 1709, Bartolommeo Christofori introduced the hammer action which sets the piano apart from earlier stringed instruments. This hammer action did away forever with the scratching sound which could not be avoided in the more primitive instruments. Beethoven was the first composer to bring about a wider use of the piano.

HOW DID SOCIAL DANCING BEGIN?

Dancing has existed in some form or other practically since the beginning of man. Primitive peoples have danced in imitation of animals or forces of nature, and religious dances have been part of the history of mankind since the earliest times.

But social dancing is quite another thing. It is done for the sheer pleasure of it. Surprisingly enough, this kind of dancing has a long history, too. In fact, the ancient Greeks were very fond of dancing as a social amusement. Aristotle, for example, thought the dance was valuable because it reflected the manners and actions of the people. Homer thought very highly of social dancing.

Cicero, however, who was a rather proper Roman orator, had this to say about dancing: "No man who is sober dances, unless he is out of his mind, either when alone or in any decent society; for dancing is the companion of wanton conviviality, dissoluteness and luxury." Imagine what he would say about our rock-and-roll!

Among the Greeks there was dancing at all the banquets and festivities. And it was so much a part of ancient Greek life that both Socrates and Plato approved of it.

Dancing as a social art was known in Egypt more than 4,000 years ago! It was the custom to entertain dinner guests with dancing at ancient Egyptian banquets. In India, too, dancing as a form of entertainment has existed since the earliest times, though many of these dances had a religious significance. Another country where social dancing has been practiced for a long time is Spain, many of whose dance steps may have been Arabian in origin.

The country where social dancing as we know it really began to develop is France. Even though many of the dances originated in other countries, they were brought to perfection in France. It was Catherine de Medici who was chiefly responsible for this at first. She loved social dancing, and the taste for it spread from the Court to private homes.

At Versailles, under Louis XIV, social dancing reached great heights. Magnificent ballets were organized and the best composers of the day created music just for the dances at the Court.

HOW DID BASKETBALL GET ITS NAME?

If you had to name the game that is watched by more spectators in the United States than any other, which would it be? Surprisingly enough, it is basketball.

Basketball is often called "the international game" because it is played in every civilized nation of the world. Yet basketball did not develop slowly over the centuries, as some of our other games have. It was invented by one man, James A. Naismith, in 1891.

Naismith wanted to provide a game to interest students of physical education at the Springfield Training School, Springfield, Massachusetts. Naismith was a Canadian and he combined the Indian game of lacrosse and the British game of soccer to make a suitable indoor game.

Instead of using a stick as in lacrosse, or kicking a ball with the foot as in soccer, Naismith devised a game by which the ball is passed from player to player, or bounced (the dribble) by a single player and shot into a goal. When he first created the game, the only thing he had to use for a goal was a wooden peach basket, so he called the game "basketball"!

In basketball, as in many other games, the special talent of a player determines what position he is chosen to play. Those who are good at scoring goals by throwing the ball through the hoop are usually stationed at forward, where they lead the team's attack on the opponents' goal.

The center is usually tall. He should be able to tip the ball to a teammate during the center jump. His height should also give his team "control of the backboard," which means being able to regain control of the ball when a shot fails to go through the hoop. The guards have to keep the opposing forwards from scoring, so they have to be agile, tricky, and able to take their part in offensive passing and shooting.

WHEN DID BOXING BEGIN?

Many people say that boxing should be outlawed. In the history of boxing this has happened many times. People have felt boxing was too cruel or barbaric, and have wanted it stopped.

Imagine how they would feel if they could see the first boxing bouts that were held! These were in ancient Greece, and the boxers performed at Olympic games and other public games. Some of the rules they observed were very much like the ones we have today. But there was one big difference: Instead of gloves, the fighters wore the *cestus*. This was a wrapping of leather studded with lead or bronze plates. A blow from a *cestus,* as you can see, could be quite damaging!

After the fall of the Roman Empire, boxing disappeared, not to reappear until it was revived in England at the beginning of the 18th century. It soon became quite a fashionable sport, and it remained so for more than 100 years.

The fights were decided with bare fists, and many of them lasted for several hours. Wrestling and throwing were allowed. A round ended only when a man was knocked down, and the time between rounds varied. This tough fight went on and on until one of the fighters was unable to walk up to a chalk mark at the center of the ring when a round began!

Naturally, this kind of brutal boxing eventually turned public opinion against prize fighting. Something had to be done to save the sport, so padded gloves began to be used. Then little by little, the old rules were made more humane. Finally, in 1867, came the big step that brought boxing back into favor. The Marquis of Queensberry introduced a set of rules that made many improvements. For example, the rounds were limited to three minutes each. The interval between rounds was one minute. These rules were adopted all over the world, and the rules governing boxing today are based on them

Until the 20th century, there was very little boxing in countries outside of England and the United States—but it has since spread all over the world.

WHEN DID CRICKET ORIGINATE AND WHERE DID BASEBALL START?

Cricket is believed to have originated in England in the fifteenth century; certainly it is known to have been played then. From old newspapers we are able to see that cricket matches were advertised in the early 1700's. The first recorded county cricket match was played in 1719. By 1750 the pitch was fixed as 22 yards (20 metres) long with a two-stump wicket, 22 inches (56 centimetres) high, and 6 inches (15 centimetres) wide. No limits were made to the bat, which was long and curved, bearing little resemblance to the modern bat. Pictures of the period show the players clad in white shirts, breeches and stockings and wearing a variety of headgear, though mainly a sort of top hat.

The Hambledon Club, founded about 1750, played an important part in the history of cricket. Hambledon was a small village in Hampshire, but its fame spread rapidly and its team defeated one representing the rest of England. Bowling was underarm, but skill in setting the field and in wicket-keeping soon developed.

Lord's Cricket Ground, opened in 1781, also had an historic role. In 1814 it moved to its present site, where the Marylebone Cricket Club (the now-famous M.C.C.) established its headquarters. The Club, founded in 1788, became the ruling body for cricket. By the 1800's the wicket was fixed at 27 inches (69 centimetres) by 9 inches (3.5 centimetres). Batsmen had a big advantage over bowlers until round-arm bowling became the vogue in the forties. Overarm bowling was not recognised until 1864.

Test Cricket began with matches in Australia in 1877 when Lillywhite's English touring side was defeated by a combined Australian team. The first test match in England was played in 1880 and with the exception of the war years, test matches have continued ever since.

In 1907 an American commission investigated the origins of baseball, intending to settle the controversy once and for all. This commission published its report in 1908, and this said that baseball was distinctly an American game, that Doubleday had invented it and that baseball had nothing to do with any foreign games.

Some people, however, thought that the commission did not really try to investigate the origin of baseball, but chose as its purpose to prove that it was an American game. A great deal of evidence has since been collected to support this criticism. Let us consider some of it. The name "baseball" itself was used to describe a popular English game that goes back to the eighteenth century. A book published in England in 1744 and reprinted in the United States in 1762 and 1787 describes a game of baseball that shows a player at the plate with a bat, a catcher behind him, a pitcher, and two bases. In fact there were many references in books published before 1830 not only to baseball but also to baseball clubs.

WHAT WAS THE FIRST MOTION PICTURE?

A curious thing about the development of motion pictures is that the first people who made it possible weren't interested in movies at all! The first inventions were by men who wanted to study the movements of animals.

Even Thomas Edison, who perfected a device called "a kinetoscope" in 1893, thought of it only as a curiosity. But there were many other people who saw great possibilities for entertainment in these inventions and they began to make movies.

At first they were only scenes of something that moved. There were waves on the beach, horses running, children swinging, and trains arriving at stations. The first film which really told a story was produced in the Edison Laboratories in 1903. It was *The Great Train Robbery,* and it caused a nation-wide sensation.

The first permanent motion-picture theatre in the United States opened in November, 1905, in Pittsburgh, Pennsylvania. This theatre was luxuriously decorated and the owners called it "the Nickelodeon." Soon, all over the country, other Nickelodeons were opened.

D. W. Griffith, a former actor, was among the most famous of the early directors and producers. He was the first man to move a camera during a scene and he perfected modern editing technique. He invented the closeup and many other parts of motion picture art. In 1914, he produced *The Birth of a Nation,* one of the most spectacular pictures of all time. This picture about the Civil War cost more than $750,000 and was the most expensive film made up to that time.

Hollywood became the movie capital of the world after Cecil B. de Mille and Jesse Lasky began making a movie there called *The Squaw Man.* Soon other companies came to Hollywood and modern movies were on their way.

WHO INVENTED TELEVISION?

Television, as you know, is a rather complicated process. Whenever such a process is developed, you can be sure a great many people had a hand in it and it goes far back for its beginnings. So television was not "invented" by one man alone.

The chain of events leading to television began in 1817, when a Swedish chemist named Jons Berzelius discovered the chemical element "selenium." Later it was found that the amount of electrical current selenium would carry depended on the amount of light which struck it. This property is called "photoelectricity."

In 1875, this discovery led a United States inventor, G. R. Carey, to make the first crude television system, using photoelectric cells. As a scene or object was focused through a lens onto a bank of photoelectric cells, each cell would control the amount of electricity it would pass on to a light bulb. Crude outlines of the object that was projected on the photoelectric cells would then show in the lights on the bank of bulbs.

The next step was the invention of "the scanning disk" in 1884 by Paul Nipkow. It was a disk with holes in it which revolved in front of the photoelectric cells, and another disk which revolved in front of the person watching. But the principle was the same as Carey's.

In 1923 came the first practical transmission of pictures over wires, and this was accomplished by Baird in England and Jenkins in the United States. Then came great improvements in the development of television cameras. Vladimir Zworykin and Philo Farnsworth each developed a type of camera, one known as "the inconoscope" and the other as "the image dissector."

By 1945, both of these camera pickup tubes had been replaced by "the image orthicon." And today, modern television sets use a picture tube known as "a kinescope." In this tube is an electric gun which scans the screen in exactly the way the beam does in the camera tube to enable us to see the picture.

Of course, this doesn't explain in any detail exactly how television works, but it gives you an idea of how many different developments and ideas had to be perfected by different people to make modern television possible.

WHO INVENTED PLAYING CARDS?

In nine out of ten homes in Great Britain today, you can find a set of playing cards. More than eight out of every ten families play card games. In fact, playing cards are so familiar to most of us that we somehow have the feeling that they have always existed.

The truth is that playing cards have been known since the very first days of man's creation of a graphic art. Their history goes back so far in time that no one can tell exactly when or where they originated.

For a long time it was claimed that the Chinese invented playing cards, because long ago the Chinese paper money and their playing cards were practically identical. We know that there were playing cards in China a thousand years ago! But now it is considered uncertain whether the Chinese, the Egyptians, the Arabs, or the Hindus invented playing cards.

The use of playing cards for fortune telling goes back to their very origin. It's even possible that they were used for this purpose before they were used for playing games or gambling. All through the Middle Ages, playing cards were used by "sorcerers" to foretell the future.

When were playing cards introduced into Europe? Some people believe the Crusaders brought them back from their travels. Others say the Saracens introduced them into Spain or Italy, or that gypsies brought them into Eastern Europe. In any case, playing cards have apparently been known in Europe since the 13th century.

Originally, there were many different types of playing cards. The tarots were picture cards and had no numbers. There were 22 tarot cards. A different type of card had numbers and there were 56 cards in this deck. The French were the first to create a deck of 52 cards. They used the number cards and kept the king, queen, and knave, or jack, from the picture cards. This 52-card deck was adopted by the English.

The earliest cards were hand-painted, but with the development of wood engraving, playing cards became cheaper and spread to the common people very quickly.

HOW DID CHESS ORIGINATE?

There is probably no game about which so much has been written for so many hundreds of years as chess. It is called "the royal game" because it is considered the king of games. It is also probably the oldest game known, some people claiming that it is about 5,000 years old!

We know that the name "chess" is derived from the Persian word *shah,* meaning "king." And we know that "checkmate" is derived from the Persian *shah mat,* meaning "the king is dead." But did the Persian originate chess? No one knows for sure.

The fact is, the origin of chess has been attributed at one time or another to the Greeks, Romans, Babylonians, Egyptians, Jews, Persians, Chinese, Hindus, Arabians, and many others! One theory is that it originated among the Buddhists in India. According to Buddhist ideas, war and the killing of one's fellow men for any purpose whatever are criminal. So chess was invented by them as a substitute for war! Most authorities now believe that chess probably did originate in India, spread to Persia, Arabia, and then to Western Europe.

As far as the individual pieces are concerned, they have undergone many changes in the long history of chess. The king at one time could be captured, which, of course, is impossible in chess as we now play it. "Castling" was a new idea added to chess about 400 years ago.

The queen in chess has perhaps the most interesting history. At one time this piece was called by a name that meant "minister" or "general"! Nowadays, when you play chess and lose your queen you feel you've lost

248

your most powerful piece. But in ancient times the queen moved only one square diagonally and thus was the weakest piece on the board! It was only about 500 years ago that she was given her present power.

The rooks and knights seem to have been unchanged down through the years. The rook, by the way, gets its name from the Indian word *rukh* and the Persian word *rokh,* meaning "a soldier."

Today, chess is played the world over, and the international tournaments, which are held regularly, are eagerly followed by millions of people.

WHO INVENTED STAMPS?

Have you ever wondered why they are called "postage" stamps? It goes back to the old days when packages and letters were carried by men across the country in relays. The stations where one messenger handed on the mail to the next messenger were called "posts." So the word "postage" meant the charge for carrying the mail.

The word "stamp" comes from the way the letters were sealed. A blob of wax was put on the letter, and before it became hard, the design of a seal or ring was stamped into it. This identified the sender of the letter.

The idea of using stamps, instead of wrappers or other devices for mail, was first suggested in the 1830's by an Englishman called Rowland Hill. He thought that by using postage stamps there would be an increase in the use of the mails and thus the government would get more revenue. He also suggested a big change in the cost of sending letters.

Before his time, the cost of sending a letter depended on two things: the number of sheets in the letter and the distance it was to travel. The farther a letter went, the more it cost for each sheet. Hill suggested that there should be a standard rate for sending letters, depending only on the weight. The distance it would travel would make no difference.

The first country to use postage stamps was Great Britain in 1840. From here the idea spread quite quickly. Zurich and Geneva, which were cantons in Switzerland then, were the next to issue postage stamps. The first country in the Western Hemisphere to issue stamps was not the United States—but Brazil! It issued postage stamps in 1843, and the United States followed in 1847. Actually, however, some local postmasters and private letter-carrying services had been issuing their own stamps since 1842, before the Government took it over.

HOW DID DOGS GET THEIR NAMES?

If you live in the country and have to take care of sheep or cattle, a tiny lap dog wouldn't be of much help to you. But if you lived in a small apartment in the city, a big, long-haired dog would certainly make a mess of it in no time! Dogs have been domesticated longer than any other animal, and man has developed more than 200 breeds of dogs to serve him in different ways for different purposes.

Did you know that the ancient Romans felt that all dogs could be divided into just three groups? These were the wise dogs, the fighting dogs, and swift-footed dogs. Today, the International Kennel Club divides dogs into six main classes: sporting dogs, which hunt by scent in the air; hounds, which hunt by ground scent; terriers, which hunt by digging into the earth; working dogs; toy dogs, for companions; and nonsporting dogs, which have many uses.

The individual breeds of dogs usually got their names because of some special feature or characteristic. For example, the bloodhound is an obvious name. It has the instinct of tracking blood by smell. The greyhound, however, gets its name in a way you'd probably never be able to guess. It was once called the *graihound,* because it originally came from *Graikoi,* which was the name for Greece!

The bulldog was used at one time to work with bulls, so that's easy. A pointer is pretty obvious, too. It points out the presence of game with his nose. The setter does it in a different way. It crouches, or "sets," over the place where game lies hidden! The terrier, which we said hunts by digging into the earth, gets its name from the Latin *terra,* "the earth."

A harrier is a dog used in hunting hares. The beagle gets its name from the Gaelic word *beag,* which meant "little." The St. Bernard dog is named after the monastery of St. Bernard in the Alps where it is bred. The Pomeranian is so called because it was bred in Pomerania, Prussia. "Mastiff" comes from the Italian *mastino,* which means "watchdog." The spaniel is a Spanish dog, as the name suggests. And the word "poodle" comes from the German *pudel,* "a puddle," because it's a water dog!

WHEN DID MAN
BEGIN TO DOMESTICATE ANIMALS?

When man began to domesticate animals he took one of his greatest steps forward on the road to civilization. Because domesticated animals supplied labor for man and made him sure of his meat supply, he no longer had to depend solely on hunting. Hence he could settle down to a fixed home site, acquire possessions, and start building a new kind of society.

Nobody knows exactly when this happened, or which animals were domesticated at which time. But we know that it was before recorded history. After the dog came tame cattle, sheep, goats, and pigs. These animals, as well as the beasts of burden, such as the camel, the yak, and the ass, were originally domesticated not in Europe but probably in central Asia.

It is not surprising that the earliest domestic animals were those which could help maintain the food supply. The dog helped man with his hunting. Cattle, sheep, goats, and pigs furnished meat or milk or both. Birds probably followed soon after. The goose was most likely the first of all poultry to be domesticated, followed by the duck. By the way, they were both common in ancient Egypt.

Pigeons, besides being good to eat, have served man since Biblical times as messengers. Prehistoric cliff dwellers in North America raised flocks of turkeys. And rabbits were probably first kept for food, too.

The animals which serve mankind as beasts of burden were domesticated later than were goats, sheep, and cattle. The ass and the camel were probably man's first beasts of burden. The horse was tamed later.

Elephants, too, were tamed and put to work by man many centuries ago. And in South America, the llama has carried burdens for uncounted ages. Cats were domesticated in Egypt about 3,600 years ago.

HOW DID THE CIRCUS BEGIN?

Didn't circuses always exist, since the day there were children in the world? The circus is so universally loved and has so much legend and magic about it, it's almost hard to believe it didn't always exist.

Actually the first circuses were quite different from the ones we're all familiar with. They took place in ancient Rome and were held in a huge arena called "the Circus Maximus." The main attraction was chariot races. Between the races, acrobats, tightrope walkers, and horsemen entertained the crowds.

The circus as it is known today comes from the van shows held in England in the early 18th century. Troupes of acrobats and jugglers traveled from one town to another in vans, which they used as dressing rooms.

They gave their performances on the village green at fairs and markets. No admission was charged, but after each performance the manager passed a hat to collect what money he could get.

The first United States circus was presented by Ricketts in Philadelphia and in New York City in the late 18th century. It was very small, but quite popular, and even George Washington attended some of its performances.

In the first half of the 19th century, many circuses sprang up in the United States. They traveled about the country in wagons, and the show

could go on only in the daytime because there was no way to light up the ring. Nine horses and seven men were considered a full troupe at that time. The band was made up of a hurdy-gurdy, a clarinet, and a bass drum.

About 1860, circuses began to resemble the kind we know today. Tents came into use, candles on a frame around the center pole made it possible to give shows at night, the number of performers and animals increased, and fresh attractions were always being added. Then along came P. T. Barnum who started to take his circus around the country by rail and "the greatest show on earth" was born!

WHO STARTED THE FIRST ZOO?

"Zoo" is short for "zoological garden." And a zoological garden is a place where living animals are kept and exhibited.

Why do we keep wild animals in zoos? The most important reason is that everyone is interested in animals. Another reason is that scientists are able to learn many important things by studying living animals. By watching the things animals do, what they eat, and how they grow, much can be learned not only about them—but about human beings, too.

So a zoo is a kind of school for learning about both animals and people. And this probably explains why the first zoo we know anything about was called an "intelligence park." It was started as long ago as 1150 B.C. by a Chinese emperor, and it had many kinds of deer, birds, and fish in it. Even though it was somewhat like our modern zoos, there was one big catch to it. It probably wasn't open to the public but was kept for the amusement of the Emperor and his Court.

Since it costs a great deal of money to put together a zoo and maintain it, zoos in ancient times were assembled and owned by kings and rich lords. Many of them had collections of rare birds, fish, and animals of all kinds.

The first real public zoological garden in the world was opened in Paris in 1793. This was the famous *Jardin des Plantes*. In it were animals, a museum, and a botanical garden.

The next big zoological garden to be opened was in 1829 in Regent's Park in London. Then came the Zoological Garden of Berlin, which was begun in 1844 and became one of the finest and best in the world.

In the United States, the first zoo to be opened was in Philadelphia in 1874, and the next year (1875) came the Zoological Garden in Cincinnati.

WHEN DID PEOPLE BEGIN TO WEAR WIGS?

Did you know that Egyptian mummies more than 4,000 years old have been found adorned with wigs? So the Egyptians must have worn them quite commonly. In ancient Greece wigs were used by men and women. It is believed that wigs were introduced from Persia and spread throughout Asia Minor.

In ancient Greece wigs were also used for the theatre, and the various masks they had for comedy and tragedy had hair suited to the character that was being represented.

In Rome wigs came into use in the early days of the empire. The fashionable ladies of Rome loved to wear false hair, and the golden hair imported from Germany was considered very desirable. Women had wigs of different colors to go with their costumes, and the wife of Marcus Aurelius was said to own several hundred wigs!

In the 16th century, wigs were worn simply to look like natural hair. But a hundred years later wigs became an important part of the costume.

The fashion started in France. In 1624, Louis XIII, who was bald, began to wear a wig and everybody copied him.

From France the fashion spread through Europe. In England, Charles II wore a peruke, which is a short wig, and this became popular. During the time of Queen Anne wigs were worn which covered the back and the shoulders and floated down over the chest!

Later on, certain types of wigs were worn by certain professions, and in time they were the only ones to wear wigs. Gradually, doctors, soldiers, and clergymen gave up the custom. Wigs are now worn as part of the official costume only in England, and only by the speaker of the House of Commons and the clerks of Parliament, the Lord Chancellor, and the judges and attorneys.

HOW DID COOKING OF FOOD BEGIN?

Why can you eat fruit and many vegetables raw, and yet have to cook meat and fish? To most of us, of course, cooked meat and fish simply taste better than when raw.

But there is another, even more important reason. And that is, when we fail to cook certain meats and fish, or don't cook them enough, organisms which live in the fish and animals may enter our body and cause disease. The best known example of this is "trichinosis," a disease human beings may get from eating undercooked or uncooked pork or pork products. Tapeworm and other infections by parasites can be caught by eating undercooked fish of certain kinds.

Of course, early man had no choice—he had to eat his food raw because he had no way of cooking it. When man at last discovered how to make fire, he used it to keep warm and to frighten away wild animals.

The possibility is that man discovered the cooking of food by accident. Some of the animals he killed may have been thrown near the embers of his fire. Or meat may have fallen into the glowing embers. When man saw the meat turn brown, and noticed how good it smelled, he tasted it and found it more satisfying than when raw. So he may have decided to cook it from then on.

There were no pots, so early man cooked on the hot stones around an open fire. The first oven was a pit lined with stones and glowing coals. Soon he began to build an oven for his cooking above the ground, with an outlet for smoke, a draft, and a stone across the front opening to hold in the heat.

Man learned how to boil food in pits lined with large hide or skin. This was filled with water and heated to the boiling point by red-hot stones. Eventually man learned to smear clay over reed baskets and let it harden. These were the first primitive kettles. They were placed over the fire for cooking foods, either with or without water.

Thus early man worked out the two main methods of cooking: by baking or roasting in dry heat, and by boiling or steaming in moist heat.

Chapter 3

THE HUMAN BODY

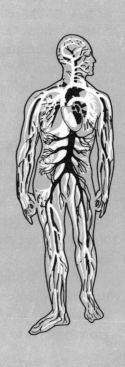

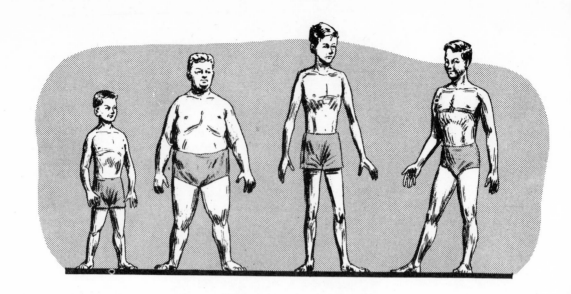

HOW DO WE GROW?

All living things grow. They grow in structure (shape, size, and how they are made), and in function (what they can do).

The most important forces that cause growth lie inside a living thing from its beginning. These forces are called its heridity. Animals, including human beings, have stages of growth. These are: embryo and fetus (not yet born), infant, child, youth, mature adult, and old age.

Some creatures have hardly any infancy. Some birds can fly as soon as they hatch. The guinea pig can take care of itself three days after birth. The human being is not an adult until he is about 20 years old.

At birth an infant already has all the nerve cells he will ever have—the cells in his brain, in his spinal cord, and those that reach out into every part of his body. The growth of the connections between these nerve cells will enable him to control his movements, to learn, and to behave like the people in his society.

So all human beings are much alike in their growth. But there are important differences. Boys and girls all follow the same general pathway of growth, but each one follows it in his own particular way and at his own speed.

People's bodies grow faster in the early weeks of life than at any other time. Even before the end of the first year, they are growing less rapidly. Through the whole period of childhood, they grow at a moderate rate. Then growth starts to speed up again.

For girls, this usually begins between ages 11 and 13, and for boys, between 12 and 14. For a while, they grow faster until they reach a top speed. Then they slow down again and grow more slowly until growth in height stops altogether. They have reached full size.

Growth in height and growth in weight often takes turns in a person. First he grows upward for a while, then sideways. For many people, there is a "chubby" period that happens somewhere around 11 or 12 years. But then their height begins to catch up in the next years and the chubbiness is gone.

WHY DO WE STOP GROWING?

The average baby is about 50 centimetres long when it is born. In the next 20 years, man triples the length of the body he was born with and reaches an average height of about 1.7 metres.

Why doesn't he just keep on growing and growing? What makes the body stop getting bigger? In the body, there is a system of glands called the endocrine glands which controls our growth.

The endocrine glands are: the thyroid in the neck, the pituitary attached to the brain, the thymus which is in the chest, and the sex glands. The pituitary gland is the one that stimulates our bones to grow. If this gland works too much, our arms and legs grow too long and our hands and feet become too big. If the gland doesn't work hard enough, we might end up as midgets.

A child is born with a large thymus gland and it continues to get bigger during childhood. When a child reaches the age of 13 or 14, the thymus gland begins to shrink. The thymus gland and the sex glands may have a certain relationship. As long as the thymus gland is working, the sex glands are small. As the sex glands develop, the thymus gland stops working. This is why, when a person has become sexually mature at about the age of 22, he stops growing!

Sometimes the sex glands develop too soon and slow up the thymus gland too early. This often makes a person below average in height. Since our legs grow later and grow more than other parts of the body, this early development makes the legs short. That's why people who develop too early are often thickset. Napoleon was an example of this kind of person.

If the sex glands develop too late, the thymus continues working and the person becomes taller than the average. Actually, we continue growing slightly even after the age of 25, and we reach our maximum height at about the age of 35 to 40. After that, we shrink about 12 millimetres every 10 years. The reason for this is the drying-up of the cartilages in our joints and in the spinal column as we get older.

WHAT MAKES US HUNGRY?

When we need food, our body begins to crave for it. But how do we know that we are feeling "hunger"? How does our mind get the message and make us feel "hungry"?

Hunger has nothing to do with an empty stomach, as most people believe. A baby is born with an empty stomach, yet it doesn't feel hungry for several days. People who are sick or feverish often have empty stomachs without feeling hungry.

Hunger begins when certain nutritive materials are missing in the blood. When the blood vessels lack these materials, a message is sent to a part of the brain that is called the "hunger center." This hunger center works like a brake on the stomach and the intestine. As long as the blood has sufficient food, the hunger center slows up the action of the stomach and the intestine. When the food is missing from the blood, the hunger center makes the stomach and intestine more active. That's why a hungry person often hears his stomach "rumbling."

When we are hungry, our body doesn't crave any special kind of food, it just wants nourishment. But our appetite sees to it that we don't satisfy our hunger with just one food, which would be unhealthy. For instance, it would be hard for us to take in a certain amount of nourishment all in the form of potatoes. But if we eat soup until we've had enough, then meat and vegetables until we've had enough, then dessert until we've had enough, we can take in the same quantity of food and enjoy it!

How long can we live without food? That depends on the individual. A very calm person can live longer without food than an excitable one because the protein stored up in his body is used up more slowly. The world's record for going without food was claimed by a woman in South Africa who said she lived on nothing but water and soda water for 102 days!

HOW DO WE DIGEST FOOD?

Taking food into our bodies is not enough to keep us alive and growing. The food must be changed so that it can be used by the body, and this process is called "digestion."

Digestion starts when food is put in the mouth, chewed, and swallowed, and it continues in the alimentary canal, which is a long, partly coiled tube going through the body. All parts of the alimentary canal are joined together, but they are different in the way they work. The mouth opens into a wide "pharynx" in the throat, which is a passage used for both food and air. The "esophagus" passes through the chest and connects the pharynx and stomach. The stomach leads into the coiled "small intestine." The last part of the alimentary canal is the "colon" or "large intestine."

Here is a quick picture of what happens to food during digestion. In the mouth, the saliva helps to break down starches (such as in corn or potatoes). When food has been moistened and crushed in the mouth, it goes down through the pharynx and along the esophagus, and finally enters the stomach.

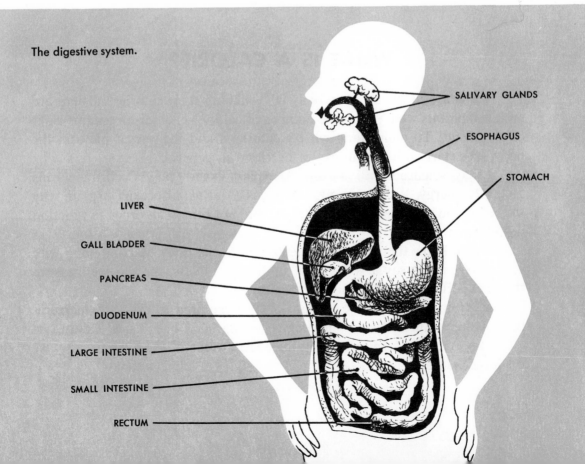

The digestive system.

SALIVARY GLANDS

ESOPHAGUS

STOMACH

LIVER

GALL BLADDER

PANCREAS

DUODENUM

LARGE INTESTINE

SMALL INTESTINE

RECTUM

It is in the stomach that most of the process of digestion takes place. Here, juices from the stomach wall are mixed with the food. Hydrochloric acid is one of these juices. Pepsin, another secretion, helps to break down proteins into simpler forms to aid digestion. The starches continue to break down until the material in the stomach becomes too acid. Then digestion of starches almost stops.

Food stays in the stomach until it is liquid. The materials in the stomach are churned about to mix digestive juices well throughout the foods. When the food is liquid it is called "chyme." The chyme moves out from the stomach into the small intestine through a valve at the lower end of the stomach, the "pylorus."

The small intestine is a tube 6.5 to 7.5 metres long, which lies in coils. In the first part of the small intestine, the "duodenum," digestion continues. Juices from the pancreas and liver help break down the foods. The breakdown of proteins is finished here, fats are split into finer parts, and starch digestion is completed here. Digested food is absorbed here into the blood and lymph. In the large intestine, water is absorbed and the contents become more solid, so they can leave the body as waste material.

WHAT IS A CALORIE?

Nowadays, it seems, everybody is "watching their calories." There are even restaurants which print the number of calories each dish contains right on the menu! To understand what a calorie is and the part it plays in the body, let's start with the subject of nutrition in general.

Today, science is still not able to explain exactly how a cell transforms food into energy. We just know it happens. And we also can't explain why the cell in the body needs certain foods, and not others, in order to function properly.

We do know that food is broken down in the body by combining with oxygen. We might say it is "burned" up like fuel. Now, the way we measure the work a fuel does is by means of calories.

A "gram calorie" is the amount of heat required to raise the temperature of one gram of water one degree centigrade. The "large calorie" is 1,000 times as great. In measuring the energy value of food, we usually use the large calorie.

Each type of food, as it "burns up," furnishes a certain number of calories. For instance, one gram of protein furnishes four calories, but one gram of fat furnishes nine calories. The body doesn't care which "fuel" is used for energy, as long as it gets enough of that energy from food to maintain life.

The amount of calories the body needs depends on the work the body is doing. For example, a man weighing about 68 kilograms needs only 1,680 calories per day if he is in a state of absolute rest. If he does moderate work such as desk work, this jumps to 3,360 calories per day. And if he does heavy work, he may need as much as 6,720 calories a day to keep the body functioning properly.

Children need more calories than adults, since older people can't burn up the fuel as quickly. Interestingly enough, we use up more calories in winter than in summer. The normal fuels of the body are carbohydrates, starch, and sugar. Suppose, however, we take in more fuels than we need? The body uses up what it needs and stores some of it away for future use. The body can store away about one-third of the amount it needs each day. The rest becomes fat! And that's why we "watch our calories."

WHAT ARE VITAMINS?

The word *vita* means life. Vitamins are substances necessary to maintain life. These substances are formed by plants or animals which must be supplied to the body in tiny quantities so that the vital processes can continue as they should.

Until late in the 19th century, a peculiar and dangerous disease called "scurvy" used to cause serious illness among the crews of sailing ships all over the world. Late in the 18th century, it was discovered that the eating of fresh fruits and vegetables cured the disease. It took scientists 100 years to find out that this happened because fresh foods contained vitamins!

Because they didn't know the exact chemical nature of these vitamins, they didn't give them names but simply called them Vitamins A, B, C, D, etc. Let us see why some of these vitamins are necessary for good health.

Vitamin A is always found in association with fat in the animal body. It is formed in growing plants and transferred to animals when they eat the plants. Vitamin A helps prevent infection. It is found in milk, egg yolk, liver, cod liver oil, and in lettuce, carrots, and spinach.

Vitamin B, or the "B complex," as it is called, was for many years thought to be one vitamin. Now it is known to be at least six different vitamins. These are called "B1, B2," etc. Vitamin B1 is necessary for the prevention of certain nervous diseases, and its absence causes a disease called "beriberi." Vitamin B1 is found in milk, fresh fruits, whole grain cereals, and fresh vegetables. Vitamin B1 must be constantly replaced in the body.

Another important vitamin is Vitamin C. Absence of this vitamin causes scurvy. The joints become stiff, teeth become loose, and the bones become weak. Oranges, cabbage, and tomatoes are rich in Vitamin C. The body is unable to store Vitamin C so it must be replaced constantly.

Vitamin D is important for infants in proper bone development and for teeth. This vitamin is found in great quantities in cod liver oil, liver, and egg yolk. Sunlight provides our body with Vitamin D, too. If you eat a well-balanced diet, you are probably getting enough of the vitamins you need.

WHY DO WE PERSPIRE?

The body could be considered a permanent furnace. The food we take in is "fuel," which the body "burns up." In this process, about 2,500 calories are being used every day in the body.

Now this is quite a bit of heat. It's enough heat to bring 23 litres of water to the boiling point! What happens to all this heat in the body? If there were no temperature controls in the body, we could certainly think of ourselves as "hot stuff." But we all know that the heat of the body doesn't go up (unless we're sick). We know that our body heat remains at an average temperature of 37 degrees centigrade.

Perspiration is one of the ways we keep our body "furnace" at a nice normal temperature. Actually, our body temperature is controlled by a center in the brain known as the temperature center. It consists of three parts: a control center, a heating center, and a cooling center.

Suppose the temperature of the blood drops for some reason. The heating center goes to work and certain things begin to happen. Special glands give out more chemical substances to burn, the muscles and the liver use up more "fuel," and soon our internal temperature rises.

Now suppose the temperature of the blood rises for some reason. The cooling center goes to work. The process of oxidation, or burning up of fuel, is slowed up. And another important thing happens. The vessels in the skin are dilated, or opened, so that the extra heat can radiate away, and also to help our perspiration to evaporate.

When a liquid evaporates, it takes away heat. For example, we feel cold after a bath because the water which remains in contact with our warm skin is evaporating rapidly and cooling us off. So perspiration is part of the process of cooling the body.

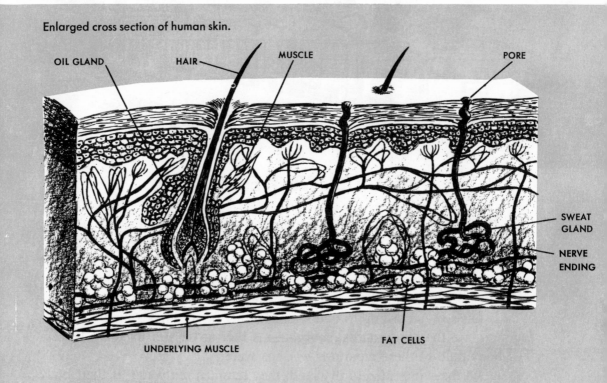

Enlarged cross section of human skin.

OIL GLAND   HAIR   MUSCLE   PORE

SWEAT GLAND

NERVE ENDING

UNDERLYING MUSCLE   FAT CELLS

Perspiration is like a shower which washes the body from within. The fluid flows out through millions of tiny openings in the skin in the form of miscroscopic drops. And these tiny drops can evaporate quickly and cool the body quickly when necessary.

On humid days, we suffer because the water on our skin can't evaporate easily. So we use fans to carry away the moist air and to help the evaporation of our perspiration.

WHY DO WE NEED SALT?

The body of a human being contains about 47 litres of water. In fact, many of our organs have an amazingly high water content. For instance, muscle is 75 per cent water, the liver is 70 per cent water, the brain is 79 per cent water, and the kidney is 83 per cent water!

But this "body fluid" is not pure water. It is actually a salt solution. Why is this so? According to one scientific theory, all land animals, including man, are the descendants of organisms that arose and lived in the sea. The body fluid of these creatures was sea water.

When they emigrated to dry land, they retained sea water as their body fluid. But the land is unable to provide enough salt in a natural way. Since salt dissolves in water, the solid land loses much of its salt into the rivers and oceans with rain water. Therefore the plants which grow in this land, do not contain enough salt.

This is why animals that feed on plants desire salt. The body loses a certain amount of fluid every day which contains salt, and plant food doesn't replace it. The animals that feed on other animals don't desire extra salt. They get all the salt they need from the body fluid of their victims. This applies to human beings, too. For instance, the Eskimos eat mostly meat, so they have very little craving for salt.

People who live inland have always had a greater desire for salt than others. In ancient Mexico, salt was considered so valuable that there was a salt god. And as we know, in ancient times in Europe people were paid for work done in salt. Our word "salary" comes from the Latin word for salt.

In the human body, salt accumulates most in the skin. If a person eats a diet without salt, the blood loses its salt through various methods of excretion. Then the skin must give up its reserves of salt to the blood, so that the blood can keep a constant concentration of salt. When this happens and the skin gives up its reserves of salt, it often has a beneficial effect on skin diseases. That's why salt-free diets are often prescribed for people with certain diseases.

Salt is eliminated chiefly by the kidneys. If the kidneys are sick, the patient is given a diet with little salt, so as not to overwork the kidneys.

WHY DO WE GET THIRSTY?

When we feel thirsty and have nothing to drink, we may suffer so much that we can think of nothing else. All of us have the experience of being thirsty at times—but can you imagine how it would feel to be thirsty for days and days? If a human being has absolutely nothing to drink for three weeks, he will die.

Our body simply needs to replenish its liquid supply—and yet between 50 and 60 per cent of our weight is water! As a matter of fact, in the course of a day the average adult loses about two-thirds of a litre of water through perspiration, and excretes about a litre of water to get rid of waste products.

On the other hand, whether we drink or not, we also take in water. When the body digests food, it obtains almost a third of a litre of liquid from this food per day. But this process of losing water and gaining it isn't enough to keep the balance of water our body needs. Thirst is the signal our body gives us that it needs more water.

Dryness in the mouth or throat is not what causes thirst, as many people believe. That dryness may be caused by many things such as nervousness, exercise, or just a slowing-up of the flow of saliva. It is possible to make the saliva flow again (for example, with a little lemon juice), but this will not take care of our thirst.

In fact, your saliva can be flowing freely, your stomach and blood stream and bladder may be full of water—and you can still be thirsty! For example, people who drink whiskey at a bar may have taken several drinks and still feel thirsty—if they happen to have munched on salty peanuts or pretzels between drinks!

The reason for this is that thirst is caused by a change in the salt content of our blood. There is a certain normal amount of salt and water in our blood. When this changes by having more salt in relation to water in our blood, thirst results.

In our brain, there is a "thirst center." It responds to the amount of salt in our blood. When there is a change, it sends messages to the back of the throat. From there, messages go back to the brain, and it is this combination of feelings that makes us say we're thirsty.

WHY DO WE GET TIRED?

Fatigue can actually be considered a kind of poisoning! When a muscle in the body works, it produces lactic acid. If we remove the lactic acid from a tired muscle, it's able to start working again at once!

In the course of a day, we "poison ourselves" with lactic acid. There are other substances the body produces in the course of muscular activity, which are known as "fatigue toxins." The blood carries these through the body, so that not only the muscle itself feels tired, but the entire body, especially the brain.

Scientists have made an interesting experiment about fatigue. If a dog is made to work until it is exhausted and falls asleep, and its blood is then

transfused into the body of another dog, the second dog will instantly become "tired" and fall asleep! If the blood of a wide-awake dog is transfused into a tired, sleeping dog, the latter will wake up at once, no longer tired!

But fatigue is not just a chemical process; it is also a biological process. We can't just "remove" fatigue; we must allow the cells of the body to rest. Damages must be repaired, nerve cells of the brain must be "recharged," the joints of the body must replace used-up lubricants. Sleep will always be necessary as a way of restoring the body's energy after fatigue.

However, there is an interesting thing to remember about the process of resting. For example, a person who has been working hard at his desk for hours may not want to lie down at all when he's tired. He'd rather take a walk! Or when children come home from school they want to run out to play . . . not to lie down and rest.

The reason is that if only a certain part of the body is tired—say, the brain, the eyes, the hands, or the legs—the best way to make that part feel fresh again is to make other parts of the body active! We can actually rest by means of activity. Activity increases the respiration, the blood circulates faster, the glands are more active, and the waste products are eliminated from the tired part of the body. But if you are totally exhausted, the best thing to do is to go to sleep!

WHAT HAPPENS WHEN WE SLEEP?

We all know what sleep does for us. It restores our vitality and makes us feel refreshed again. Sleep is needed by the tired organs and tissues of our body.

Yet it is a curious fact that science is still unable to explain exactly how the process of sleep takes place. It is believed that deep in the brain there is a very complex area which is known as the "sleep center." This center is regulated by the blood. In the course of the day, activity by the nerves and muscles in our body sends calcium into the blood. This calcium finally stimulates the sleep center to work, and we go to sleep.

We know that if calcium is injected directly into the sleep center, an animal will go to sleep immediately. But if calcium is injected into the blood stream, this doesn't happen. So it seems that the sleep center must first be "sensitized" by certain chemical substances, produced when we are tired, before it will react to the calcium and put us to sleep.

The sleep center does two things when it makes us sleep. It blocks off the brain so that we have no will power or consciousness. This is "brain sleep." And it blocks off nerves leading from the brain so that our internal organs and limbs fall asleep. This is "body sleep." Normally, when we are asleep, both reactions have taken place.

It is possible, however, for these reactions to take place separately. For instance, the brain can sleep while the body is still awake! A very tired soldier can keep on marching with his legs, and his brain may be sleeping! Sleep-walkers do the same thing!

There are different types of sleep that we experience. A shallow sleep is less restful than a deep sleep. The reason a short nap often seems so restful is that a short sleep is usually a deep sleep!

WHAT CAUSES OUR DREAMS?

Let us begin by saying what does not cause our dreams. Our dreams do not come from "another world." They are not messages from some outside source. They are not a look into the future, nor do they prophesy anything.

All our dreams have something to do with our emotions, fears, longings, wishes, needs, memories. But something on the "outside" may influence what we dream. If a person is hungry, or tired, or cold, his dreams may include this feeling. If the covers have slipped off your bed, you may dream you are on an iceberg. The material for the dream you have tonight is likely to come from the experiences you will have today.

So the "content" of your dream comes from something that affects you while you are sleeping (you are cold, a noise, a discomfort, etc.) and it may also use your past experiences and the urges and interests you have now. This is why very young children are likely to dream of wizards and fairies, older children of school exams, hungry people of food, homesick soldiers of their families, and prisoners of freedom.

To show you how what is happening while you are asleep and your wishes or needs can all be combined in a dream, here is the story of an experiment. A man was asleep and the back of his hand was rubbed with a piece of absorbent cotton. He dreamed that he was in a hospital and his sweetheart was visiting him, sitting on the bed and stroking his hand!

There are people called psychoanalysts who have made a special study of why we dream what we dream and what those dreams mean. Their interpretation of dreams is not accepted by everyone, but it offers an interesting approach to the problem. They believe that dreams are expressions of wishes that didn't come true, of frustrated yearnings. In other words, a dream is a way of having your wish fulfilled.

During sleep, according to this theory, our inhibitions are also asleep. We can express or feel what we really want to. So we do this in a dream and thus provide an outlet for our wishes, and they may be wishes we didn't even know we had!

HOW DOES THE BLOOD CIRCULATE?

In very simple terms, the blood circulates because the heart "pumps" it and the veins and arteries act as "pipes" to carry it. The blood circulates to carry oxygen from the lungs and food materials from the organs of digestion to the rest of the body, and to remove waste products from the tissues.

The "pipes" are two systems of hollow tubes, one large and one small. Both are connected to the heart, the "pump," but do not connect with each other. The smaller system of blood vessels goes from the heart to the lungs and back. The larger goes from the heart to the various parts of the body. These tubes are called "arteries," "veins," and "capillaries." Arteries move blood away from the heart; the veins carry blood back to the heart. The

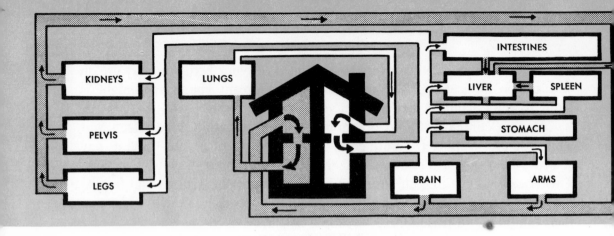

capillaries are tiny vessels for carrying blood from arteries to veins.

Now a word about the "pump"—the heart. It is like a double two-story house, each with a room upstairs, called the right and left "auricles." The downstairs rooms are the right and left "ventricles."

If we were to trace a drop of blood as it circulated through the entire body, this is the course it would follow. The blood with oxygen from the lungs goes to the left auricle (upstairs room), then to the left ventricle (downstairs room), and then to the "aorta." This is the great artery, and it and its branches carry the blood to all parts of the body.

Through the capillaries it goes from the smallest arteries into the smallest veins. It flows through the veins which become larger. Finally, it reaches the right auricle of the heart. Then into the right ventricle, and from there into arteries which carry it into the lungs. Here it gives up carbon dioxide and some water and takes up oxygen. Now it's ready to come back to the left auricle of the heart and start off on its journey again!

The heart squeezes and relaxes about 100,000 times each day and pumps about 13,630 litres of blood in 24 hours in an adult male!

HOW CAN BLOOD BE TYPED?

It is hard to believe that everyone's blood isn't exactly the same, and in fact, this wasn't known by science for a long time. Blood transfusions used to be given from man to man without any thought to blood types. But it was discovered that in about half the cases the patient got worse instead of better, and in fact, often died.

So investigation began and it was found that there are different kinds of blood. This is what happens when different types of blood are mixed. If

272

a drop of one blood type is added to the blood or serum of another type "foreign" to it, the blood cells become clumped together. This is known as "agglutination."

When agglutination takes place, the destruction of blood cells usually follows, and this is why the typing of blood is so important. By means of agglutination tests, it has been found that the blood of human beings can be divided into four groups: O, A, B, and AB.

The cells of group O are not agglutinated by the serum of any other group. In other words, type O blood can be given to any person in a transfusion. People with type O blood are known as "universal donors.' In group AB, the serum does not agglutinate any cells, so that people with this blood type can receive any other type of blood.

Every person inherits a certain blood type and it never changes. An interesting thing about blood types is that they seem to be distributed over the world in a certain way. As you move from west to east, the percentage of people with blood type A decreases, while the B group grows larger. In England 43 per cent belong to group A, in Russia 30 per cent, and in India only 15 per cent. When it comes to group B, exactly the opposite is true. By the way, there seems to be no relationship between the blood type you have and whether you are generally a healthy or sick person.

WHAT IS A BLOOD TRANSFUSION?

The need for blood can arise from many reasons. A soldier may be wounded. A worker in a factory may have a serious accident. A person may be dying because of internal bleeding. Or a weakened patient may require a serious operation.

The blood is needed to replace what was lost or to build up resistance in advance. One or two litres of new blood transfusion into his veins means new life to the patient!

The idea of blood transfusion is not new. As far back as 1654, an Italian doctor called Francesco Folli tried blood transfusions from one living animal to another. Later, there were attempts to transfuse blood from animals to man, but the results were unfavorable.

Now we know that the animals of one species do not tolerate blood from another species. In fact, it acts as a poison and usually causes death. During World War I, much progress in blood transfusion was made. It was already known that blood from certain persons could not be safely given to others. This led to classifying blood into four groups, which could be determined in advance by laboratory methods.

Since blood from a donor, or blood-giver, in one group cannot safely be given to a person with blood of another group, so the practice now is to have donors "typed" in advance. Hospitals also now have "blood banks," in which blood is kept at low temperatures, instantly available. These banks operate like money banks, receiving blood "deposits" and paying out blood instead of money. It means that when there is an emergency and blood of a certain type is needed, the bank has a supply on hand.

Today, blood banks don't only store blood, they store "plasma." The liquid, or plasma, portion of the blood is separated from the blood cells and frozen. Then a drying process reduces the plasma to powder. This is packed in a sealed package accompanied by another container which has sterilized water. When blood is needed, the water restores the plasma to its original fluid state, ready for injection! Since plasma contains no blood cells, blood type does not matter and any plasma can be used for any patient anywhere.

WHAT IS THE SKIN?

When we think of the human body, it is easy for us to think of the heart, or the liver, or the brain as "organs." They have certain jobs to do and they do them. But did you know that the skin is an organ, too?

Where other organs take up as little space as possible, the skin is spread out as thinly as possible to form a thin coat. In fact, this coat covers an area of 20,000 square centimetres. The number of complicated structures that are in each of these square centimetres is fantastic, ranging from sweat glands to nerves.

The skin consists of two layers of tissue. One is a thicker deep layer called the "corium,"and on top of it is the delicate tissue called the "epidermis." These are joined together in a remarkable way. The bottom layer has "pegs" that project into the upper layer, and this is moulded over them to bind them closely together. Because these "pegs" are arranged in ridges, they form a kind of pattern which we can see in certain places on our skin. In fact, your fingerprints are made by these ridges.

The top layer of your skin, the epidermis, doesn't contain any blood vessels. It actually consists of cells that have died and been changed into "horn." We might say that the human body is covered with horn shingles. This is very useful to us, because horn helps protect us. It is insensitive, so it protects us from pain. Water has no effect on it, and it is even a good electrical insulator.

The very bottom layers of the epidermis are very much alive, however. In fact, it is their job to produce new cells. The new cells are pushed upward by the mother cells. In time, they are separated from their source of food and die to become horn.

Billions of the upper dead horn cells are removed every day in the natural course of our activities. But luckily, just as many billions of new cells are manufactured every day. This is what keeps our skin always young.

There are 30 layers of horn cells in our skin. Every time a top layer is removed by washing or rubbing, a new one is ready underneath it. We can never use up all the layers, because a new layer is always pushing up from the bottom. In this way, we are able to remove stains and dirt from our skins and keep it clean.

WHY DO PEOPLE HAVE
DIFFERENT-COLORED SKIN?

People with the whitest skin are found in northern Europe and are called Nordics. People with the blackest skin live in western Africa. People in Southeast Asia have a yellowish tan to their skin. The majority of men, however, are not white, black, or yellow, but represent hundreds of shades of light, swarthy, and brown men.

What is the reason for these differences of color in the skin of people? The explanation really lies in a whole series of chemical processes that take place in the body and the skin. In the tissues of the skin there are certain color bases called "chromogens," which are colorless in themselves. When certain ferments or enzymes act on these color bases, a definite skin color results.

Suppose an individual either does not have these color bases, or his enzymes don't work properly on these bases? Then the person is an "albino" with no pigmentation at all. This can happen to people anywhere in the world. There are albinos in Africa, "whiter" than any white man!

Human skin itself, without the presence of any coloring substance, is creamy white. But to this is added a tinge of yellow, which is due to the presence of a yellow pigment in the skin. Another color ingredient found in skin is black, which is due to the presence of tiny granules of a substance called "melanin." This substance is sepia in color, but when it appears in large masses it seems black.

Another tone is added to the skin by the red color of the blood circulating in the tiny vessels of the skin.

The color of an individual's skin depends on the proportions in which these four colors—white, yellow, black, and red—are combined. All the skin colors of the human race can be obtained by different combinations of these color ingredients which we all have.

Sunlight has the ability to create melanin, the black pigment, in the skin. So people living in tropical areas have more of this pigment and have darker skin. But when you spend a few days in the sun, the ultra-violet light of the sun creates more melanin in your skin, too, and this results in the "sun tan"!

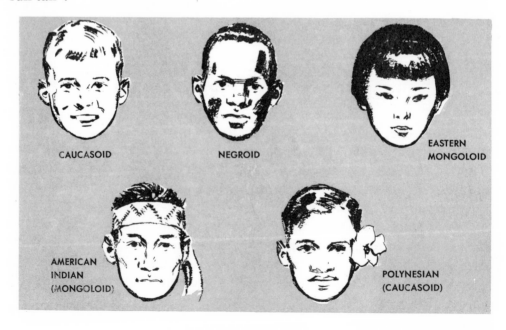

CAUCASOID

NEGROID

EASTERN MONGOLOID

AMERICAN INDIAN (MONGOLOID)

POLYNESIAN (CAUCASOID)

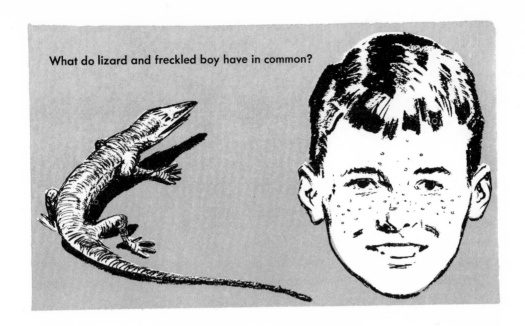

What do lizard and freckled boy have in common?

WHAT ARE FRECKLES?

To understand what freckles are and how they appear, we have to understand what gives skin its color in the first place.

The most important pigment in deciding the color of the skin is melanin. You might say that the different skin color of various races depends entirely on the difference in the amount of melanin.

In lower forms of life, by the way, it is the melanin which enables certain fish and lizards to change their colors. In the human being, its most important function, apart from controlling the color, is to protect us against the harmful effects of too much exposure to sunshine.

Melanin is produced by a whole network of special cells that are scattered through the lower layer of the epidermis, which is the thin, outer part of our skin. These cells are called "melanocytes." Now we come to the question: What are freckles? Well, freckles are simply a bunching-up of these melanocytes in spots. That's why freckles have that brownish color, the color of the pigment melanin. Why do some people have freckles and others don't? The reason is heredity. Our parents decide whether we'll have freckles!

The color of freckles (really the color of the melanin in them) can vary from light tan to dark brown, depending on exposure to sun and heat. Sunshine not only can darken them, but can cause new melanin to form.

WHAT CAUSES WARTS?

Practically everyone you know has some "special way" for getting rid of warts. People will tell you all kinds of fantastic things and promise that the warts will surely disappear if only you follow their instructions exactly.

Because warts are apt to appear suddenly and disappear suddenly, many people actually believe that some sort of magic charm must be responsible. In fact, as long ago as ancient Roman times, people had superstitious ideas about warts. A Roman called Pliny wrote this in his *Natural History*: "You are to touch the warts with chick peas on the first day of the moon, wrap the peas in cloth and throw them away behind you."

Warts are not caused by touching a frog or toad, as many people still believe today. Warts are a growth of the skin, or mucous membrane. Many warts are present from birth, others first appear in childhood or in later life. Many disappear in time.

A complete scientific explanation of what causes warts simply doesn't exist. We just don't seem to know enough about them yet! Some medical men who have studied warts believe they are caused by a filterable virus. This means a germ so tiny that even the finest filter can't stop it. Others believe they are brought on by friction and irritation.

In fact, when a wart appears on the hands or fingers of an adult, it is usually brought on by some irritation, which may be slight but is often repeated. Because the irritation is so slight, we don't notice it and a wart often results.

There are many cases of warts appearing on the hands of people who do special kinds of work. For instance, men who work in slaughter houses often get warts on their wrists or knuckles. These are called "butchers' warts," and they may be caused by tuberculosis germs.

Men who work in coal tar, petroleum, and around X-rays often get warts. These often become cancerous, which means the wart becomes cancer of the skin. It is because there is always the danger that warts might become serious infections, that they should never be tampered with by "home methods." Either leave the wart alone, or have it removed properly and completely by a doctor. Any time you agree to do anything to a wart because someone has convinced you he has a "cure" for it, you are running the risk of having it become a serious infection!

WHY DO WE HAVE MOLES?

There is an old superstition about moles. It says that when the mother is frightened or has some exciting experience before the birth of a child, the child will have a mole on his body. And this mole was often supposed to have a special outline according to what frightened the mother!

Well, a superstition is all this is. There is simply no explanation known to science as to why moles appear, or how to prevent them. They are often called "birthmarks" because they are present at birth, or appear shortly after birth.

Do you know that practically every human being has at least one mole? The average number of moles a person has is about 14! Moles can appear on almost any part of the body, including the scalp. A mole consists of the growth of the tissue in which it has formed. It may consist of the tissues of blood vessels, or cells containing pigment, or hair-follicle cells, or connective tissue. So each mole may be quite different.

There are two reasons why moles are not very desirable. One is the possibility that a mole may become transferred into a cancerous growth. This is quite rare, and most people have no reason to worry about it.

The second reason, of course, is that moles may not look very attractive, especially if they are large and on the face. But since most moles never cause any serious disturbance, the best thing to do is to leave them alone. When a mole is located in such a place that it may be irritated often or injured, then it may be desirable to have it removed. For example, moles on the soles of the feet, palms of the hands, on the collar-line of the neck or belt-line of the waist are apt to be subject to irritation. In these cases, it is best to have them removed before the person reaches teen-age.

Also, any mole which shows an increase in size, change of color, scaling, itching, or bleeding should be removed. And this is very important: Moles should be removed by a surgeon only, never by anyone else!

WHAT IS THE EYE MADE OF?

The human eye is like a camera. It has an adjustable opening to let in light (the pupil); a lens which focuses the light waves to form an image; and a sensitive film (the retina) on which the image is recorded.

Inside each human eye are about 130,000,000 light-sensitive cells. When light falls on one of these cells, it causes a quick chemical change within the cell. This change starts an impulse in a nerve fiber. This impulse is a message that travels through the optic nerve to the "seeing" part of the brain. The brain has learned what this message means so we know we are seeing.

The eye is shaped like a ball, with a slight bulge at the front. At the center of this bulge is a hole called the "pupil." It looks black because it opens into the dark inside of the eye. Light passes through the pupil to the lens. The lens focuses the light, forming a picture at the back of the eyeball. Here, instead of film as in a camera, is a screen of light-sensitive cells, called the "retina."

Around the pupil is the iris. It is a doughnut-shaped ring colored blue or green or brown. The iris can change in size like the diaphragm of a camera. In bright light, tiny muscles expand the iris, so that the opening of the pupil is smaller and less light passes into the eyeball. In dim light, the pupil is opened wider and more light is let in.

The entire eyeball is surrounded by a strong membrane called the "sclera." The whites of the eyes are part of the sclera. The sclera is transparent where the eyeball bulges in front. This part is called the "cornea." The space between the cornea and the iris is filled with a clear, salty liquid called the "aqueous humor." The space is shaped like a lens. It is, in fact, a liquid lens.

The eye's other lens is just behind the pupil. You can see what happens when this lens changes shape. When you look at near things, the lens becomes thicker in shape. When you look at distant objects, the lens becomes thinner.

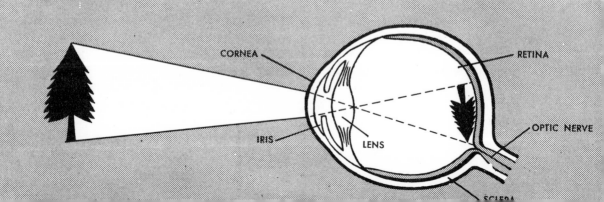

HOW DO WE SEE COLOR?

When a camera takes a color photograph, this is a physical process. But when we "see color," we are really having a psychological experience! The eyes receive an impression but do not "see." It is the brain that sees. So when the image is brought to the brain, the brain cells have to interpret this and make a judgment.

While we "see" in our brain, and therefore also "see color" in our brain, the brain still has to receive certain images from the eye. Our eyes are so constructed that they can perceive seven colors in the spectrum: red, orange, yellow, green, blue, indigo, and violet.

The rod cells on the edges of the retina can only distinguish brightness and darkness. The cone cells in the center pick up the individual wave length of the colors.

How do the eyes actually pick up the colors? Science has not yet figured this out to everybody's satisfaction, but there is a theory that seems to explain it. It is called the "Young-Helmholtz theory of color vision." According to this theory, the eye contains three sets of nerves. These respond to the primary colors of light: red, green, and blue-violet.

Now, if all three sets of nerves are stimulated in equal amounts, we receive the sensation of white. If mostly green light reaches our eye, the "green" nerves are stimulated more than the others, and we receive the sensation of green. When yellow light reaches the eye, the "green" and "red" sets of nerves are both stimulated, and we see yellow.

WHAT IS COLOR-BLINDNESS?

All the colors can be made by mixing three primary colors: red, green, violet, or yellow, blue, and red. For instance, the colors of flowers are created by combinations of granules of pigments having the three primary colors of red, blue, and yellow.

Because of the cone cells in the retina of the eye, which are sensitive to red, green, and violet, our eyes are able to reproduce all the colors in nature for us.

What happens when a person is color-blind? Certain colors strike the eye and fail to create the sensations which they reproduce in normal eyes.

For example, rays of red light strike the eye and not only stimulate the parts of the retina that are sensitive to red, but also stimulate those parts that are sensitive to green!

The green light acts in the same way. It also stimulates parts of the retina that are sensitive to red! What does a person see when this happens? He doesn't see either red or green, but instead a sort of yellowish-grey. This is because when you combine red plus green, you get white.

Such a person is color-blind only for red and green. He can still see blue, yellow, and violet. But red and green always appear as various shades of yellow-grey. In fact, a color-blind person can use these shadings to tell red and green apart.

A person may be slightly color-blind, and this can be unknown to anyone, including himself. A person who is red-green color-blind can learn at an early age to tell the two colors apart, even though he sees both colors as greyish-yellow. He doesn't do it by color, as people with normal vision do, but by judging the tone and luminosity of what he sees. Red and green have quite different luminosity.

HOW DOES THE EAR WORK?

The ear is one of the most wonderful instruments in our body. Without our having to do any "tuning," it can pick up the tiny tick of a watch one moment and the roar of an explosion the next.

The ear, however, is not the only thing we need to be able to hear. The process of hearings begins with sound. Waves of air, which we call "sound waves," strike on the eardrum. We can neither see nor feel these waves, but the ear is so delicate that the slightest vibration is caught and passed on to the brain. Only when such waves reach the brain do we actually hear.

The ear is made up of three main parts: an outer ear, a middle ear, and an inner ear. Certain animals can move their outer ear forward to catch sounds more easily. But since we cannot move our outer ear, it doesn't really help us much in hearing.

When sound waves enter the outer ear, they travel down a canal. At the end of this canal is a thin skin, stretched tightly across a tube. This skin separates the outer from the middle ear, and it acts as a drum membrane. From the inner side of this drum a short tube, called the "Eustachian tube," leads to the throat. Enough air enters this tube by way of the throat to equalize the pressure caused by the vibrations on the other side of the drum membrane. Otherwise the membrane might be broken by loud sounds.

Directly behind the drum membrane in the middle ear are strung three curious little bones called the "hammer," the "anvil," and the "stirrup." They touch both the drum membrane and the inner ear. When sound waves strike the membrane, they start the three bones vibrating.

These bones, in turn, set up a series of vibrations in the fluid of the shell-shaped inner ear. In this shell, called the "cochlea," tiny cells transfer the sound to certain nerves. These nerves send them to the brain, which recognizes them, and that recognition we call "hearing."

In the inner ear there are also three semicircular canals which have nothing to do with hearing. They are also filled with a fluid, and they give us our sense of balance. If they are out of order, we become dizzy and cannot walk straight.

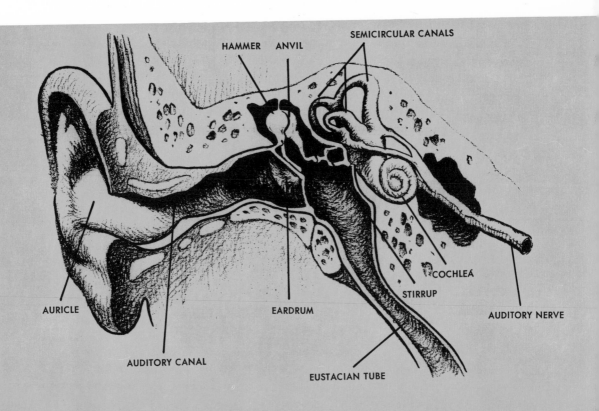

WHAT CAUSES DEAFNESS?

We should never make fun of people who are deaf or hard-of-hearing. They are suffering one of the greatest misfortunes that can happen to anyone. Just imagine how much of the beauty and joy of life they are forced to miss!

Deafness and hard-of-hearing are not the same thing. Deafness means nearly complete or total loss of hearing. A person can be born deaf, or be born with normal hearing and become deaf because of an accident or illness. Hard-of-hearing applies to those who lose some of the ability to hear later in life.

Deafness itself cannot be prevented. A person has some inborn defect and deafness results. But poor hearing is often the result of things which might have been avoided, or at least did not have to happen.

For example, poor hearing is often caused by severe infections. These infections, or diseases, may damage part of the hearing system during childhood. Head colds, tonsilitis, measles, scarlet fever, mumps, and meningitis are some of the diseases which may bring on poor hearing.

A less common cause of poor hearing is a bony growth in the ear. These growths make it difficult for the sound wave to be conducted into the ear.

Sometime poor hearing is caused by sound itself! If a person is exposed continuously to the sound of loud explosions, or violent vibrations, or even the noises of heavy industrial machines, a slow and gradual loss of hearing may take place. In fact, this kind of experience ranks third among all the causes of poor hearing!

What happens in such cases is that the violent sound waves affect part of the hearing mechanism so that high tones can no longer be heard. After the age of 50, changes may take place in the auditory nerve and lead to a partial loss of hearing.

HOW ARE TEETH FORMED?

One way to learn about things as they are today is to go back to their beginnings. Now maybe you've never thought of going far, far back to discover something about your teeth, but here is what happens if you do.

The human tooth is actually a transformed fish scale! Fishes that existed hundreds of millions of years ago were covered by projecting scales. Some of these scales, those located on the jaws, were used to hold and tear prey and in the course of time they became teeth. Today, for example, the human tooth and a shark's scale are similar in their basic structure.

A tooth is thus really a projection of the skin. The part of the tooth which is situated within the socket of the jaw is known as the "root." The part that projects beyond the gums is the "crown," and the part between them is called the "neck."

Teeth are not embedded in our jaws like plants in the earth. A truer way to think of them is as if they were buried flowerpots. Each tooth is fixed in its own "flowerpot" of bone, which is the socket of the tooth.

How does a tooth get its food? At the base of the root there is an open passage called the "root canal." Through this root canal pass the nerves and the blood and lymph vessels. They enter the cavity of the tooth, which is called the "pulp," and carry necessary substances in and out of the tooth.

Most of the tooth, however, is composed of a bony substance called the "dentine." The part of the tooth we see is the outer surface of the crown which is called the "enamel."

WHY ARE THERE DIFFERENT TYPES OF HAIR?

The kind of hair you have is a matter of inheritance. But the question is: Why are there so many different types of hair that might be inherited?

The general structure of the hair varies very little among human beings. But its form, its color, its general consistency, and the way a section of it looks under a microscope vary quite a bit. And because these differences occur in certain patterns, the hair is one of the best ways known to determine the race of a person. In other words, the hair you have inherited bears the stamp of your race.

There are three main classifications of hair by the way it's constructed. The first is short and crisp, the kind we call "woolly." A cross section of this hair shows it is elliptical or kidney-shaped. The color is almost always jet black, and it is the hair of all the black races with two exceptions.

The second type of hair is straight, lank, long, and coarse. A cross section of it look round. The color is almost without exception black. This is the hair of the Chinese, the Mongols, and the Indians of the Americas.

The third type of hair is wavy and curly, or smooth and silky. A section

The texture of a man's hair is an important clue to his race.

of it is oval in shape. This is the hair of Europeans. It is mainly fair with black, brown, red, or towy varieties.

There is also a fourth type, known as "frizzy," which is the hair of the Australian natives. Curly hair is generally hair that is quite flat in structure. The rounder the hair, the stiffer it is.

When it comes to color, some types have a range of colors, some do not. Wavy types of hair vary most in color. That's why, among Europeans, you can find the deepest black hair side by side with flaxen hair. But fair hair is more common in northern Europe and much rarer in the south. Among the races with straight hair, fair hair color is very rare. Races with frizzy hair have red hair almost as often as those with wavy hair. But red hair is related to the individual only—there are no races with red hair!

CAN SHOCK CAUSE GREY HAIR?

The answer to this question is yes. But strangely enough, how and why shock and nervous disorders cause grey hair is still something that cannot be entirely explained. We still don't even have a full explanation as to why old age brings on grey hair! But let's see if we can get some idea of what might be involved.

A hair is really a growing-down of the skin. It strikes root there, and then, like a tulip bulb, shoots upward. As the hair cells move out and away from the skin they become changed into a horny material. And on the outside surface of the hair, the cells become flattened and lie on top of one another like shingles. This is what gives the hair its "metallic" appearance.

Now among the cells of the root of the hair, there are certain cells that contain pigment, or coloring matter. These cells also multiply and move upward with the other hair cells. But when they move upward with the growing hair shaft, they finally die and the granules of pigment which they had are left in the hair.

The horn substance of the hair itself is yellow. The pigment granules are all shades of brown, from a reddish color to a deep black-brown. So the color of the horny material and the pigment granules mingle, and this is what gives us all the shades of hair we know, from blond to black. The kind of pigment granules a particular person may have depends on the genes he inherited.

Now, one explanation for the appearance of grey hair is that age and disease (or shock or worry) cause less pigment to be deposited in the hair, and the color becomes gray. Another explanation is that air cavities or bubbles begin to appear, and these air bubbles replace the pigment granules. We know that nervous excitement, worries, and sorrow can cause these air bubbles to appear among the hair cells and make the hair look grey. But how and why this happens, we still don't know.

WHAT ARE FINGERNAILS MADE OF?

If every time you bit your nails you suffered pain, you'd probably never bite them. Or for that matter, if it hurt us to cut our nails there would be a great many people with very long nails!

But cutting, biting, filing our nails don't hurt us because the nails are made up of dead cells. The nails are special structures that grow from the skin. Most of the nail is made up of a substance called "keratin." This is a tough, dead form of protein, and a horn-like material.

At the base of the nail, and part of the way along its sides, the nail is embedded in the skin. The skin beneath the nail is just like any other skin except that it contains elastic fibers. These are connected to the nail to hold it firmly.

Most of the nail is quite thick, but at the point near the roots beneath the skin it is very thin. This part is white in appearance and has the shape of a semicircle or half-moon. It is called the "lunule." The fingernails grow about 50 millimetres a year.

Women, of course, have made the fingernails an object of beauty with nail colors and polishes. But to a great many people, the nails present all sorts of problems. One reason for many nail disorders is that the nails become injured. A burn or frostbite, for example, may injure nails so that they'll never grow again.

Nails that are very brittle, or hard, or that tend to split may be the result of many things: infections, a disturbance of the nutritional system, poor circulation of the blood, or even glandular disturbances.

Women who complain of peeling off of the nails at the tips may in many cases only have themselves to blame. They simply let their nails grow too long. Long nails are subject to shocks and this can result in damage to the nails.

ARE ALL FINGERPRINTS DIFFERENT?

In movies, TV shows, plays, and books, there are often situations in which a person leaves a fingerprint on something—and is later caught as a result of it. A fingerprint is considered positive proof—a mistake is impossible if a person has left his fingerprint. Here is why this is so.

If you look at the tips of your fingers, you'll see a network of ridges. These ridges contain the "touch" receptors of the skin. These ridges (their pattern makes a "fingerprint") are different for every person and cannot be changed. If the skin of the fingertips is burnt several times in succession, the same fingerprints appear each time after the burns heal!

There are the same kind of characteristics in everyone's fingerprints— a certain kind of arrangement in the center, along the edges, at the tip, and so on. But for each person, there is a completely different arrangement of these characteristics!

Now, it is easy for an expert to find a hundred different characteristics on a fingerprint. This means a fingerprint has a hundred different types of arrangements of the ridges. Now suppose we take the index finger. In order to find two people whose fingerprints of the index finger have just two characteristics that are alike, we'd have to examine 16 people. To find two people whose fingerprints are alike in three characteristics (out of a hundred), 64 persons must be examined.

This goes on until we say: we want to find two people who have the same print on the index finger—the same for all 100 characteristics. We would have to examine all the people who would live in the world during a period of four billion years! And this is just for the print on one finger to be the same! And, of course, we have 10 fingers.

It is really one of the miracles of nature that each one of us has his own individual pattern of fingerprints and that it remains ours alone, unchanged, as long as we live.

HOW DO WE TALK?

The ability of man to speak is due a great deal to the way in which the larynx is made. This is a hollow organ, shaped something like a box. It is really an enlarged part of the windpipe. The walls of this "box" are made of cartilage and they are lined inside with mucous membrane.

At one place on each side, the mucous membrane becomes thicker and projects from the wall into the center of the box. These projections are the "vocal cords." Each cord is moved by many small muscles. When air goes from the lungs into the mouth, it passes between the two vocal cords and makes them vibrate. This produces a sound.

What kind of sound? It depends on the position and tension of these vocal cords. The muscle system that controls them is the most delicate muscle system in the entire body to make possible all the kinds of sounds we produce. Actually, the vocal cords can assume about 170 different positions!

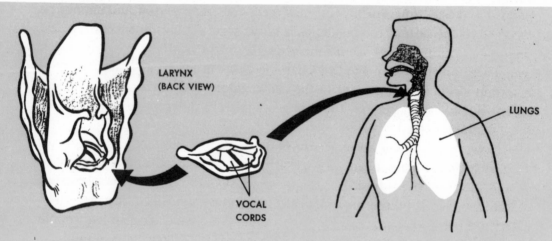

LARYNX
(BACK VIEW)

VOCAL
CORDS

LUNGS

When the vocal cords vibrate, the column of air that is in the respiratory passage is made to vibrate. What we really hear is the vibration of this column of air. If the vocal cords are not too tensed, long waves are produced and we hear deep tones. If the vocal cords are tensed, they vibrate rapidly, so short waves are produced and we hear high tones. When boys reach the age of about 14, the cords and the larynx become thicker and this makes the pitch of the voice lower. This change in pitch is called "change of voice."

So we see that the pitch of the sound we make is controlled by the tension of the vocal cords. Now how about the tone? This is determined by the resonating spaces, just as the tone of a violin is determined by the vibrations of the entire instrument. In speaking or singing, the resonating spaces involved include the windpipe, the lungs, the thorax, and even the spaces in our mouth and nose. The vibration of air in all of them helps decide the tone.

But that isn't all. Our abdomen, chest, diaphragm, tongue, palate, lips, teeth also get into the picture! All of them are involved in producing sounds and letters. So you see that the process of speaking is like playing on a very complicated and difficult musical instrument. It is only because we learned it early in childhood and practice it continuously that we are able to do it so well!

WHAT CAUSES US TO REMEMBER THINGS?

No one can as yet explain how the brain is able to store away memories and how we are able to recover these memories from the brain. But we do know quite a bit about different kinds of remembering, and methods that seem to help us remember.

Memory is the ability to keep in the mind what one has learned or experienced. Everything that happens to a person leaves some kind of "trace" or record in the brain. This record seems to fade slowly unless it is traced again by a similar experience, or by reviewing it, or by repeating it.

There are several ways to remember. One is by "recall." If, a few days after a party, someone asks you to name the other people who were there, you'll try to recall their names or what they looked like.

Recall is different from "recognition," which is another way to remember. If someone asks you if Bill Johnson was at the party, you might recognize the name as that of someone who was there. Or, if you meet him on the street, you might recognize him as having been at the party.

It is harder to recall than to recognize. If the teacher asks you to recall what was spoken about in class last week, it will be harder to remember than if she names a subject and asks you if it has already been spoken about.

Still another way to remember is by "images." You may remember last summer's vacation by having mental pictures of the cabin in the mountains. You see them again in your "mind's eye." This is called "visual imagery."

You may also be able to hear music after you have stopped playing a record. This is called "auditory imagery."

Another way of remembering is "association." When you have an experience, you usually experience something else also at the same time, or just before, or just after. These experiences become linked or "associated," and when you remember or recognize one of the events, it will cause you to recall the other.

WHY ARE SOME PEOPLE LEFT-HANDED?

Many parents of left-handed children worry about this condition and wonder if they shouldn't try to correct it. The answer given by most authorities is: No! If there is a strong preference for the left hand, and the person is able to perform well with it, there should be no interference.

About four per cent of the population is left-handed. In the course of history, many of the greatest geniuses have been left-handed! Leonardo da Vinci and Michelangelo, the greatest sculptors of all times, were both left-handed.

Of course, we live in a "right-handed society"—that is, most of the things we use are made for right-handed people. Our doorknobs, locks, screwdrivers, automobiles, musical instruments—even the buttons on our clothes—are arranged for right-handed people. This may cause a certain amount of adjustment to be made by left-handed people, but most of them can manage quite well.

There is no single accepted explanation of what makes most people right-handed and a small minority left-handed. Here is one theory: The body is not "symmetrical," that is, it is not exactly the same on both sides. The right side of our face is a little different from the left. Our legs differ in strength. Our feet may differ a tiny bit in size. And this "asymmetry" goes through our whole body.

Now when we come to the brain, we discover that while it has a right half and a left half, these two halves don't function the same way. It is believed that the left half of the brain is "predominant" over the right half.

The nerves from the brain cross over at the level of the neck and go to the opposite side of the body. The right half of the brain supplies the left half of the body, and vice versa.

Now since the left half of the brain predominates, the right half of the body is more skilled, better able to do things. We read, write, speak, and work with the left half of the brain. And this, of course, makes most of us right-handed, too. But in the case of left-handed people, there is an "inversion." The right half of the brain is predominant, and such a person works best with the left side of his body!

WHY DO WE LAUGH?

Have you ever told a joke, and discovered that the other person didn't laugh? And don't you know some people who never seem to laugh, while others are always smiling or laughing? We laugh not because of any mechanical process in our body, but to express our feelings. These feelings may be sheer joy, lightness of heart, amusement.

Yes, there is one "mechanical" cause of laughter—and that is tickling. But this is only a reflex action on the part of our body to a certain kind of stimulation. It is not at all related to the other kind of laughter we enjoy.

When we laugh, we are spontaneously expressing certain feelings that are brought on by seeing, remembering, imagining, or thinking of something. Now, that "something" has to provoke laughter in us. Why does it create that reaction in us?

This is really a question for psychologists to answer, men who study human behavior. And while they have come up with many theories, no one seems to have the complete answer yet.

One such idea is that laughing is a kind of "social" act. If you're watching TV alone and see something funny, you might not laugh very loud. But if there are a group of friends watching with you, you might all laugh loudly together. Or take this example: a group of people are sitting together telling stories. They laugh and smile. You may hear what they're saying, but since you're not a member of their group, you probably won't laugh.

We all know, in a general way, the kind of things that make us laugh. If somebody does something awkward, like dropping something or slipping and falling, we might laugh. This may be because it makes us feel superior at the moment, and we are so pleased about it that we express our feeling by laughing.

Even the kind of laughter we engage in may vary, depending on the cause. Humor creates one kind of laughter, the ridiculous another, the comic another. It is even possible for us to laugh scornfully at someone. So, you see, laughter is an expression of our feelings, a way of reacting to something.

WHY DO WE CRY?

Most of us imagine that the only time we cry is when we are sad. Did you know that we actually cry about 250,000,000 times in the course of a lifetime?

Let's see how this is possible. Our eyelids are folds of skin that are lowered and raised like stage curtains by means of muscles. This curtain moves so quickly that it doesn't disturb our vision. We don't even know it's happening. In fact, the eyelids open and close automatically every six seconds during our lifetime.

In each eye there is a tear gland, located over the outer corner of the eye. There are also ducts which carry the tears to the upper eyelid and canals which carry off the tears from the front of the eye.

Every time we blink our eyelids, suction is exerted on the opening of the tear ducts which takes out some fluid. The purpose of this is to irrigate the cornea of the eye and prevent it from drying out. But, mechanically speaking, this is no different from crying. It is exactly what happens when we cry!

Have you noticed how when people laugh a great deal, tears begin to flow? The reason is that when we laugh hard, the muscles squeeze those glands where the tears are stored and they begin to flow.

Everyone knows how onions can make us cry without our feeling sad at all. That's because the onion gives off a volatile substance. When it reaches our eyes, we protect ourselves from the irritation of this substance by making tears flow. The tears "wash" the irritating substance away. The same thing happens with smoke. We "cry" automatically to protect and cleanse our eyes.

What about crying when we are sad? Man, of all living creatures, is the only one who cries to express emotion. Only a thinking and emotionally sensitive person cries. Babies yell, but they do not cry until they have learned to think and feel.

What happens then is that our emotion, instead of finding expression in words, is channeled into the mechanism that produces tears. It is a reflex action that happens despite ourselves. But the reason it happens is that the body has found it can express itself in this way when we can't, or won't, use words to convey what we feel.

WHAT CAUSES HICCOUGHS?

In England, there was an old superstition about how to get rid of hiccoughs. It goes like this: "To cure the hiccoughs, wet the forefinger of the right hand with spittle, and cross the front of the left shoe three times, saying the Lord's Prayer backwards."

You've probably heard of dozens of other "prescriptions" for getting rid of hiccoughs, most of them just about as effective as this old superstition!

Hiccoughs really have nothing mysterious about them. They are the result of an action the body takes to protect itself. Let's see how this is so.

The body, as you know, has many reflexes. A reflex is a response on the part of the body to some sort of specific stimulation. This response is always the same, and seems to take place because certain nerve connections have been built up in our nervous system. We don't "decide" what action to take; the nerve connections spring into action without our control when there is a reflex action.

Now there are whole series of reflexes that have to do with getting solid and liquid food into our system and with getting rid of these or other foreign objects from air passages into which they sometimes go. For example, there are a whole series of reflexes connected with swallowing food. When food goes "the wrong way," the gagging and choking are reflex actions trying to expel the food.

Sneezing and coughing are actually normal reflexes in which a blast of air is used to help the body get rid of material it doesn't want. Vomiting is a very strong reflex action of this same type. And hiccoughing can be considered a sort of half-hearted and ineffective effort to vomit!

Hiccoughs can start because hot food has irritated some passage inside, or when gas in the stomach presses upward against the diaphragm. The diaphragm separates the chest from the stomach. The diaphragm tightens and pulls air into the lungs. But air can't get through and we feel a "bump" at the moment the air is stopped. So hiccoughs are a reflex action of the body trying to get food or gas out of the stomach, thereby irritating the diaphragm, which in turn affects the passage of air in and out of the lungs. We feel this as a "bump" and say we have the hiccoughs!

WHAT MAKES PEOPLE SNEEZE?

For some strange reason, the act of sneezing has long been considered more than just a physical action. All kinds of ideas and legends have grown up about sneezing, as if it had special significance.

Actually sneezing is the act of sending out air from the nose and mouth. It is a reflex act, and happens without our control. Sneezing occurs when the nerve-endings of the mucous membrane of the nose are irritated. It can also happen, curiously enough, when our optic nerve is stimulated by a bright light!

The irritation that causes sneezing may be due to a swelling of the mucous membrane of the nose, as happens when we have a cold; it may be due to foreign bodies that somehow get into the nose; or it may be due to an allergy. The act of sneezing is an attempt by the body to expel air to get rid of the irritating bodies.

From earliest times, however, people have wondered about sneezing, and it has universally been regarded as an omen of some kind. The Greeks, Romans, and Egyptians regarded the sneeze as a warning in times of danger, and as a way of foretelling the future. If you sneezed to the right, it was considered lucky; to the left, unlucky.

The reason we say "God bless you" after someone sneezes cannot be traced to any single origin, but seems to be connected with ancient beliefs. The Romans thought a person expelled evil spirits when he sneezed, so everyone present would say "Good luck to you" after a sneeze, hoping the effort to expel the spirits would succeed.

Primitive people believed that sneezing was a sign of approaching death. When anyone sneezed, therefore, people said "God help you!" because the person sneezing was in danger.

There is a legend that before the days of Jacob, a person died after sneezing. Jacob interceded with God, according to this tale, so that people could sneeze without dying—provided a benediction followed every sneeze!

During the sixth century there was a plague in Italy, and Pope Gregory the Great ordered that prayers be said against sneezing. It was at this time that the custom of saying "God bless you!" to persons who sneezed became established.

RAGWEED GOLDENROD

WHAT IS HAY FEVER?

If you don't suffer from hay fever, watching someone who does presents quite a mystery. Here you are living side by side, breathing the same air, and you go about feeling perfectly fit, while the other person sneezes constantly and suffers a great deal!

Hay fever is a form of allergy. It belongs to a group of maladies, including hives, asthma, and certain skin problems, that are caused by something called "protein sensitization."

Let us examine what this means. Protein, as we know, is found in foods. But it so happens that the pollens of plants are also protein. At a certain time of the year, many kinds of grasses, such as ragweed, send their pollens into the air in great amounts.

They reach human beings through the nose, mouth, and eyes. If the person whom they reach is not protein-sensitive, nothing happens. But when a person is abnormally sensitive to these proteins, they act upon certain muscles and tissues and cause those reactions that make them feel miserable.

A person may be sensitive to several different pollens, which is why the treatment of hay fever is a bit complicated. All the causes of the attack of hay fever have to be identified. Some patients are helped by injections of pollen or protein extracts which seem to build up an immunity. Other patients simply try to live in some other section of the country where the troublesome pollens don't exist.

WHY DO SOME PEOPLE GET ALLERGIES AND NOT OTHERS?

To have an allergy means to be affected by or be sensitive to one or more common substances. The substances might be food, chemicals, plant and animal products of any type. It could even be household dust, or dander from cats, dogs, and horses.

The substance that causes an allergic reaction is called an "allergen." Now why does an allergen affect one person and not another? Medical science simply can't explain it! Many doctors and scientists think that heredity has a part in deciding who will be allergic. There are families in which grandparents, parents, and children are sensitive or allergic to the same substance.

However, there are cases in which only one member in the family is allergic. It is also believed that emotions play an important part in the development of allergy. In some unknown way, the emotions of fear, rage, and worry seem to lead to an allergic attack.

What happens in the body when a person has an allergy? It is believed that the substance responsible, when it enters the body, causes special cells in the tissues of the body to make a chemical called "antibody." Now, antibodies happen to be one of our main defenses against infection. But when an allergy is involved, they produce unpleasant reactions.

It is believed that the allergic substance combines with its antibody to cause the release in the body of something known as "histamine." It is the histamine, acting on the blood vessels and lungs, that causes the allergic symptoms. But the amount of histamine produced is either small or is found only in certain parts of the body because histamine has not been found in the blood of a person suffering an allergic attack.

So you see we still have quite a bit to learn about allergies—this reaction that can make so many people feel so miserable!

WHAT IS PAIN?

Do you ever wish you couldn't feel pain in your body? Well, you should consider yourself lucky that you can feel pain! Pain is your protector. If you didn't feel the pain of a toothache, you might not care for that tooth in time to save it. If you didn't feel pain from touching something hot, you might cause yourself serious injury.

Did you know that there are some people who have a disease which prevents them from feeling certain kinds of pain? It's called "syringomyelia." A person with this disease can touch hot things without feeling it, or stick a nail in his hand without feeling it. But what happens to such people is that they often do themselves great harm—burning away tissue, receiving wounds without taking care of them, all because they didn't have pain to tell them something was wrong.

Strangely enough, science still cannot explain fully how pain arises. It is believed that pain is due to an injury to the free nerve endings in the skin. For this reason, a very weak stimulus will not produce pain. In other words, these nerve endings in the skin will pick up something as a "sensation"—but unless there is a great deal of energy involved, we do not feel it

as pain. In a very hot object, the molecules are moving with great energy, and so when we touch it we feel pain.

As far as we know, the body doesn't have any special "receptors" for pain. But there do seem to be special nerves that lead from where the stimulus is received up the spinal cord to the brain.

The points on the skin that respond to stimuli with a sense of pain are known as "pain spots." These pain spots are not distributed over the body equally, because there are some places where practically no pain spots exist. But on the average there is one pain spot for every part of the skin as big as this letter "o." So there are about 3,000,000 spots on the skin where pain can be produced!

There are different types of pain—burning, cutting, gnawing, boring, and so on. What you feel as pain is probably a combination of sensations, including pressure, higher temperature, etc. So pain is a "composition" of unpleasant sensations.

WHAT HAPPENS WHEN WE GET DIZZY?

Every living creature on earth must have a sense of balance. Since gravity pulls everything downward, every living thing must have an idea of its relation to the earth in space or it would collapse or fall down.

In human beings, the organs that give us a sense of balance (or equilibrium) are called the "semicircular canals." They are three elongated tubes in the form of three semicircular arcs, and are located behind the ear.

Why are there three? Because space has three dimensions: length (backwards and forwards), breadth (right and left), and height (up and down). The three canals are placed approximately at right angles to each other in the three dimensions of space.

There is a fluid (lymph) in these canals, and at one end of the tubes they are enlarged into a bulb-shape, called the "ampulla." In these ampullae, there are sensitive cells out of which grow stiff hairs. The hairs stick up into the space of the ampulla and are connected to nerve fibers.

Now, whenever the fluid in the canal moves, it makes the hairs move or bend, and this sends a message to the brain and to the muscles. Since the canals occupy three different planes, if we move in any direction some hairs will move as a result. For example, when we move forward in an automobile, the hairs in two of the canals won't register anything, but the canal which responds to motion in a forward or backward direction will cause the hairs in it to bend backward. The lymph in the canal causes this.

Now suppose we revolve rapidly in a circle. The lymph in the horizontal semi-circular canal bends the sensory hairs backward. When we stop, the lymph keeps going around because of inertia. This causes the hairs to now bend in the opposite direction. And this makes us feel we are revolving in the opposite direction—even though we are not. Since we know we are not revolving (our legs are still), we find ourselves assuming that the world is revolving around us in the reverse direction. In other words—we are dizzy!

WHAT CAUSES HEADACHES?

The answer to this question might be: anything and everything! A headache can start for any one of hundreds of reasons. You see, a headache is not a sickness or a disease. It is a symptom. It simply is a way of knowing that there is some disorder somewhere—in some part of the body or the nervous system.

Of course we know something about the "mechanism" of a headache, that is, what happens in the body or nervous system to produce the pain of a headache. The pain itself comes from certain structures in the skull. The large veins and others in the brain that drain the surface of the brain are sensitive to pain. It is not the brain substance itself but the coverings of the brain and the veins and arteries that are sensitive. When they "hurt," you have a headache. Also, when your sinuses, teeth, ears, and muscles hurt, the pain may spread to the brain area and produce a headache. If the muscles that are over the neck and near the head are contracted, this can also produce headaches.

When you listen to people talk about their headache problems, you hear them give personal reasons. But most of these are conditions that apply to many people. For example, some people get a headache when they're hungry, others say going without their "morning coffee" produces a headache, or it may be from a "hangover." What is really happening in all these cases is that the arteries in the skull are being dilated (or enlarged)—and this produces a headache in practically anybody. It's known as a "vascular headache."

Or suppose somebody suddenly had a vigorous jolt or twisted his head and began to complain of a headache. There's nothing special about such cases. What happened was that certain pain-sensitive structures in the brain were pulled or tightened and pain resulted. A person may be undergoing great emotional tension and this will cause muscles to contract or tighten over the back, lower part of the head, and neck Result? A headache!

"Migraine" headaches are a special kind of headache and quite different from these. But as you can see, the symptom of disorder we call a "head-ache" has many, many causes!

WHAT IS A "COLD"?

Almost everybody knows the joke about the doctor who tells the patient who has a cold: "If you only had pneumonia, I could cure you." The cold is not only one of the most annoying afflictions man has to bear, but one of the most mysterious, as well.

More than 90 per cent of the people in the United States get a cold every year, and more than half of them get several colds during the year. You probably know the symptoms of a cold as well as your doctor does. There's a "running" nose, you sneeze a lot, you might have a sore or tickling throat, and sometimes a headache. Later on, a cough or fever may develop.

In an adult, a cold is seldom serious. But in children, the cold symptoms may actually be the early symptoms of more serious childhood diseases, such as measles or diptheria. That's why colds in children should have prompt medical attention.

A cold takes from one to three days to develop. There are three stages of the common cold. The first is the "dry" stage, which doesn't last long. Your nose feels dry and swollen, your throat may have a tickle, and your eyes may water a bit. In the second stage, you get the "running" nose. And finally, that nose is really "running" and you may have fever and be coughing.

Now as to the great mystery. What is the common cold? What causes it? We can describe it as an acute inflammation of the upper respiratory tract—but that doesn't help much. Medical science simply doesn't know the specific cause of the common cold!

It is generally believed, however, that the infection is caused by a virus of some kind. But here's the strange thing: That virus is probably in your throat most of the time. It simply doesn't attack until your body resistance is lowered. There may also be other bacteria present and they don't attack either until your resistance is low. So it seems that the cold virus weakens the tissues so that other germs can infect them.

The best way to avoid a cold, therefore, is to keep your resistance high with a good diet, plenty of rest and sleep, proper dress, and avoiding contact with people who have colds.

WHY DO WE GET FEVER?

The first thing your doctor, or even your mother, will do when you don't feel well is take your temperature with a thermometer. They are trying to find out whether you have a temperature.

Your body has an average temperature of 37 degrees centigrade when it is healthy. Disease makes this temperature rise, and we call this higher temperature "fever." While every disease doesn't cause fever, so many of them do that fever is almost always a sign that your body is sick in some way.

Your doctor or nurse usually takes your temperature at least twice a day and puts it on a chart, showing how your fever goes up and down. This chart can often tell the doctor exactly which disease you have. A fever chart for pneumonia, for instance, goes up and down in a certain way. Other diseases have other patterns or "temperature curves" on the chart.

The strange thing is that we still don't know what fever really is. But we do know that fever actually helps us fight off sickness. Here's why: Fever makes the vital processes and organs in the body work faster. The body produces more hormones, enzymes, and blood cells. The hormones and enzymes, which are useful chemicals in our body, work harder. Our blood cells destroy harmful germs better. Our blood circulates faster, we breathe faster, and we thus get rid of wastes and poisons in our system better.

But the body can't afford to have a fever too long or too often. When you have a fever for 24 hours, you destroy protein that is stored in your body. And since protein is mighty necessary for life, fever is an "expensive" way to fight off disease!

WHAT IS MEASLES?

Measles is a disease that occurs in every part of the world and didn't originate in any particular country. German measles is quite distinct from real measles, and has a different effect on the body.

Measles is generally a childhood disease, but grown-ups who never had it may get it, too. It is caused by a virus, a living germ too small to see in the ordinary microscope.

Measles is contagious, as it spreads very easily. The infection is spread by droplets in the air when a sick person coughs. It is also spread by direct contact with someone who is already infected with the virus but who isn't sick yet. The reason adults don't get measles is that most people have had it as children, and no one has the disease more than once.

About 10 to 12 days after contact with the virus, red spots appear in the throat and mouth. The temperature rises, the nose begins to run, and a cough develops. One or two days later, a red rash breaks out all over the body. A high fever is usually present. The whites of the eyes become inflamed and the eyes are sensitive to light.

This sounds pretty terrible, doesn't it? But just about when the rash has covered the entire body, the temperature drops suddenly and the child feels much better. Sometimes other germs infect the ears or the lungs of the sick child—and these infections are more serious than the infection with the measles virus.

Epidemics (when there are many cases) usually appear in large cities every two to four years. When there is an epidemic in a city, measles is caught by most of the children who have not had it. Babies up to the age of about five months don't get measles if the mother has had the disease. Infections with measles virus are most common in the spring.

There is no special treatment known for this disease. A serum can be used to weaken the force of the infection. But what the sick child chiefly needs is a lot of rest and he should be kept in a dark room.

WHAT IS VACCINE?

A living organism such as the body has the power itself to resist and overcome infections. This is known as "immunity."

The body has to be helped to acquire this immunity. In the case of many diseases produced by viruses, immunity is created by a person's having the disease and recovering from it. Smallpox, measles, and chicken pox, for example, give the body a lasting immunity. This means, once you have one of these diseases, you won't get it again.

With a disease such as influenza, repeated attacks may occur. To produce immunity artificially, a virus can be injected that has been weakened. The person thus gets only a slight case of the disease. When he recovers, he remains immune for varying lengths of time. The injection of the weakened virus is known as "vaccination." And a vaccine consists of the disease organisms, which have been made harmless, and which produce immunity by causing the formation of antibodies. Antibodies neutralize the viruses and are produced by the body itself. The vaccine stimulates the body to produce them.

The vaccine may be obtained by infecting some animal with the disease and isolating the virus. The process is repeated until the virus is so weakened that it won't produce the disease in man, yet it will produce immunity. Vaccines can also be made from large amounts of "killed" or inactivated virus. When a large amount of this vaccine is injected, it stimulates the body to produce antibodies to fight the disease. Vaccines for sleeping sickness and for influenza have been produced by this method. Sometimes immunity is produced by injecting an active virus into the skin, and the immunity is created because such a virus normally enters the body in some other way.

WHAT IS NICOTINE?

Nowadays we see advertising everywhere for cigarettes that talks about their having "less tars and nicotine." What is nicotine? Why are people concerned with how much there is in cigarettes or cigars?

People who smoke get a great deal of satisfaction from it. A certain amount of smoking has a calming effect on the nervous system. It also "hides" the sensation of fatigue, so that it seems to make people feel less tired. It even stimulates the imagination to a certain extent, so that some people can work better when they smoke.

One of the chief constituents of tobacco is nicotine. Pure nicotine, if it is taken out of the tobacco, acts as a poison. But, of course, when people smoke they do not take pure nicotine into their body.

Let us see what actually happens during the smoking process. Smoking is a process of "dry distillation." This means that dry substances are transformed into vapor. Now, in a lit cigarette, the hottest part, where there is maximum heat, is the part that glows. This heat chemically destroys 25 per cent of the nicotine.

Behind the glowing zone, the tobacco is heated to a medium temperature. Here, gases containing nicotine arise from the leaves and 30 per cent of the nicotine disappears into the air. The rest of the cigarette has cold tobacco particles. As the nicotine passes over them, nicotine is deposited on them. As a result, only about 15 per cent of the total quantity of nicotine enters the mouth. Filter types of cigarettes are attempts to catch even more of this nicotine before it enters the mouth.

The shorter the path from the "glow" where the distillation is taking place to the mouth, the more nicotine enters the mouth. That's why short, fat cigars and cigarettes are usually not as "mild" as long, thin ones. It is also probable that smoking a cigar or cigarette to the very end enables more nicotine to enter the mouth. When a person re-lights a cigar or cigarette that has gone out, it doesn't burn as well the second time, and this also allows more nicotine to be taken in.

Even though about 15 per cent of the total nicotine enters the mouth, only traces of this fraction enter the blood through the mucous membrane of the oral region. But when the tobacco smoke is breathed into the nose the amount is doubled, and when it is taken into the lungs about four times as much enters the body.

WHAT IS CANCER?

As you probably know from the appeals being made for funds to fight cancer, and from all the research that is being done on this subject—cancer is a great menace to the health and life of mankind. We will only discuss cancer in general terms, so you can have an idea of what happens in a body that has cancer.

A cancer is a continuous growth in the body which doesn't follow the normal growth pattern. The cells forming the cancer spread through the body to parts which may be far from the spot where the cancer began. Unless it is removed or destroyed, the cancer can lead to the death of the person.

Cells in the body are growing all the time. As they wear out and disappear, their places are taken by new cells of exactly the same kind. But cancer cells look and act differently from normal body cells. They look like the young cell of the part of the body where they started—but different enough to be recognized as cancer when seen through a microscope.

When these cancer cells divide and increase in number, they don't change into the fully grown form and then stop reproducing. Instead, they remain young cells and continue to increase in number until they are harmful.

As the cancer cells grow, they do not remain in one spot, but separate and move in among the normal cells. They may become so numerous that the normal cells in this part of the body cannot continue to work or even remain alive. When the cancer gets into the blood, it is carried to distant parts of the body. There it may grow to form large masses which interfere with the activities of the normal cells.

Unless the growth and spread of the cancer is stopped, the patient will die. That's why it's important to have periodic examinations to detect and treat cancer before it has spread too far.

Cancers are not spread from man to man by contact. No drug has been found that cures completely and is useful for all kinds of cancer. One of medicine's greatest goals is to understand fully the nature and cause of cancer, and to find a way to prevent and cure it.

WHAT IS AN ANESTHETIC?

The chief purpose of an anesthetic is to control pain. Man has been attempting to find ways to do this since ancient times.

A medical book written in the first century A.D. describes sleep-producing drugs, and we know such drugs were used in the Orient even before that time. Various herbs, gases, oils, and even hypnotism were also tried in the past.

Before the use of modern anesthetics, every operation brought agony to the patient, and often death from pain and shock. Modern surgery became possible only when a method was found to reduce pain and quiet the patient.

There are two ways in which this is accomplished. One is to produce a state of unconsciousness known as "general anesthesia." The other is to block the passage of nerve impulses to the area requiring surgical treatment, which is called "local anesthesia."

Most general anesthetics are gases. When they are inhaled, the person becomes unconscious. Examples of these gases are nitrous oxide, chloroform, ether, and ethylene. There are also anesthetics which are drugs that can be injected into the blood stream.

These are most useful in operations where it isn't necessary to relax the patient completely. Sometimes, these are used as a preliminary anesthetic because they act quickly to produce unconsciousness. Then, to maintain unconciousness, anesthetics which are inhaled are given.

Local anesthesia is produced by injecting a narcotic drug either at the place of the operation, or at a place that will block off sensory nerves supplying the area. Such drugs may also be injected at different levels of the spine into the spinal fluid. Spinal anesthetics are sometimes used in childbirth.

Another kind of anesthesia is called "continuous caudal anesthesia," and has also been used in childbirth. In this case, the anesthetic is injected at the point where the nerves emerge from the base of the spinal column. The anesthetic does not go into the spinal canal.

Examples of local anesthetics are cocaine, novacaine, eucaine. Nowadays, these drugs have made even the extraction of a tooth a painless experience.

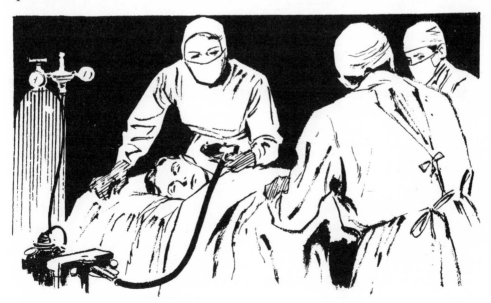

CAN A PERSON BE HYPNOTIZED AGAINST HIS WILL?

Hypnotism is a fascinating subject to many people. We see astonishing things being done when it is performed on other people, and from time to time we even read about hypnotism being used by doctors to help patients.

When a person is hypnotized, it doesn't mean that he is not aware of anything. He is aware, but on another level. This is called "unconscious" or "subconscious" awareness. Sometimes, because the person hypnotized concentrates on his task so intensely, he is able to do things in this state of awareness that he can't under normal behavior.

In order for a person to become hypnotized, he must be a willing, co-operative, and relaxed subject. The hypnotist can persuade him by repeatedly suggesting that he will become tired and sleepy, that his eyes will close, that he will begin to lose his interest in the outside world, and that he is going to be in a state of sleep where he will have that unconscious awareness.

One of the amazing things that happens when a person is hypnotized is the way he accepts suggestions. By accepting suggestions from the hypnotist, a person can become deaf, dumb, blind, or perform strange acts. But it is important to remember that these suggestions are acceptable to the person hypnotized. If not, he rejects them.

A person can also be made to perform certain things after the hypnotic trance ends. He may be instructed to read a certain chapter in a certain book on a certain day, and he will do it without knowing consciously why he is doing it.

Can a person be hypnotized against his will, or without his knowledge? Remember we pointed out that a person must cooperate with the hypnotist? That's why it is impossible to hypnotize a person against his will. Sometimes people really want to cooperate, but they hide this by acting unwilling, and so it seems they are being hypnotized against their will!

310

Chapter 4

HOW OTHER CREATURES LIVE

CAN ANIMALS UNDERSTAND EACH OTHER?

If we mean can animals communicate with each other, that is, pass on certain messages by signs and sounds, the answer is yes. If we mean can they talk to each other as we do, the answer is no.

Even among human beings, all communication is not by means of words. We have expressions to indicate anger, a shrug of the shoulder to indicate indifference, nodding and shaking the head, gestures with hands, and so on. Many animals make noises and signs to do the same thing.

When a mother hen makes a loud noise or crouches down, all her chicks understand this as a warning of danger. When a horse neighs or paws the ground, the other horses "get the message." Some animals can follow very slight signs or signals given by other animals. When a bird merely flies up to a branch to look around, the other birds don't move. But if a bird flies up in a certain way, they can tell it's about to fly off and they may follow.

Dogs communicate in many ways. They not only bark, but they howl, growl, snarl, and whine. They lift a paw, or bare their teeth. Other dogs can understand what these sounds and actions mean.

Animals communicate with each other not only with sounds and movements, but with smell. Most animals that live in herds depend on smell to keep together. And, of course, we know how dogs recognize each other by smell.

Apes are supposed to be among the most intelligent of animals, yet they really have no better "language" than other animals. They make many sounds and expressions of the face to communicate their feelings of anger or hunger or joy, but they have nothing like the words of human speech.

By the way, unlike human beings who have to learn how to talk, apes and other animals know their "language" by instinct. They will make the right kind of cries and sounds and expressions even if they have never seen another animal like themselves before.

Birds, however, learn their way of singing, at least in part. That's why a sparrow brought up among canaries will try to sing like one. It has been learning the wrong "language"!

DO ANIMALS LAUGH OR CRY?

If you have a pet, such as a cat or a dog, you may become so attached to it that in time you almost feel it's "human." That is, you begin to think it can express the way it feels in terms of human emotions, such as crying, or perhaps even laughing.

But this isn't really so. Crying and laughing are human ways of expressing emotions and no animals have this way. Of course, we know that animals can whimper and whine when they are hurt, but crying involves the production of tears with this emotion, and animals cannot do this.

This doesn't mean that animals don't have the tear fluid in their eyes. But it is used to irrigate the cornea of the eye. A creature must be a thinking and emotionally sensitive person to cry. Even children begin to cry only when they learn to think and feel. An infant yells, but he is not crying.

Crying is a substitute for speaking. When we cannot say what we feel, we cry. It is a reflex that happens despite ourselves and that helps us "get out" what we feel.

Laughter is also a human phenomenon. Some animals may give the impression that they laugh, but it is not at all like human laughter. The reason is that man always laughs at something, and this means that a certain mental process or emotion is involved. Animals are incapable of having such a mental process or emotion.

For example, when we laugh at a joke, or at a "funny" sight, our minds or our emotions make it seem laughable. In fact, there are many kinds of laughter and many reasons why we laugh. We may laugh at the ridiculous (a big, fat man with a tiny umbrella), or at the comic (a clown, for example), or at the humorous (a joke), and so on. We may even laugh in scorn.

Psychologists also believe that laughter is a social phenomenon. We laugh when we are part of a group that finds something amusing. Animals, of course, cannot resort to laughter for any of these reasons.

CAN ANIMALS TASTE?

Our sense of taste is a source of great pleasure to us. It makes the enjoyment of food possible. But we have a sense of taste not just to give us pleasure, but to protect us, too. It often prevents us from eating things that might harm us.

What is the process of tasting? It is the ability to perceive the impact of molecules. These moving molecules stimulate the taste nerves and we identify the message we receive as having a certain taste. Only substances that are in solution, where the atoms move about freely, can be tasted. A piece of glass, for example, has no taste. Everything that makes the molecules move about more intensifies the taste. That's why hot things have more taste than cold things.

The sensation of taste is first received by taste buds, which are really nerves constructed like buds. They have the special ability to pick up certain sensations which we call taste.

These taste buds are located, in man and the higher animals, on the tongue. The number of taste buds varies greatly, depending on the taste needs of the particular species of animal. Man, for example, is only a moderate taster. We have about 3,000 taste buds. A whale, which swallows whole schools of fish without even chewing, has few or no taste buds.

A pig, oddly enough, is more particular in its tastes than man, and has 5,500 taste buds. A cow has 35,000 taste buds, and an antelope has as many as 50,000 taste buds! So you see that not only can animals taste, but many of them are more sensitive tasters than man.

Animals that live in the sea often have taste buds all over their body. Fish, for example, taste with the whole surface of the body, right down to their tails! Flies and butterflies can actually taste with their feet. When the last joint of a butterfly's leg touches something sweet, its snout stretches out immediately so it can suck it up.

Snakes and lizards use their tongues for tasting, but not as we do. The tip of the tongue flickers out and picks up particles. It brings them to a special organ in the roof of the mouth which smells or tastes them!

CAN ANIMALS SEE IN COLOR?

The world is so bright with color everywhere we turn that it's hard to imagine that other creatures don't see it as we do. But how can we find out whether animals can see color when they can't tell us?

Scientists have made many experiments to get the answer. The bee has been the subject of hundreds of these tests, because we have been curious to know whether the bee tells flowers apart by their color. In one experiment, a bit of sirup was put in front of a blue card, and no sirup in front of a red card. After a while, the bees would come to the blue card, no matter where it was placed, and even if it had no sirup in front of it. This proved they could tell colors apart.

Two strange things were found out about the bee's ability to see in color. The first is that a bee cannot see red as a color. For a bee, it's only dark grey or black. The second is that bees can see ultraviolet as a color, while for human beings, it is just darkness!

Male birds have bright colors. Can female birds see those colors? In experiments done with hens, it was proven that they can see all the colors of the rainbow! But now comes a surprise. The animal that is probably closest of all to man as a friend, the dog, is color-blind! So far all experiments that have been made prove that the dog can't tell one color from another. Many times when we think the dog is responding to a color, he is really responding to some other clue or sign—smell, size, shape. Dog lovers should not be too disappointed by this because the dog's sense of smell is so great that it probably compensates for the inability to see in color. Cats, by the way, seem to be color-blind, too!

Monkeys and apes have a very good sense of color, but most other mammals are color-blind, including bulls!

The reason for color-blindness in mammals is connected with the fact that most of them hunt by night and don't depend on color, and also that they themselves are usually dull in color, so it isn't important in their lives.

WHAT IS THE FASTEST FOUR-LEGGED ANIMAL?

Man is very proud of his speed. After all, doesn't he zoom through space faster than sound itself can travel? Don't we fly from one coast of our country to another in a few hours?

What man should really be proud of in these cases in his brain, which has enabled him to develop machines that can go at fantastic speeds. For when it comes to his body, he is very far indeed from being the speed champion among mammals. In fact, he ranks quite low.

Let's take a look at the speeds at which some four-legged creatures can travel. We must remember, however, that many animals capable of great speed cannot sustain this speed for a long time. Man himself, who can run 22 to 25 miles (35 to 40 kilometres) per hour, can hold this during a race such as a 200 metre dash, but not in a longer race! Also, these speeds are not scientifically exact. They are based on reports and observations which various people have made at different times. But they give you a pretty accurate idea of how animals compare in speed.

The champ of them all is the cheetah, a kind of leopard; it has reached 70 miles per hour! The black-buck comes next at about 65 miles per hour. At about 60 miles per hour, we have the Mongolian gazelle and the Pronghorn antelope. Any of these animals mentioned would outdistance all other mammals in a race of over a mile or so.

The lion, surprisingly enough, can charge after his enemy at a speed of 50 miles, but he can't keep it up. A deer, which most of us consider a very fast animal, only goes at about 45 or 50 miles an hour, and that's about the speed of a race horse!

Another animal that is used in racing, the greyhound, goes at about 35 to 40 miles—only a few miles faster than a grizzly bear! And an elephant has been known to make a dash at 25 miles an hour!

WHAT ANIMALS LIVE THE LONGEST?

There are many legends and stories about various animals that have lived to an amazing old age. Most of them are exaggerated, however. Let us consider some of the longest-lived animals and see what the records actually show.

Among mammals, the elephant is generally believed to live the longest. There are stories of elephants that lived 150 or 200 years, but this has never been proven. It is probable that there has been an occasional elephant that lived about 100 years, but as far as verified records go, the oldest was an elephant that died at a little over 60.

The horse shares honors with the elephant for a long life. There are many cases of horses that lived over 50 years. Here are some verified records of the long life of other mammals: hippopotamus, 41 years; rhinoceros, 40 years; bears, 34 years; monkeys, over 20 years; cats, about 23 years; dogs, 22 years. These are records set by individual animals and do not represent the average.

Among birds, it is sometimes claimed that parrots and eagles have lived more than 100 years. But this again has never been proven. As far as the

records show, the longest certain species of birds have ever lived are: condor, 52; parrot, 54; eagle, 55; white pelican, 51. Among the smaller birds, these are the records: starling, 17; canary, 22; English sparrow, 23; cardinal, 30.

A great many legends exist about various fish that have lived to a ripe old age. But when the facts are checked, no proof exists. The carp is a fish that has a long life, but the oldest carp on record was only about 25 years. One fish, called "the European catfish," has been known to live for more than 60 years in a lake in England. The American eel has been known to reach an age of 50.

We now come to the champion as far as long life is concerned—the tortoise. One famous tortoise, called "the Mauritius tortoise," definitely lived for 152 years, and according to some biologists, probably lived for 200 years. There is evidence that a tortoise known as "the Carolina tortoise," which lives in the United States, may live for 123 years!

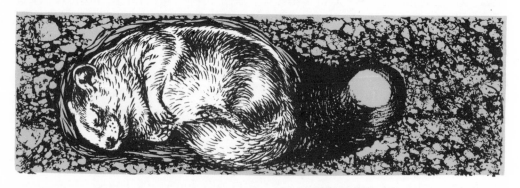

WHY DO ANIMALS HIBERNATE?

Let's look at the woodchuck as a typical hibernating animal. Unlike the squirrel, it doesn't store up a food supply for the winter. It depends on plant food, and when winter comes its food supply is gone. But the woodchuck has stored up a reserve supply of fat on its own body. So when it can no longer find food, it crawls deep into its burrow and goes to sleep. It sleeps through the cold winter and lives on the fat which it has stored up. The word "hibernate" comes from the Latin and means "winter sleep."

Many mammals, like the bear, do not really hibernate. They do sleep more in the winter than in summer, but it is not the deep sleep of hibernation. On warm and pleasant days in the winter, the bear, the squirrel, the chipmunk will wake up and come out into the open.

But the sleep of a true hibernator is almost like death and is quite unlike ordinary sleep. While an animal is hibernating, all its life activities nearly stop. The temperature of its body decreases until it is only a little warmer than the air of its den.

Because of this, the animals burn the food stored in their bodies very, very slowly. Since they burn less fuel, they need less oxygen, and as a result, their breathing is slower and their hearts beat only faintly. If the temperature in the den becomes very low, the hibernating animal wakes up, digs itself in a little deeper, and goes to sleep once more.

When spring comes, the animals are awakened by the change in temperature, moisture, and by hunger. They crawl out of their dens.

Did you know that many cold-blooded animals hibernate, also? Earthworms crawl down into the earth below the frost line; frogs bury themselves in the mud at the bottom of ponds; snakes crawl into cracks in the rocks or holes in the ground; and a few fish, such as the carp, bury themselves in the muddy bottom. Even some insects hibernate by hiding under rocks or logs!

WHEN WAS THE COW DOMESTICATED?

A great many city people are confused by the names given to domestic cattle, so let's get that straight first. The young male animal is first called a bull-calf and grows up to become a bull. The young female is first a heifer-calf, grows into a heifer, and after two or three years, becomes a cow.

The oxen (which include domestic cattle) were among the earliest of all animals to be domesticated. The reason for this is that the males were very docile and therefore could be used for doing heavy work, and the females were able to supply more milk than was needed for their own offspring. In time, these animals began to be used for food, but this was not the chief reason they were domesticated. In fact, among many people their flesh was considered unfit for human consumption, sometimes for religious reasons. The breeding or raising of cattle for the purpose of supplying meat is a modern development.

While we can't be sure of the exact date when the ox was first domesticated, there is evidence that man living in the Stone Age already had domesticated cattle. We know that the Egyptians had them about 6,000

years ago, and the Babylonians probably much earlier.

The ox is probably descended from a species of bison called "aurochs" or wild oxen called "urus," which existed in Europe, Asia, and northern Africa in prehistoric times. The earliest known domesticated ox in Europe was a small, slenderly built animal, with short horns. It was probably brought into Europe from Asia by men of the Stone Age during their migrations.

Later on, during the Bronze Age, a new and larger type of cattle appeared in Europe. Today, there are many breeds and sub-breeds of cattle all over the world. In Europe alone, there are about 50 distinct breeds. One of the oldest of these is the Brown Swiss. The Holstein has been bred for dairy qualities for about 2,000 years!

WHY DOES A COW CHEW ITS CUD?

Many thousands of years ago, there were certain animals who couldn't protect themselves too well against their stronger, fiercer enemies. In order to survive, these animals developed a special way of eating. They would snatch some food hastily whenever they could, swallow it quickly without chewing, and run away to hide. Then when they were in their hiding place, sitting calmly, they would chew the food at their leisure!

Our "cud-chewing" animals are descended from these and are called "Ruminantia." It so happens that nearly all the mammals that are most useful to man are Ruminantia. These include cows, sheep, goats, camels, llamas, deer, and antelopes.

Here is what makes it possible for a ruminant like a cow to chew its cud. A ruminant has a complicated stomach with five compartments. These compartments are: the paunch or rumen, the honeycomb bag or reticulum, the manyplies or omasum, the true stomach or abomasum, and the intestine.

Each of these compartments of the stomach does something different to the food. When the food is swallowed, it is made into a coarse pellet and goes into the paunch, the largest of the five compartments. There it is moistened and softened and then passes into the honeycomb or reticulum. Here it is made into balls, or "cuds" of a convenient size.

After a ruminant has eaten, it usually lies down or rests quietly somewhere. At this time it regurgitates the food from the reticulum back into the mouth. Now the ruminant chews the cud for the first time. After chewing, it swallows the food again and it goes into the manyplies, or third stomach. From here the food goes into the true stomach where the process of digestion takes place. Camels, by the way, differ from other ruminants in not having a third stomach.

Cows have no teeth in the upper jaw. Instead, the gum is in the form of a tough pad. This pad holds the grass down across the edges of the lower front teeth. When a cow grazes, it uses a sideways motion of the head to cut off the grass in this manner.

WHY DO COWS GIVE MILK?

People have used milk for food from ancient times, and have developed certain animals to supply large amounts of milk. We depend on cows to supply most of our milk, but in Spain, for example, the sheep is one of the chief milk-producing animals.

Many desert tribes depend on the camel for milk, and in Egypt, they use water buffaloes. In Peru, the llama is a milk-producing animal. People in many countries use goat's milk.

Milk is the fluid secreted by the mammary glands of the animal as food for their young in the period immediately after birth. It takes the place of the blood which supplied the young with nutrition before it was born. In fact, it is exactly like blood, only without the red blood cells and the blood pigment.

The composition of milk varies quite a bit, depending on the species of the animal which produces it. But milk always contains fat, protein, carbohydrate, and minerals. Goat's milk, for instance, contains twice as much fat as cow's milk, and the milk of reindeer contains five times as much fat as cow's milk!

The milk of every animal also contains various salts according to the needs of its young. The more rapid the growth of the newborn, the more salts in the mother's milk. A cow doubles its original weight at birth in 47 days, but a human being does it in 180 days. That's why cow's milk is too rich in proteins and salts and must be diluted for feeding newborn children.

The milk produced by cows varies depending on many factors. One, of course, is the breed of cow and the constitution of the individual cow. Another is the time between milkings. The last milk to be drawn at each milking is richer in fat than the rest. So, if a cow has not been completely milked, it will probably have fatter milk next time.

Since green food is the main source of vitamins for the cow, summer milk is usually richer than winter milk, when the cow can't walk about in the pasture. About 110 grams of food solids are contained in each litre of milk. The most important solids are the butterfat, the casein, the milk sugar, and the minerals.

HOW LONG HAVE DOGS BEEN DOMESTICATED?

Hundreds of thousands of years ago, giant mammoths still roamed the earth and the world was covered with dense forests. Men lived in caves and dressed themselves in the skins of wild beasts. It was then that the dog first became man's friend.

At first the dog followed men on their hunting expeditions, to get whatever share he could of the kill. Then the instinct for companionship made him adopt man as his leader. Soon the men trained the dogs to help them in the hunt, to carry their burdens, and to guard their firesides. All this happened long before there was any recorded history. Actually, we can only

guess at the story from finding the bones of primitive dogs with the bones of men in the caves of Stone Age.

Since the history of the dog goes back many hundreds of thousands of years, it is impossible to trace it clearly. Some scientists believe that dogs are the result of the mating of wolves and jackals. Other scientists say that some dogs are descended from wolves, other dogs from jackals, others from coyotes, and some from foxes. A widely held theory is that our modern dogs and the wolves are descended from a very remote common ancestor.

This theory helps to explain the differences in size and appearance of the various breeds of dogs and also explains their habits. When a dog turns around three times before he settles down to sleep, it may be because his remote ancestors had to beat down a nest among the forest leaves or jungle grasses. Other evidence of the wild ancestry of dogs is the build of their bodies, which is naturally adapted for speed and strength. This, together with their keen scent and quick hearing, were qualities they needed when they were wild hunters.

From the time there have been any permanent records of man's history, the dog has been mentioned. There are pictures of dogs on Egyptian tombs that are 5,000 years old. The Egyptians even considered the dog sacred, and when a dog died in an Egyptian home, the whole family went into mourning.

Though the dog has been loved and respected by most peoples of the world, there are some exceptions. The Hindus still consider the dog unclean and the Mohammedans despise dogs.

HOW ARE SEEING-EYE DOGS TRAINED?

Today hundreds of young, healthy, blind people have won new freedom to work, to live, to come and go as they please through the help of guide-dogs.

Training such a dog is a long and careful process. The guide-dog must be taught to obey his master's orders. He must also be taught to disobey when an unsafe order is given. No seeing-eye dog will walk in front of a speeding car no matter how firmly his blind master says, "Go!"

A seeing-eye dog is usually a German shepherd, though boxers and Labrador retrievers are also used occasionally. It takes three months to train a guide-dog. First come the obedience exercises—come, sit, lie down, stand, and fetch. These are repeated as daily "setting-up exercises."

Then the guide-harness, a U-shaped leather harness, is buckled on. The dog learns to walk at the left of his trainer, a little more than halfway forward. The trainer acts as a blind man would, bumping into things. The dog learns to guide his master away from these obstacles. He is taught to stop and wait at the curb. He watches traffic and lets cars pass. Regardless of commands, he goes ahead only when it is safe.

Before the dog is passed on to a blind master, the trainer makes a final check. He blindfolds himself and has the dog lead him through the thick of traffic to make sure that the dog is a safe guide.

Next the blind master and his dog train together for four weeks. Daily

N.B. In Britain "Alsatian" is more commonly used to describe the German Shepherd dog.

the two practice the dog's obedience commands. The dog lives for his master's praise. Next come brisk walks, the master grasping the U-shaped guide-harness. They get used to each other's movements and signals.

Soon they are ready to try the noise and traffic of a city street—at first under the watchful eye of an instructor. The dog picks his way skillfully through the crowds, swings aside from all trouble spots, stops at each curb. Now the two are working smoothly as a team. They go home together to start a newer, freer life for the blind man!

WHEN WERE CATS DOMESTICATED?

The cat has been around for a long, long time. Fossils of cats have been found which are millions of years old!

The domesticated cat we know today is the descendant of the wildcat, but just which wildcat we don't know, because it happened so long ago. Probably our varieties, or breeds, of domesticated cats all came from two or three of the small wildcats that existed in Europe, North Africa, and Asia thousands of years ago.

The best guess we have is that about 5,000 years ago these wildcats were domesticated for the first time. We know that 4,000 years ago the Egyptians had tame cats. In fact, the Egyptians worshipped the cat as a god. Their goddess Bast, or Pacht, was shown in pictures with a cat's head, and sacrifices were offered to cats.

The cat represented their chief god and goddess, Ra and Isis. When a house cat died, the Egyptian family and servants shaved their eyebrows and went into mourning. The death of a temple cat was mourned by the whole city. Many mummies of cats have been found, prepared in the same way as the mummies of kings and nobles. The penalty for killing a cat was death!

In Europe, however, there were probably no tame cats until after A.D 1000. In ancient times, the Europeans had quite a different attitude toward the cat than the Egyptians did. They thought of it as an evil spirit rather than a god. The devil was often pictured as a black cat, and witches were supposed to take the shape of cats.

The various breeds of domestic cats and individual cats vary from each other as much as the different breeds and individual dogs do. Probably the most easily recognized groups are the short-haired cats and the long-haired cats. The Angora and the Persian are the best-known long-haired cats.

CAN CATS SEE IN THE DARK?

Perhaps you have a cat as a pet in the house. You love to hold it and play with it and you feel it's almost a member of the family. But a cat is one of the strangest creatures on earth. Even though it has lived with man for thousands and thousands of years—it always seems to be just one step removed from the jungle!

A cat is closely related to such animals as the lion, tiger, and leopard, and in its own way it behaves like them. For instance, cats lie in wait for their victims, and then spring on their back, just the way a lion might kill an enemy.

A cat can make a tremendous leap in the air, as much as two metres straight up. A cat has padded feet so that it can stalk its prey in absolute silence. It has 18 claws on its feet that it can pull out and draw back again.

What makes a cat able to see in the dark? It has eyes that can adjust themselves to different amounts of light. When there's a bright light, the pupils of the eyes become narrow slits. When it's dark, the pupils become wide, almost the size of the entire eye. This doesn't mean a cat can see in absolute darkness, but it needs much less light than most animals. Because a cat's eyes round out from the head, it collects light from a wide angle. When a cat's eye reflect all this light, it seems to glow.

Cats may live to be 19 or 20 years of age, but the average age is about 14 years.

FROM WHAT ANIMAL IS THE HORSE DESCENDED?

Many of the animals on earth today are descended from creatures much larger than themselves. But the horse seems to have developed in the opposite way.

The first known ancestor of the horse was a little creature no larger than a cat, which lived ages ago. It had four toes on its front feet and three on the hindfeet. It has been called "the Eohippus," or "dawn horse." Fossils of this ancestor of the horse have been found in many parts of the world, including Wyoming and New Mexico.

A much later ancestor was larger. Only one toe touched the ground, though the other toe was visible on each side of the main toe. This gradual development of one toe enabled the horse to travel faster. It could then escape from its enemies and survive. The present foot of the horse is the remaining middle toe. The hoof is really the nail, greatly enlarged.

The horse was common in Asia, North Africa, Europe, and North America in prehistoric times. The American variety died off many thousands

Our present-day horse and two of its ancestors.

of years ago. The present-day American horse is that which was brought from Europe by the Spaniards and, later, by other colonists.

It is almost certain that the horse came from the East to the civilized countries of Asia Minor and the Mediterranean. It first appeared in Babylonia about 3000 B.C. It was brought into Egypt about 1675 B.C. This horse had probably already been tamed by the wandering tribes of central Asia.

In prehistoric times, the horse was a source of food long before anyone thought of using it for riding. The earliest pictures and carvings of horses were made by European cave men about 15,000 years ago. These portraits show a horse very like the existing Mongolian pony.

In fact, in Mongolia and Chinese Turkestan may be found the last remaining species of wild horse. It is called "Przhevalski's horse," after the man who discovered it in the 1870's. It is believed that Przhevalski's horse may be the direct ancestor of our present-day horse.

WHY IS THE LION CALLED "KING OF BEASTS"?

Throughout the history of man, the lion has been considered the symbol of strength. We say "strong as a lion" or "lion-hearted." In courts throughout the world, the lion was used on shields and crests and banners to indicate power.

Probably this was not because anybody could prove that a lion could defeat all other animals in combat, but because lions strike such terror in man and in other beasts.

The ancient Egyptians believed the lion was sacred, and during the time when Christ was born, lions lived in many parts of Europe. By the year 500, however, they had all been killed. Today, the only places where lions are plentiful are in Africa and in one region of India.

Lions are members of the cat family. The average length of a grown-up lion is about 3 metres and they weigh between 180 and 225 kilograms. The males are larger than the females. People who hunt lions can always tell whether they are tracking a male or female by the size of the tracks. The male has larger front feet than the female.

The lion's voice is a roar or a growl. Unlike other cats, it doesn't purr, and rarely climbs trees. Unlike other cats, too, it takes readily to deep water. Lions feed on grazing animals, so they live in more or less open country and not in forests. And because they drink once a day, they always live near some supply of water.

Lions rest by day and do their hunting by night. Lions may live singly, or in pairs, or in groups of four to a dozen which are known as "prides." The main food supply of lions comes from zebras, gazelles, and antelopes. Sometimes a lion will attack a giraffe, but it won't attack an elephant, rhinoceros, or hippopotamus. When a lion isn't hungry, he pays no attention to other animals.

When hunting, a lion may lay hidden until an animal passes close by, or it may crawl and wiggle up to its victim and then make a sudden rush. When it makes that rush, it can go as fast as 40 miles an hour!

ARE ALL APES EQUALLY INTELLIGENT?

At one time the name "ape" was given to any monkey. But now it is used to designate the tail-less manlike apes found only in the tropical forests of Africa and Asia. These include the huge gorilla and big chimpanzees, the shaggy red orangutan, and the long-armed gibbons.

These animals are called "the anthropoid," or manlike, apes because in many ways they are similar to man. Their skeletons are similar to that of man, and they have the same number and kind of teeth. The deeply wrinkled brains of the apes, though smaller, are like the human brain in shape and arrangement. Their faculties are similar, with the exception of speech. Their blood, too, is much like human blood.

Gorillas are the largest apes, being as tall as a man and much heavier and more powerful. Gibbons are the smallest and least manlike.

The one that is most like man is the chimpanzee. This ape is smaller

GORILLA   CHIMPANZEE   ORANGUTAN   GIBBON

than either the gorilla or the orangutan. It is more intelligent than either of the others, imitates human ways more readily, and is more responsive to training. Its body is quite similar to that of man, except that the chimpanzee has 13 pairs of ribs and man usually has only 12 pairs.

The chimpanzee's flesh-colored skin is covered, except on the hands and face, with coarse black hair. As the ape grows older, gray hairs appear about the mouth and the skin becomes dusky or black.

Chimpanzees are captured quite easily and seem to adapt themselves to living in zoos. Unfortunately, they also acquire man's diseases, such as tuberculosis, and some have died in captivity of cancer. Chimpanzees are sociable animals and quickly learn to imitate man. Some become so attached to favorable keepers in zoos that they will cry for them when ill and will refuse to take medicine from any other!

Scientists have been able to list at least 20 separate sounds as "chimpanzee language"!

WHY DO BIRDS HAVE FEATHERS?

The science of evolution explains it this way: Ages and ages ago, birds belonged to the reptile family. Then a period came in their development when they left the reptile family and gradually their scales became feathers. The fact is, feathers are merely another form of the substance that in some animals appears as hoofs, horns, and nails!

A feather is made up of a tapering rod. The upper, more slender portion is called "the shaft" and the lower portion, "the quill." The quill is hollow and is pierced at the tip with a hole through which nourishment passes during growth. The shaft is filled with pith.

The colors of feathers on birds are produced by pigments deposited in the substance of the feather. Some colors are produced by the surface formation of the feather, which reflects the light in special ways. The food a bird eats may also determine its colors! For example, certain canaries produce deep orange feathers instead of yellow when fed a little cayenne pepper with their food after they are hatched.

Birds lose all their feathers at least once a year and replace them with new ones. During this process, called "molting," most birds give up only a few feathers at a time. Feathers grow rapidly, and when new are brushlike in appearance.

There are two types of feathers. Those which form the outline of the body are called "the contour feathers." The soft, fluffy feathers underneath are "the down." When a bird comes out of the egg, its body is covered with a coat of down. This is soon cast aside to make way for the regular feathers which grow from the same cell openings as the down.

The texture and size of the feathers which a bird has depends on the type of life it leads. The feathers of the owl, for instance, are soft and downy, and enable it to fly quietly, but not swiftly. Those of the hawk, on the other hand, are shorter and lie closer to the body so there is little resistance to the air and it can fly swiftly. Feathers of birds that take to the water are furnished with oil from special glands, which make them waterproof!

WHY DOES A MALE BIRD HAVE BRIGHTER COLORS THAN THE FEMALE?

To understand why this is so, we must first understand why birds have colors at all!

Many explanations have been given for the coloring of birds, but science still doesn't understand this subject fully. You see, the reason it's hard to explain is that some birds are brilliantly colored, others dully. Some birds stand out like bright banners; others are difficult to see.

All we can do is try to find a few rules that hold true for most birds. One rule is that birds with brighter colors spend most of their time in treetops, in the air, or on the water. Birds with duller colors live mostly on or near the ground.

Another rule—with many exceptions!—is that the upperparts of birds are darker in color than the underparts.

Facts like these make science believe that the reason birds have colors is for protection, so that they can't easily be seen by their enemies. This is called "protective coloration." A snipe's colors, for instance, blend perfectly with the grasses of marshes where it lives. A woodcock's colors look exactly like fallen leaves.

Now if the colors are meant to protect birds, which bird needs the most protection, the male or the female? The female, because she has to sit on the nest and hatch the eggs. So nature gives her duller colors to keep her better hidden from enemies!

Another reason for the brighter colors of the male bird is that they help attract the female during the breeding season. This is usually the time when the male bird's colors are brightest of all. Even among birds, you see, there can be love at first sight!

WHY DO BIRDS SING?

The song of birds is one of the loveliest sounds in nature. Sometimes when we are out in the country and we hear birds singing, it seems to us they are calling back and forth, that they are telling one another something.

The fact is that birds do communicate with one another, just as many other animals do. Of course, at times the sounds birds make are mere expressions of joy, just as we may make cries of "Oh!" and "Ah!" But for the most part, the sounds that birds make are attempts at communication.

A mother hen makes sounds that warn her chicks of danger and causes them to crouch down motionless. Then she gives another call which collects them together. When wild birds migrate at night, they cry out. These cries may keep the birds together and help lost ones return to the flock.

But the language of birds is different from language as we use it. We use words to express ideas, and these words have to be learned. Birds don't learn their language. It is an inborn instinct with them. In one experiment, for example, chicks were kept away from cocks and hens so they couldn't hear the sounds they made. Yet when they grew up they were able to make those sounds just as well as chicks that had grown up with cocks and hens!

This doesn't mean that birds can't learn how to sing. In fact, some birds can learn the songs of other birds. This is how the mockingbird gets its name. If a sparrow is brought up with canaries, it will make great efforts to sing like a canary. If a canary is brought up with a nightingale, it can give quite a good imitation of the nightingale's song. And we all know how a parrot can imitate the sounds it hears. So we must say that while birds are born with the instinct to sing, some learning takes place, too.

Did you know that birds have dialects? The song of the same kind of bird sounds different in different parts of the world. This shows that in addition to their instinct, birds do quite a bit of learning in their lifetime when it comes to singing.

HOW DO BIRDS FIND THEIR WAY HOME?

One of the strangest and most mysterious things in nature is the ability of certain creatures to find their way home, sometimes from great distances. As you know, birds are not the only ones who can do this. Bees, eels, and salmon are able to return to a particular place after long journeys, too.

Many experiments have been made with birds in an attempt to find out what guides them on their way home. In one case, seven swallows were taken 400 miles from home. When they were set free, five of them returned to their nests. In another case, a certain kind of sea bird was taken from its nest off the Welsh coast to Venice by plane. When it was released, it made its way home to its nest, a distance of 930 miles if it flew in a straight line.

Migrating birds offer an even more amazing example of this ability. There are swallows that migrate from England to South Africa every year. They not only return to England the next spring, but many of them come back to nest in the very same house where they nested the year before. And do you know the distance they have to fly back? Six thousand miles!

By the way, did you know that certain types of butterflies migrate, too, and find their way home over long distances? In the tropics, one can sometimes see great mass flights of butterflies all flying steadily in one direction.

They may go a thousand miles and more, and then return again in another season.

Despite all the efforts that have been made to explain how these creatures find their way home, we still don't know. Since many of the birds fly over great bodies of water, we can't explain it by saying they use landmarks to guide them. Just to say they have an "instinct" doesn't really explain it, either. The reason they do it may be to obtain food or to reproduce under the right conditions. But the signals and guideposts they use on their flights are still a mystery to man!

WHAT IS THE LARGEST FLYING BIRD?

The largest of all living birds cannot fly at all. This is the African ostrich, which measures up to 2.5 metres in height and may weigh more than 135 kilograms. This would be a big burden for a bird to lift into the air!

The two groups of flying birds that have the largest wingspread are the albatrosses and the condors. They weigh up to about 13 kilograms.

The wandering albatross leads the parade of largest flying birds with a wingspread of over 3.5 metres. Next comes the condor, which has a wingspread of up to 3.5 metres. Next comes the king vulture, which is found in South America, Mexico, and Central America. It has a wingspread of up to 3 metres.

The white pelican comes after with a wingspread of over 2.5 metres. It is found in Canada and points south, and in winter is seen along the Gulf Coast of the United States. The great bustard, a large gooselike game bird related to the cranes, is next. It is found in parts of Europe, Asia, and Africa, and has a wingspread of over 2.5 metres.

The U.S. bald eagle is the next largest flying bird, having a wingspread up to 2.5 metres. The golden eagle is about the same size, as is the whooping crane. Then comes the sandhill crane, with a wingspread of 2 metres.

the brown pelican, which is the same size, and the buzzard, which also has this wingspread. These are the largest flying birds.

Incidentally, there is a great variation in the speed of flying birds. The fastest flight of birds ever measured was that of two swifts who flew over a course of two miles in India. It was found that they covered this distance in from 36 to 42 seconds, or at the rate of 171.4 to 200 miles an hour!

After the swifts, probably the fastest flying birds are the duck hawks and their relatives. They have been known to fly at 165 to 180 miles an hour! Homing pigeons fly at about 60 miles an hour, and hummingbirds at about 50 to 55 miles an hour.

WHY DO GEESE FLY IN FORMATION?

You hear a distant call in the sky, "Honk! Honk!" You look up and see a V-shaped formation of geese passing overhead and going south.

That V-shaped formation of geese actually goes at the express train speed of about 50 miles an hour. We can make a guess as to why they fly in this formation. We know that airplanes fly in this formation, too, so that each plane can see the other and follow a leader. The geese also follow a leader on their flights, a wise old gander which knows the way perfectly, day or night. The V-formation is as good for them as it is for planes.

Altogether, there are approximately 40 different species of geese. Only 10 or 12 are found in the United States, and practically all of these are only winter visitors. The goose might be considered a Canadian bird.

The best known of these geese is actually called the "Canada goose." It flies over nearly all of North America while migrating. Its head and neck are black with a broad white patch extending across its throat and sometimes up across both cheeks.

The Canada goose usually keeps the same mate for a lifetime. Its favorite food in spring and summer are grasshoppers, but it also eats other insects and earthworms. Much of the time, however, it feeds on wild plants, wild rice, the roots of rushes. It builds its nest on the ground, as do other geese, and lines the nest with down from its own breast.

The Canada goose is delicious to eat, and until laws were passed to protect it, thousands were killed every year. A grown goose weighs about 5 to 6 kilograms.

WHAT KEEPS A DUCK AFLOAT?

When we use the word "duck," we are really referring to a very wide variety of birds. It ranges from the familiar barnyard type to the wild traveler in the skies. In fact, the duck family includes swans, geese, the mergansers or fishing ducks, the tree ducks, the dabbling ducks, the diving ducks, and the ruddy ducks.

Most of the wild ducks breed from the Canadian border states to the limit of trees in the Far North. It is only in the winter that they travel to the Central and Southern States. But they stay in the South for only a short time. As soon as the ice breaks up in the North, they head for home, the ponds, streams, marshes, lake shores, and seacoast where they like to live.

Ducks have no problem living in icy waters. The reason they are able to stay afloat is that their outer coat of closely packed feathers is actually waterproof. A gland near the duck's tail gives off an oil which spreads over the feathers. Underneath this coat, a layer of thick down protects them further. Even the webfeet of a duck are designed to protect them from the cold water. There are no nerves or blood in the webfeet, so they don't feel the cold.

The ducks' feet and legs are set far back on the body, which helps them greatly in swimming. It also gives them that peculiar waddle when they walk. A duck can move through the air pretty rapidly, too, and in short flights ducks have been known to go as fast as 70 miles an hour!

Most ducks build their nests on the ground near water. They line the nest with delicate plants and with down from the duck's own breasts. This warm down covers the eggs when the female is away from the nest. A duck lays about six to fourteen eggs, and only the female sits on the eggs.

Ducks molt, or shed their feathers, after the breeding season. Since their wing quills are gone at this time, ducks cannot fly during their molting period. To protect themselves from their enemies, they stay very quiet so as not to attract attention.

There are about 160 different types of species of ducks in the world, and they are found on every continent except Antarctica.

WHY IS THE OWL CONSIDERED WISE?

When a bird or animal has something unusual about its appearance or its habits, superstitions usually spring up about it. The owl is both a strange-looking bird and one that behaves quite differently from other birds.

The result is that all kinds of legends have grown up about it. Did you know that in ancient times it was considered an unlucky bird? The Romans hated the owl so much that when it was seen and caught in the city in the daylight hours, it was burned and its ashes publicly scattered in the Tiber!

Yet in England and elsewhere, it is often referred to as "the wise old owl." This is probably due to its appearance—and not to any superior intelligence. Its great, staring eyes seem to be looking at you as if the owl were thinking very hard. Actually, those eyes are very sensitive to daylight. And they are so placed that the owl has to turn its whole head in order to change the direction of its glance.

Owls of one species or another are found in all parts of the world, even in the Arctic districts where their plumage is snow-white. The owl hunts only at night, but its eyes and ears are remarkably keen. In the night an owl can both see and hear the movements of a mouse, its favorite food.

It captures its prey with its feet. Its claws are needlelike and close over its victim like the jaws of a trap. Animals as large as the squirrel and rabbit are hunted.

Clumsy as the owl may seem, its flight is swift. Its feathers are soft and fringed so that it can fly noiselessly. The plumage is loose and fluffy, making the bird seem larger than it really is. It is one bird whose face isn't at all birdlike!

CAN A HUMMINGBIRD STAND STILL IN MID-AIR?

Have you ever seen a hummingbird as it was poised over a flower for a few minutes? It seemed to be absolutely still in the air, its beak pressed into a flower, and then suddenly it was gone.

What did the hummingbird rest on? Nothing. It was standing still in mid-air because it was beating its wings so rapidly. Those tiny wings were moving so fast that all we could see was a kind of haze.

A hummingbird doesn't fly in the same way other birds do. It beats its wings at an average of about 55 strokes a second! Just take your finger and try to move it up and down as quickly as you can. You'll probably be able to move it two or three times a second.

The hummingbird had to develop this remarkable wingpower because of its eating habits. It feeds on the nectar of flowers and on the tiny insects which are found in the center of flowers. But these flowers are usually so small and delicate that if the hummingbird tried to rest on them, the flowers wouldn't support its weight. But by beating its wings so rapidly, the hummingbird (which gets its name from the humming sound the wings make) can stand still in the air and reach in with its beak to get the nectar and insects.

The hummingbird seen most commonly in North America, the ruby-throat, measures somewhere between 8 and 10 centimetres from the end of its bill to the tip of its tail. Even though it is such a tiny bird, it will put up quite a brave fight to protect its nest. Hummingbirds have been known to chase away hawks and crows that tried to attack the nest.

This nest of the hummingbird is a tiny little gem. It is made of plant down, spiderwebs, and moss, and shaped like a little cup. The eggs are pure and white and there are never more than two.

HOW DO FISH BREATHE?

Hundreds of thousands of years ago, long before man appeared on the earth, there were already fish swimming about in the oceans. At that time, fish were the most highly developed form of life in existence. In fact, fish were the first backboned animals to appear.

Since that time, fish have developed in a variety of ways, so that today only a very few even faintly resemble the first primitive fish of the oceans.

As a general rule, fish are long and tapering in shape. Man has copied this shape in his construction of ships and submarines because it's the best shape for cutting through water quickly.

Most fish use their tails as a power engine and guide themselves with tail and fins. Except for a kind of fish called "lungfish," all fish breathe by means of their gills. A fish takes in water through its mouth. The water flows over the gills and out through the opening behind the covers of the gills. This water contains oxygen which the fish thus obtains to purify its blood, just as human beings take oxygen out of the air to purify their blood.

When the water is contaminated in some way, fish will sometimes attempt to come to the top and breathe in air, but their gills are not suited for using the oxygen in the air.

The blood of fish is cold, but they have nervous systems like other animals and suffer pain. Their sense of touch is very keen, and they taste, as well as feel, with their skin.

Fish are able to smell, too. They have two small organs of smell, which are located in nostrils on the head. Fish have ears, but they are inside the head and are called "internal ears."

The reason fish are usually dark on top and light underneath is that this helps protect them from enemies. Seen from above, they look dark like the ocean or river bed. Seen from below, they seem light, like the light surface water. There are more than 20,000 different kinds of fish, so you can imagine in how many different ways they live!

CAN ANY FISH LIVE OUT OF WATER?

A fish carries on its life processes like any other animal, and has a complete set of organs to help it do so. People are always asking, for example, do fish have hearts, can they hear, can they smell?

Fish have a stomach, intestines, heart, nervous system, and can suffer pain and discomfort. Their sense of touch is very keen, and they taste, as well as feel, with their skin. They have organs of smell, and they have internal ears.

As we know, fish breathe by means of gills through which water is constantly passing from the mouth. But there are some types of fish that spend quite a bit of time out of the water.

The flying fish, while it doesn't spend much time out of the water, is an interesting one. It swims rapidly through the water, moving its tail vigorously. It then spreads its fins and the speed lifts the fish out of the water. A flying fish may glide through the air for several hundred metres.

Even more curious are the climbing perch. They are found in the Far East. They may vary in length from about 8 to 20 centimetres. They can actually get about on land by spreading the rows of movable spines on their gill covers. This braces them on the ground. By pushing with their tails and front fins, they can "walk" on land! According to some reports, these fish can actually climb trees! Many have been found in trees 1.5 metres above the ground. The gills of these fish have become modified so that they can breathe in the air for some time.

The mud skipper, a fish that looks somewhat like a tadpole, can use its front fins to skip about on land and climb trees, too. The lungfish of Africa has developed a lung that enables it to live out of the water. It burrows into the mud during dry spells, forms a cocoon about itself, and can spend the whole summer sleeping out of the water!

HOW DO FLYING FISH FLY?

If there were fish which actually "flew" through the air the way birds do, they would obviously do it by flapping their "wings," or fins. There are no fish which fly that way.

But flying fish do manage to get about in the air and this is how they do it. The "wings" of the flying fish are the front fins, but greatly enlarged. When the fish in in "flight," it spreads out these fins and holds them at an angle to the body. In some cases, the fish also spread the rear fins.

The fish gets into the air by swimming rapidly through the water with part of its body breaking the surface. It goes along this way for some dis-

tance, gathering speed by moving its tail vigorously. Then it spreads the fins and holds them stiffly, and the speed of its motion lifts it into the air!

A flying fish may sail or glide for a distance of several hundred metres in this way before it drops back into the water. Sometimes it strikes the crests of the waves and moves its tail in order to pick up additional power while it is in flight. By the way, the flying fish doesn't just skim over the water. It can fly high enough to land on the decks of large ocean liners.

WHY DO SALMON GO UPSTREAM TO SPAWN?

There are many things that creatures do to produce and protect their young that seem quite miraculous to us. After all, isn't it rather amazing the way birds build nests, or the way certain animals will fight to save their young from enemies?

The instinct that takes the salmon on the long trip upstream must be there because this is the best way new salmon can be born and grow. Not all salmon go to the headquarters of a stream to spawn. Some stay quite close to lower stretches of rivers. The pink salmon is an example of this. It spawns only a few miles above salt water. But in contrast there is the king salmon. It may travel as much as 3,000 miles up a river from the sea!

When the salmon enter fresh water, they are in fine condition, healthy and strong and fat. But as soon as they reach fresh water, they stop feeding. Sometimes they wear themselves out trying to reach the exact place they want to go deposit their eggs.

Since many of the rivers they have to ascend have rapids and falls and jagged rocks, the salmon are often very thin and straggly looking by the time they have spawned. But whether they are worn-out or still in fair condition, the Pacific salmon die after spawning.

When the fish reach the spawning spot (which is usually the very same spot where they were hatched!), the female digs a sort of hole in the gravel or sand with her body, tail, and fins. The eggs are deposited in this "nest" and are fertilized by the male. Then the female covers the eggs.

Now their job is finished and the salmon seem to lose all interest in life. They drift downstream more or less with the current, and then they soon die. Then life begins for the newly hatched fish, which may be about 60 days later.

The young salmon remain in fresh water for a few months or a year, then descend the streams and enter salt water. And so the cycle begins all over again!

HOW CAN A SNAKE MOVE WITHOUT LEGS?

There is probably no creature that ever lived that has fascinated man as much as the snake. There are actually more than 2,000 different kinds of snakes. They are found in practically every part of the world except the polar regions. And they live on land, in the earth, in water, and in trees!

As you watch a snake move, you can't detect a single muscle or bone in motion. The snake has no legs, and yet it can crawl over stones, up trees, and glide through holes!

On the underside of the snake there are broad scales. These are moved forward in such a way that the rear edge of each scale pushes against something in the ground. When the scales are pushed against these rough and irregular spots in the ground, the whole snake moves forward.

But the really strange thing about the snake's "walking" is how those scales are made to move. The snake has a great number of ribs. An African viper, for instance, has 145 pairs of ribs! Each rib is attached to a section of a backbone. And each section of the backbone is joined to the next one in a way that makes the backbone very flexible.

The tips of each pair of ribs are attached with muscles to the broad scales on the underside of the snake. The snake can actually move each scale on its underside independently! So the "legs" of the snake are really its ribs, and the "feet" are the scales.

When the snake wants to make speed, it throws its body into an S-shaped curve, this curve or loop pushes against anything it touches, and the snake glides forward swiftly. Oddly enough, in the skeletons of certain snakes like the boas, we can see traces of hindlegs, which they lost in the process of evolution. So maybe at one time snakes did have real legs!

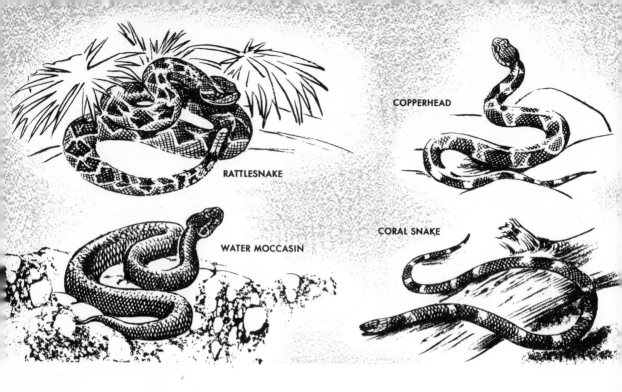

RATTLESNAKE

COPPERHEAD

WATER MOCCASIN

CORAL SNAKE

WHICH SNAKES ARE POISONOUS?

Man seems to have always had a fear and horror of snakes. Their appearance, the way they move about, and the fact that many people have died of snakebite, is responsible for this fear.

There are more than 2,000 species or kinds of snakes. They live on land, in the earth, in water, and in trees. And they can be found in practically all parts of the world except the polar regions and some islands.

The poisonous snakes possess poison fangs, which are hollow teeth, with an opening at the tip. These poison-conducting teeth, or fangs, are in the upper jaw and connect with poison glands in the head. A poison-snake cannot be made permanently harmless by the removal of its fangs, because new fangs will be grown.

Snakes with poison fangs usually inject the poison into their prey to kill it or make it unconscious before it is eaten.

There are about 120 species of non-poisonous snakes in the United States. Poisonous snakes of the United States consist of only four types. One is the coral snake, of the cobra family. It occurs only in the South.

The other three types belong to the pit viper family, of which the rattlesnake, the copperhead, and the water moccasin are members. There are about a dozen kinds of rattlesnakes. All rattlesnakes may be considered as a type, and are easily recognized by the rattle on the end of the tail.

The viper of South-West Asia, like the Rattlesnake, really is a viper. Both are called sidewinders because they can move sideways as well as in a forward direction. About 600 snakes are poisonous but only a quarter of these have a bite fatal to man. Vipers are the only poisonous snakes in Europe. Britain has only three snakes, the Smooth Snake, the Grass Snake, and the Adder. Of these only the Adder (or Viper) is poisonous. There are no snakes in Ireland. English snakes live in fields, heaths and woods.

DO RATTLESNAKES RATTLE BEFORE THEY STRIKE?

A rattlesnake is certainly something to be afraid of. And because people are afraid of it, they have developed an idea that makes it seem a little less dangerous—that a rattlesnake will warn you before it strikes by rattling its tail.

Unfortunately, this isn't completely true. When a rattlesnake does rattle, it's usually because it has become frightened. This makes it vibrate its tail rapidly which causes the rattles to strike together. But studies of the rattlesnake have shown that about 95 per cent of the time this snake gives no warning at all before it strikes!

By the way, this idea of rattlesnakes and other poisonous snakes "striking" rather than biting isn't quite true, either. The fact is poisonous snakes both strike and bite, but some snakes bite more than others.

A snake with long fangs, like the rattlesnake, has its long, hollow, movable fangs folded inward against the roof of the mouth when the mouth is closed. When the snake is about to strike, it opens its mouth, the fangs fall into biting position, and the snake lunges forward. As the fangs penetrate the skin, the snake bites.

This biting movement presses the poison glands so that the poison flows out, then goes through the hollow teeth and into the wound. Other snakes, such as the cobra, which has shorter fangs, hold on for a time when they bite, and chew. This chewing motion forces the poison into the wound.

As a matter of fact, the cobra is a much more dangerous snake than the rattlesnake. The cobra is more aggressive, more likely to attack. And while a rattlesnake has more poison, the venom of the cobra is more deadly. People have been known to die from the bite of a cobra in less than an hour!

HOW DOES THE RATTLESNAKE RATTLE?

A rattlesnake may strike without rattling, and even without coiling. Moral: Stay away from rattlesnakes!

Just what is this "rattle"? The rattles are made of hard, horny, cup-shaped joints. They fit loosely into one another. When a rattlesnake becomes excited, its tail begins to vibrate. This vibration causes the joints, or rattles, to strike together. The sound that is produced is a kind of sharp, whirring noise. It can be heard as far as 18 metres away!

A new rattle is formed on the snake's tail each time it sheds its skin. But that doesn't mean you can tell the age of the snake from the number of rattles, since a snake sheds its skin two to four times a year. Also, as a rattlesnake grows older, the rattles at the end of the tail break off.

Pit vipers have a small pit on either side of the face between the eye and nostril. The pits are sensitive to heat. Since rattlesnakes hunt at night and eat warm-blooded animals, the pits are helpful in locating food.

If you imagine a rattlesnake strikes by leaping forward a great distance, that's wrong, too. It can only strike as far as it can raise its head. Even coiled, it can strike only one-third to one-half of its body length. Since even the largest rattlesnake is seldom longer than 2.23 metres, you can see it's not too difficult to stay out of range.

Did you know that all rattlers give birth to young that are alive? They have a button on the end of their tails at birth. And their fangs are ready to use!

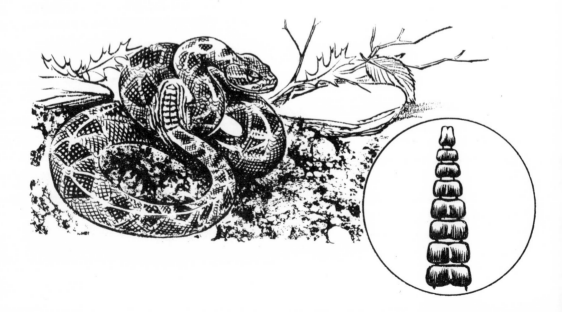

WHAT IS THE LARGEST SNAKE IN THE WORLD?

There are more than 2,000 different kinds of snakes. Snakes are such fascinating and frightening creatures that people have developed all kinds of wrong ideas about them. One of these is that there are huge, terrifying snakes 18 and 21 metres long!

The truth is that snakes never grow to quite that length, though some are certainly big enough. The largest known snake is the regal python, which may have a length of merely 10 metres. (Measure that out in your living room and it'll give you an idea of how long this really is.) This creature is found in the Malay Peninsula, Burma, Indochina, and the Philippine Islands.

The second longest snake is the anaconda, which lives in tropical South America and may reach a length of about 7 metres. That's no "shortie", either! Next comes the Indian python, found in India and the Malay Peninsula, which may grow to 6 or 7 metres. The African rock python is about the same length. The diamond python of Australia and New Guinea often grows to 6.5 metres.

Then we come to a snake that, for some reason, is believed by many people to be the world's largest. It's the boa constrictor, and the most it ever measures is about 5 metres. This nasty creature makes its home in Southern Mexico, and Central and South America.

The king cobra, another unpleasant member of the snake family, reaches a maximum length of about 5.5 metres. What about the United States? What are the largest snakes we're ever likely to run into there? The longest of these is the Eastern diamondback rattlesnake, and it only grows to a length of about 2 metres. The black chicken snake, bull snake, gopher snake—all found in the United States—also grow only to maximum lengths of under 2 metres.

By the way, while the regal python is the longest snake known, it is not the heaviest. The anaconda, which is shorter, may weigh as much as 160 kilograms, which is about 45 kilograms heavier than the heaviest python

The longest poisonous snake is the king cobra, and the heaviest poisonous snake is the Eastern diamondback rattlesnake.

DO SHARKS EAT PEOPLE?

There are more than 150 species, or kinds, of sharks, and while some are quite fierce, the surprising thing is that most sharks are harmless!

Sharks differ from other fish in many ways. Where other fish have movable coverings over the gills, the sharks have slits in the skin. Their backbone is made up of cartilage, or gristle, instead of bone. Another unusual thing about sharks is their teeth. Instead of being true teeth set in the jawbone, the shark has denticles which grow in rows in the gums and mouth. The skin in which the denticles are set keeps growing slowly outward, carrying the rows of teeth with it. As one row of teeth wears out, it drops out and is replaced by a fresh row just behind it.

The shark's mouth is placed on the underside of its head. Below the surface of the water, it eats mouth down. But to seize food on the surface, it rolls over on its back.

Sharks vary in size from 0.3 metres to the great whale shark, which can reach 15 metres long. The most common species, such as often follow ships, are usually so harmless that even other fish aren't afraid of them.

There are at least two species of sharks, however, which are quite dangerous. One is called "the tiger shark." It lives in tropical waters and may get to be as big as 270 kilograms. The tiger shark can swallow a sea lion and has been known to attack human beings. The most ferocious of all sharks is the great white shark. It is sometimes 12 metres long, and probably the most dreaded of all fishes. It will have no hesitation at all about making a meal of a man, and it, too, has been known to swallow sea lions at a gulp!

Curiously enough, the biggest shark of all is completely harmless. This is the whale shark. It may grow to 15 metres long and weigh 18 tonnes. Its ￼od consists of tiny organisms known as plankton, and its teeth, or denticles, are only 3 millimetres long.

WHY DOES A WHALE SPOUT?

Whales are not fish but mammals. They are warm-blooded creatures whose young are not hatched from an egg but are born live. And the baby whale is fed on its mother's milk like other little mammals.

But whales, like all water mammals, are descended from ancestors that lived on land. So they had to adapt themselves for life in the water. This means that over millions of years certain changes took place in their bodies so that they could live in the water.

Since whales have no gills but breathe through their lungs, one of the most important changes had to do with their breathing apparatus. Their nostrils used to be up in the forward part of the head. These have moved back to the tops of their heads. They now form one or two blow-holes which make it easier for them to breathe at the surface of the water.

Under water these nostrils are closed by little valves, and the air passages are shut off from the mouth so that they are in no danger of taking water into the lungs.

Whales usually rise to breathe every five or ten minutes, but they may remain under water for three-quarters of an hour! On reaching the surface, they first "blow," or exhale the used air from their lungs. As they do this, they make a loud noise which may be heard for some distance. What does this spout consist of? It is not water, but merely worn-out air, loaded with water vapor.

They blow several times until they have completely changed the air in their lungs, and then they dive deeply, or "sound." Some whales have been known to dive 600 metres deep! Sometimes big whales, in sounding, throw their tails up into the air or even jump completely out of the water!

WHAT HAPPENS TO FROGS IN THE WINTER?

If you happen to live near a pond, you've probably noticed how quiet it becomes as winter approaches. The croaking of the frogs is gone. Are the frogs gone, too?

The answer is no. They're probably there, but you can't see or hear them. A frog, as you know, belongs to that group of cold-blooded creatures that live both in water and on land. Such creatures are called "Amphibia," which means "double life."

The adult frog has lungs, but it does not breathe air into them as we do. It sucks air into its mouth through two nostrils, at the same time lowering its throat. Then the nostrils are closed, and the frog lifts his throat and pushes the air into its lungs.

In northern countries, when cold weather sets in, some frogs dive into a pond, bury themselves in the mud, and stay there all winter. Ponds do not freeze solid, even when winters are very cold. So the frog doesn't freeze, either.

However, it certainly becomes very cold. Now when an Amphibia becomes cold it needs very little oxygen, because it is burning little food. This explains why the frog can stay under water all winter without breathing air.

There is some oxygen in water and what little the frog needs during the winter it gets from the water through its skin. The frog sometimes spends the winter in a hole in a soft bank or buried under loose stones and earth.

Frogs vary quite a bit in shape, color, and size. Some little tree frogs are no more than 25 millimetres long. Leopard frogs are about 50 to 100 millimetres long. Bullfrogs are the giants among frogs. Some bullfrogs are 20 centimetres long and have legs 25 centimetres long.

A fully developed bullfrog is usually dark green or brown in color so that it can scarcely be seen on a muddy bank or among weeds.

WHAT'S THE DIFFERENCE
BETWEEN FROGS AND TOADS?

Many people wonder if there is a different between frogs and toads. While there are certain differences, in most important things, they are very much alike. They both belong to that group of cold-blooded creatures that live both in water and on land.

Most frogs and toads resemble each other very closely, and it's often hard to tell them apart. Frogs, however, are smooth and slippery, long and graceful. Most toads are dry, warty, and squat. Also, most frogs have teeth while most toads have none.

Almost all Amphibia lay eggs, so in this, the frogs and toads are alike. The eggs of both frogs and toads look like specks of dust floating on top of the water in a jellylike substance. The eggs hatch into little tadpoles, which look more like fishes than frogs or toads.

The tadpoles breathe through gills and have a long swimming tail, but no legs. The eggs develop into this tadpole stage in from three to 25 days. In about three or four months, the tadpoles lose their gills and their tails and develop legs and lungs. But it still takes about a year for the tadpole to become a frog or toad. Frogs and toads often live to a good old age, sometimes even as long as 30 or 40 years!

A toad lays fewer eggs than a frog, which means anywhere from 4,000 to 12,000 eggs every year, while a female bullfrog may lay from 18,000 to 20,000 eggs in one season! There are certain kinds of toads in which the male plays an important part in hatching the eggs. One kind of male toad found in Europe, for example, wraps the long string of eggs about his feet

FROG

TOAD

and sits in a hole in the ground with them until they are ready to hatch. He then carries them back to the pond.

A weird-looking toad which lives in South America hatches out its eggs in holes in its back! These holes are covered with skin, and are filled with a liquid. The young remain in these holes while they pass through the tadpole stage.

Toads which live in temperate regions are usually brown and olive, while those in the tropics are often bright-colored. It is not harmful to handle toads.

HOW DO SNAILS GET THEIR SHELLS?

You've probably seen a snail peeking out of its shell, the feelers moving about from side to side. How would you like to eat one? No? Well, in certain parts of the world (such as France) snails are considered one of the greatest delicacies!

Snails belong to the mollusk family, a kind of animal without backbones. Some snails live in gardens, others in ponds, and some even in the ocean. But there are two chief types of snails: those which have shells, and those which are covered only by a thin mantle. Members of this second group are usually called slugs. The land snail measures about 3 cms in the shell. The slug is about 7 centimetres long.

All snails have one large foot on the underside. That's why they are called "gastropods," or stomach feet. These creatures are equipped with one or two pairs of feelers. They have a pair of eyes, which may be at the end of feelers or at their base, and a mouth. The mouth often extends into the trunk. At its end, there are little sharp teeth with which the snail can scrape off pieces of plants.

Some snails eat animal food. The oyster drill, for example, is a yellow-shelled sea snail which drills into oyster shells and feasts on their flesh!

Snails and slugs breathe either by means of single lungs or by gills. Their shells, which are often beautifully formed, are secreted, or given off, by the mantle. They are usually built up coil after coil as the animal grows.

Most snails lay eggs; in a few species, however, the young are born alive. Snails and slugs leave slime behind them in a glistening trail. This helps them to walk and also keeps them moist. This slime dries up in winter, closing the mouth of the shell. The snail hibernates, or passes the winter, in a crack or hole.

WHAT IS A SHELL?

How many different kinds of shells can you think of? A nut has a shell; so has an egg, and a turtle and a snail and a crab and a lobster and so on! So when we talk about shells, we must consider a wide variety.

A shell is the hard outside covering of a living thing. It is made by the creature itself, or its parent. Shells are made from any of several substances. Nut shells are made of woody material called "lignin." Some shells are made of calcium carbonate (lime). Others are made of "silica," which is the material glass is made of.

The shell cover protects the life inside. Nuts and eggs are entirely enclosed, and the living part inside, such as a seed or baby bird, must grow and break the shell to get out.

Crabs and lobsters are almost entirely enclosed by their shells, but the shell is not made all in one piece. It is made up of plates joined together with soft material. This allows the animal to move and bend.

Some creatures, such as beetles, grow inside their shells until they fit too tightly. Then the shell splits open down the middle and the creature crawls out. Underneath there is a new skin which is soft and stretchy. After a while this skin hardens and becomes the new shell.

Still other creatures have shells that are a part of their bodies. Turtle shells are made of bone covered with scales. The upper shell is made of the turtle's ribs and backbone, and the lower shell is also made of bone. A turtle could not live without its shell any more than a human being could live without his backbone and ribs.

The largest group of animals with shells is the mollusks. Snails are one group of mollusks. Oysters, clams, and scallops are mollusks with two shells and are called "bivalves." They can close their shells completely for protection.

WHAT IS A SPONGE?

The sponge you buy in the store today and use to help clean up in the kitchen is not a real sponge. It is made of synthetic materials to look and act like a sponge, and it seems to work very well.

But real sponges come from the sea—and not from chemical laboratories. For a long time, no one was sure what a sponge was. It was thought that a sponge was a plant. Then in 1825, a man called Robert Grant proved that sponges were animals!

He watched a sponge in water through a microscope. He saw streams of water enter certain openings and come out through others. But for many years, scientists still didn't know what kind of animals these were. It was thought they were tiny, one-celled animals that lived together in a great colony.

Now we know sponges to be the dried-out skeletons of marine animals belonging to a class known as "Porifera." This is a major group in the animal kingdom. And although the sponge is one of the lowest forms of animal life, its structure is quite complicated.

The outer layer of living tissue surrounding it is made of flat, scalelike cells. The cells lining the canals are unlike those found in any other animal. They are column-shaped, and each ends in a long "lasher." These lashers beat the water in and out of the sponge. In this way, it obtains oxygen and millions of tiny organisms for food. The waste products go out with the outgoing water, and this is why fresh sponges have a bad odor. But it protects the sponge, because it discourages animals from eating it!

In the middle of the sponge is a clear, jellylike mass in which there are wandering cells. They probably digest food and take part in breathing and in giving off waste materials.

Sponges have many shapes and are often brilliantly colored. They are obtained by divers, and the most valuable sponges are found in deep water 50 to 80 miles out from shore.

HOW DO INSECTS BREATHE?

All living creatures must breathe in order to sustain life. Breathing is simply the taking-in of air in order to get oxygen, and the exhaling of a changed kind of air. The air we breathe out has had oxygen taken out of it and it has increased amounts of carbon dioxide and water.

The oxygen taken in is needed to "burn" certain food products so the body can use them. Waste products, including water and carbon dioxide, are eliminated by the body in part by being breathed out.

The simplest form of breathing is probably carried on by jellyfish and many worms. They have no breathing organs at all. Dissolved oxygen soaks through their skins from the water in which they live. Dissolved carbon dioxide soaks out. That's all there is to their "breathing."

An earthworm, which is more complicated, has a special fluid, the blood, to carry oxygen from the skin to the internal organs and bring carbon dioxide out. The frog sometimes breathes this way, too, using its skin as a breathing organ. But it has lungs for use when its body needs greater amounts of oxygen.

In insects, breathing takes place in a most unusual and interesting manner. If we examine an insect closely on the abdomen or belly, we see a large number of little openings or pores. Each of these pores is the entrance to a tube called a "trachea." This trachea works in the same way as man's breathing tube or windpipe! So an insect breathes the way we do, except that it may have hundreds of windpipes in its belly to take in air. In a creature as small as an insect, these tubes don't take up too much space. But can you imagine what would happen if man's breathing system were like the insect's? There would hardly be room for any other organs!

By the way, the rate of breathing (how often air is taken in) depends a great deal on the size of the creature. The larger it is, the slower the breathing rate. An elephant breathes about 10 times a minute, but a mouse breathes about 200 times a minute!

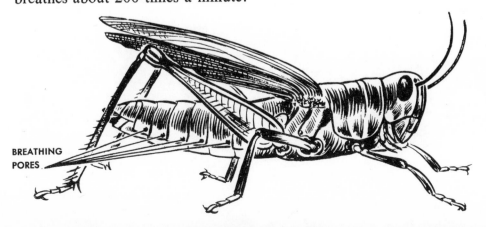

BREATHING
PORES

HOW MANY KINDS OF FLIES ARE THERE?

The answer to this question could be: "Just one kind—annoying!" The fact is, every kind of fly is rather a nuisance when it isn't a danger, and there are 40,000 known species of flies! There's hardly a corner of the world that isn't bothered by flies, although improved pesticides and use of refrigeration have reduced the fly nuisance in temperate zones.

If it surprises you that there are so many kinds of flies, it's because we are speaking scientifically. All two-winged insects are called flies, and the scientific name for them is "Diptera."

The orders of Diptera, therefore, includes the mosquito, too. But that's just the beginning. There is the common housefly, the green-headed horsefly with the painful bite, and the bee fly, that looks like a bee and feeds on flowers.

Here are a few more interesting kinds of flies. The black flies of the North Woods in the spring swarm in such countless numbers that their bites sometimes kill man and beast. Certain midges in the Southern United States by their bite transfer the germ of a disease called "pink eye." The moth fly is tiny enough to pass through mosquito netting and lives by sucking blood. The tsetse fly carries the deadly germ of sleeping sickness in Africa. The big robber flies of Australia prey on other flies, sucking their juices. Incidentally, the dragonfly and the May fly are not true flies because they have more than two wings.

The most familiar fly of all, of course, is the housefly. Did you know that what we call "the feelers," or antennae, of the housefly are organs of smell, not of feeling? These antennae can detect odors at great distances. The mouth parts of this fly are combined into one organ which we mistakenly call "the tongue."

The fly walks on tiptoe on two claws attached to the underpart of the foot. Sticky pads under the claws allow the fly to walk upside down with ease.

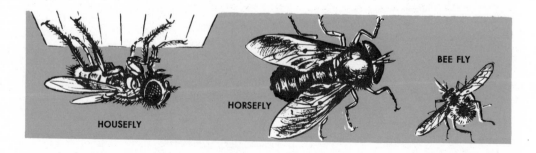

HOUSEFLY

HORSEFLY

BEE FLY

WHAT IS THE FRUIT FLY?

You've probably noticed that when fruit is left to stand a few days so that it starts to decay, little flies often appear as if from nowhere. Where do they come from, and what kind of flies are they?

There are actually two different kinds of "fruit flies." The Mediterranean fruit fly looks somewhat like a housefly with orange and black markings. It is one of the most destructive pests.

The female of this fly lays her eggs in unripe fruit and vegetables. As the young are born, they eat into the pulp. In this way, whole crops are often destroyed.

The tiny fruit fly we see hovering over decaying fruit in our home is called the "drosophila," and it is harmless. The females of this species fly about through the air looking for decaying fruit. They will lay their eggs only in fruit that has begun to rot or decay. When the young are born, they feed on the fermentation which the decaying fruit produces.

The drosophila, or tiny fruit fly, happens to be one of the most useful insects known to science because it is used in the study of heredity, which means the passing-on of characteristics from parents to offspring. If we want to study certain problems in heredity using people, we have to wait a long time for each generation to develop. For instance, to study 30 human generations would take 500 years or more. But by using the fruit fly, we can study 30 generations in a single year!

Here is how science uses the fruit fly for this purpose. The flies are raised in a laboratory on a special mixture called "a medium." In about nine days, a fruitfly is hatched and becomes an adult. By about the tenth day, it is ready to mate and produce new fruit flies!

The flies can be mated in any combination the scientist desires. In a few hours, a number of female fruit flies can lay enough eggs to produce a thousand new adults, all emerging on the same day! They can be studied with the naked eye, and surgical operations can be performed on them under a microscope. Most of our present knowledge of heredity has been gained from the study of fruit flies!

WHAT IS THE PURPOSE OF A FIREFLY'S LIGHT?

Is there anyone who hasn't been mystified by the light of the firefly? Children love to catch them and put them in bottles, or hold them in their hands while the little creatures flash on and off. Now, one thing that may surprise you is that scientists, too, have been mystified by the firefly's light. And they are still mystified—because there are many things about it they can't explain.

The light of the firefly is very much like other kinds of light—except that it is produced without heat. This kind of light is called "luminescence." In the firefly, luminescence is produced by a substance called "luciferin." This combines with oxygen to produce light.

But this reaction won't take place unless another substance, called "luciferase," is present. Luciferase acts as a catalyst; that is, it helps the chemical reaction take place but is not a part of it. To put it another way: fireflies have luciferin and luciferase in their bodies. The luciferase enables the luciferin to burn up and produce light.

Now, scientists can produce this same kind of light in the laboratory. But in order to do so, they must obtain the ingredients from the firefly! Chemists cannot produce them synthetically. It remains a secret of nature!

What is the purpose of this light in the firefly? Well, there are some explanations for it, of course. One is that perhaps this helps the fireflies find their mates. Another purpose might be to serve as a warning to night-feeding birds so that they will avoid the fireflies.

But scientists still feel that they don't really know why these lights are necessary to the firefly, since the above reasons don't seem important enough. They think the light may just be a byproduct of some other chemical process that goes on in the firefly's body. A light happens to be produced, but it's not a vital process. Well, whatever the reason for the light, I'm sure most of us are glad it's there—because of the pleasure of seeing these little insects as they move about at night.

HOW MANY BEES IN A BEEHIVE?

The honeybee has a social organization that in some ways is as complicated and as well organized as that of man! No other wild species of creature can equal it. The honeybee, in fact, can only survive for any length of time if it is a member of a colony. An individual honeybee cannot survive long living alone.

The honeybee colony consists of one queen, thousands of worker bees, and during certain seasons, a few hundred to several thousand drones or males. The colony must have some kind of shelter. The hive may be anything: a hollow log, a crude box, or a modern factory-built hive.

The queen lays all the eggs, but she cannot care for them. She may lay more than 1,500 eggs per day and about 250,000 in a season. An occasional queen may lay 1,000,000 in a lifetime, although most queens live only one to two years. She lays fertilized eggs that develop into worker bees or queens, depending on the needs of the colony, and unfertilized eggs that develop into drones.

The colony may have only a few thousand worker bees, but at the height of its development, it can have 60,000 bees! So, you see, a hive is quite a busy and crowded place during certain seasons.

With so many bees working together, division of labor is necessary in a honeybee colony. Each worker bee develops a whole variety of skills without any previous training. He is able to perform very complicated jobs as he gets older. At first, a worker bee does only cleaning and polishing of the cells. Later on, it takes on the job of feeding the larvae of bees that will soon emerge. Eventually, it becomes a field bee and goes out to gather pollen which will become honey!

HOW DO BEES MAKE HONEY?

The reason bees make honey is that it serves them as food. So the whole process of making honey is a way of storing up food for the bee colony.

The first thing a bee does is visit flowers and drink the nectar. Then it carries the nectar home in the honey sac. This is a baglike enlargement of the digestive tract just in front of the bee's stomach. There is a valve that separates this section from the stomach.

The first step in the making of the honey takes place while the nectar is in the bee's honey sac. The sugars found in the nectar undergo a chemical change. The next step is to remove a large part of the water from the nectar. This is done by evaporation, which takes place because of the heat of the hive, and by ventilation.

Honey stored in the honeycombs by honeybees has so much water removed from the original nectar that it will keep almost forever! The honey is put into the honeycombs to ripen, and to serve as the future food supply.

By the way, when bees cannot obtain nectar, they sometimes collect sweet liquids excreted by various bugs, or secretions from plants other than nectar.

Honey is removed from the hive by various methods. It may be squeezed from the comb by presses, or it may be sold in the combs cut from the hive. Most honey, however, is removed from the combs by a machine known as "a honey extractor." This uses centrifugal force to make the honey leave the comb.

Honeys vary greatly, depending on the flowers from which the nectar came and the environment where the hive is situated. Honey contains an amazing number of substances. The chief ingredients are two sugars known as levulose and dextrose. It also contains the following: small amounts of sucrose (cane sugar), maltose, dextrins, minerals, numerous enzymes, numerous vitamins in small amounts, and tiny amounts of proteins and acids.

Honeys differ in flavor and color, depending on the source of the nectar. In those areas where honey is produced, there are usually only a few plants that produce enough nectar to be a source of supply. Thus, in the Northeast United States, most honey comes from clover; in the West, it may come from alfalfa; in Europe, from heather; and so on.

HOW DO BEES COMMUNICATE?

When a worker bee finds flowers with nectar, how does it tell the other bees what it has found? How does it tell them what the flower is, how far away it is, and in which direction to go?

The way bees communicate this information is one of the most amazing wonders of nature. To begin with, the language of bees is an instinct. It doesn't have to be learned. When worker bees reach a certain age, they know this language automatically.

The bees' language is a language of smells and dancing. When a bee has discovered nectar or pollen and returns home, it begins to dance. It goes around and around in narrow circles. The dance excites other bees and tells them the dancing bee has discovered nectar or pollen. The other bees can tell from the smell of the returned bee what it has found, so they know from this what to look for.

If the bee does a really lively dance, this says that a great deal of food is obtainable, and more bees are excited to go out and seek it. So far then, the bee has been able to communicate several things. The dance says that there is nectar or pollen to be obtained. The scent on the bee itself tells what kind of flower should be looked for, and whether it's for nectar or pollen. The liveliness of the dance tells about the amount of food.

But all this applies only to flowers within about a hundred yards from the hive. When a bee finds flowers with food farther away, it comes home and performs another kind of dance. This time, instead of doing a round dance, it does a tail dance. It does a figure 8, connecting the two loops of the 8 with a straight line, meanwhile moving abdomen or "tail" from side to side.

In addition to all the other information, the tail dance tells the bees how far to go and in which direction to fly! The number of turns per minute indicate distance. The farther away, the fewer the figures 8 made. For instance, 11 turns per minute mean 2,700 metres distance! The line a bee makes between the two loops of the 8 give the exact direction of the flowers. It makes this line in relation to the position of the sun in the sky so the others can set off at the correct angle instantly!

DO BEES DIE AFTER THEY STING?

The average person regards a bee as his natural enemy—at least when he meets one face to face! The first thing we think of when we see a bee is, "Oh! Oh! It's going to sting us."

What we don't realize, of course, is that there are thousands of different species, or kinds of bees, and many of them don't sting at all. But one thing we can say about all bees is: They are all beneficial to man! The reason for this is that all bees distribute pollen during their flower-visiting, and thus help in the raising of crops for man. In fact, more than 50 agricultural crops are dependent on the pollination of bees!

Like all insects, a bee has six legs. It has three distinct body regions—the head, thorax or midsection, and abdomen. On the head are found two antennae or feelers, two large compound eyes and three single eyes, biting jaws, and a sucking or lapping tongue.

The thorax supports three pairs of legs and two pairs of wings. In all species, the legs function in gathering pollen, and some bees have legs with baskets for carrying the pollen!

Most female bees have a sting that may be thrust from between the end segments of the abdomen. Bee stings, of course, make you feel very uncomfortable, but they are rarely serious. Perhaps it's because we feel so angry when a bee has stung us that we think it's going to die soon afterward. Actually, this isn't so at all!

Most kinds of bees can use their stinger many times. In the case of the worker honeybee, the stinger is barbed. So when it sticks it into your skin—it stays there!

362

EGGS

PUPA OR
CHRYSALIS

CATERPILLAR

BUTTERFLY

HOW DOES A CATERPILLAR BECOME A BUTTERFLY?

Have you ever heard people say that a butterfly never eats? This happens to be true of some butterflies—and the reason lies in the story of how a caterpillar changes into a butterfly.

During her life, a female butterfly lays from 100 to several thousand eggs. She is very careful to lay these eggs near the kind of plant that will be useful to her offspring later. If there is only one such plant in a certain area—that's where she'll lay the eggs!

From these eggs hatch out tiny, wormlike grubs, called "caterpillar larvae." They begin at once to feed and grow, and as they grow they shed their skins several times. All the caterpillars do during this time is eat and eat—because the food they store away now may have to last them for the rest of their lives when they become butterflies! The food is stored as fat, and is used to build up wings, legs, sucking tubes, and so on, when the caterpillar becomes a butterfly.

At a certain time the caterpillar feels it's time for a change, so it spins a little button of silk, to which it clings. It hangs head down, sheds its caterpillar skin, and then appears as a pupa or chrysalis. The chrysalis clings to the button of silk by a sharp spine at the end of its body.

The pupa or chrysalis may sleep for some weeks or months. During this time, however, it is undergoing a change, so that when it comes out it is a full-grown insect. When it emerges from its chrysalid skin, it is a butterfly—but it doesn't do any flying at first. It sits still for hours to let its wings spread out and become dry and firm. It waves them back and forth slowly until it feels they are ready to use for flying—then off it goes on its first flight in search of nectar!

By the way, the life history of the moth is almost exactly the same as that of the butterfly. And did you know that there are many more different kinds of moths than there are butterflies?

HOW DO SILKWORMS MAKE SILK?

Thousands of years ago China had learned the secret of making silk cloth from the fine web spun by a certain caterpillar in making its cocoon. This secret was jealously guarded, and anyone who carried silkworms or their eggs out of China was punishable by death!

Today, of course, silkworms are raised in China, Japan, India, France, Spain, and Italy. The best silk is produced by the caterpillar of a small grayish-white moth which feeds on the leaves of the white mulberry.

In the early summer, each female moth lays 500 or more eggs. These eggs are carefully kept on strips of paper or cloth until the next spring when the mulberries open their leaves. Then the eggs are placed in incubators where they hatch out tiny black worms. The worms are placed in trays filled with finely chopped mulberry leaves and are fed constantly for about six weeks.

When the worms begin to move their heads slowly back and forth, they are ready to spin their cocoons. Little twigs are put in the trays to support them. The worms loop about themselves an almost invisible thread which they pour out through little holes in their jaws. The cocoon, which may contain as much as 460 to 1,100 metres of thread, is finished in about 72 hours.

Inside the cocoon is a shrunken chrysalis, which may develop into a moth in about 12 days. So the cocoons are exposed to heat to kill the chrysalises. The cocoons are placed in troughs of warm water to soften the silk gum which holds the filaments of the thread together.

Filaments from several cocoons are brought together into a single thread as they are unwound from the cocoons and wound on a reel. The threads from the reel are twisted into a skein of raw silk. This thread of 10 or 12 filaments is called a "single" thread of silk.

When you buy silk stockings marked "two-thread" or "three-thread," the markings are based on this thread of silk. Today, nylon has become so popular and so cheap that it has replaced silk in many uses. But silk will always be appreciated for its beauty, richness, and softness.

WHY AREN'T SPIDERS CAUGHT IN THEIR OWN WEBS?

"Won't you come into my parlor?" said the spider to the fly. The tricky spider is pretty clever, isn't he? He knows the fly will be caught and he'll be able to scamper along and have himself a nice meal!

But if the sticky web clings to the fly and traps him, why doesn't it cling to the spider? The answer to this will surprise you. It does! A spider can be caught just as easily in his own web as a fly is.

The reason this doesn't happen is that the spider is "at home" in his own web. He knows his way around. And when the web was spun originally, the spider made sure that there would be "safe" threads to use, threads he could touch without sticking to them.

There are many kinds of silk that a spider produces. The sticky kind is used in the web to catch prey. But there is also a non-sticky kind, and this is used to make the strong, supporting spokes of the web. The spider knows which is which, and he simply avoids the sticky ones! He can do this because he has a remarkable sense of touch.

WHAT IS THE SPIDER'S WEB MADE OF?

To most of us, the most fascinating thing about spiders is the webs they spin. But actually a spider is an amazing creature in many other respects, too. Here are just a few of the remarkable facts about spiders.

They are found in every kind of climate, and live in the air, on the water, on the ground, or in the ground, depending on the species. They vary in size from 8 centimetres to some that are barely visible. Some spiders can go for a whole year without water. One type of spider, the large tarantula, eats birds and can live as long as 15 years. Yet most spiders live for only one year! And just one more important fact, spiders are not insects. They belong to a group called "arachnids," and differ from insects in that they have eight legs, usually eight eyes, no wings, and only two parts to their bodies.

The silk that spiders use in making their webs is manufactured in certain abdominal glands. The silk is forced through many tiny holes from the spinning organs at the tip of the abdomen. It comes out as a liquid which becomes solid on contact with the air.

There are many kinds of silk: the sticky silk used in the web to catch prey; the strong supporting spokes which are not sticky; and the silks of the cocoon, in which the eggs are laid. Some of these are soft and fluffy; others, hard and fibrous.

Spiders make all kinds of webs. The wheel-shaped orb web is used only for catching prey. It is made by first laying down an irregular rectangle of outer heavy lines as a foundation. The spokes of the wheel are constructed next, followed by a scaffolding of three to four spirals. The final closely spaced sticky spiral is built last.

Other webs are called "sheet webs," and they are flat, funnel-shaped, or dome-shaped sheets of silk. The spider lives back at one side of it. "Trap-door" spiders make a bottlelike burrow. There is a lidlike opening at the top. It fits the burrow snugly and is disguised by sticks and dirt. "Wolf" spiders build a tunnel into the ground and line the tunnel with silk.

The European water spider builds a bell-shaped home entirely under water! The spider fills this with air brought from the surface in the hairs of the abdomen. Here she lays eggs and rears the young till they can build for themselves. By the way, not all spiders build webs. Some just make a one-roomed house in a leaf or piece of bark.

WHAT DO WASPS USE TO BUILD NESTS?

One might ask the question: What don't wasps use to build nests? For there is probably no other insect that has so many different forms of interesting architecture for its nest, and that uses so many different materials.

Wasps belong to the same family as the bees and the ants. There are many species, which can be divided into two groups: social wasps and solitary wasps. The social wasps, which include the hornets and the yellow jackets, live in colonies like those of the bees, but their colonies don't last year after year. Each year, almost the whole colony is wiped out by the cold of winter.

All social wasps make their houses of a sort of paper which they manufacture by chewing up wood and plant fibers. The hornets and yellow jackets cover the cells of their houses with wrappings of paper. Other types of wasps attach their nests to the walls of houses, to branches of trees, or to stones.

Solitary wasps do not make their nests of paper, but they have many other schemes. The digger wasps, for example, dig long narrow burrows in the earth. Carpenter wasps prefer to make their homes in wood. They dig out long tunnels in the wood, stock it with the juicy body of some insect, lay an egg on it, and then fly away to tunnel another cell.

Potter wasps lay their eggs in little jug-shaped cells of clay. Each of these is attached to some convenient twig. Mud wasps make little cup-shaped cells of mud and plaster them over the sides of buildings or on stones. One type of digger wasp is actually the only insect that uses a tool in building its nest! She covers up the cell and then stamps the earth down carefully with a tiny pebble which she holds in her jaws.

Wasps take very good care of their young, and the females will travel long distances to find just the right insect for its babies!

WHAT DO ANTS EAT?

About the only place in the world where you won't find any ants is on the summits of the very highest mountains. So as you might imagine, there are thousands of different kinds of ants and how they live and what they eat depend on the species you are considering.

Let us see what are some of the unusual eating habits of certain ants. The harvester ant gathers seed from some grass common to the region and carries them into the nest. Here the seeds are sorted and stored away as the food supply.

Other ants are dairy farmers. They keep herds of plant lice, or "aphids," as they are called. They milk them by stroking their sides until the sweet liquid which they secrete oozes out. The ants relish this honeydew, or milk, so much that they take excellent care of their "cows."

Other ants grow fungi and live on nothing else. The fungus which they eat must have something to grow on. So the ants make a paste on which to raise the fungus, or mold.

Some ants are millers. One variety of ant has a special kind of worker with a huge head. The head holds powerful muscles to work its jaws and do the grinding. This worker ant is really the miller of the colony. It grinds up the grain that is brought in by the ordinary workers. After the harvest season is over, the millers are killed and their heads are bitten off. The reason this is done is the ants want no extra mouths to feed.

One kind of ant maintains living storehouses of food. As the worker ants bring in the nectar from the flowers, special ants in the colony take it and swallow it. During the winter, the other ants come to them and receive from their mouths enough nectar to feed themselves and the colony until the next season.

HOW DO EARTHWORMS EAT?

Earthworms have been called the most important animals in the world! Important, of course, from the point of view of human beings, because the activity of the earthworms prepares the soil for vegetation, upon which life depends.

Earthworms turn the soil over and break it up by eating it. In half a hectare of garden, the worms will pass about 16 tonnes of soil through their bodies in one year! Worms let air and water get to the plant roots. They turn under decayed plant and animal matter, and they even plant seeds. This is done when they drag leaves into their burrows and thus pull fine seeds from trees and plants below the surface, too.

The manure of earthworms, which is called "worm casts," contains lime which makes the soil rich. The importance of this can be seen when we consider what scientists discovered about the Nile Valley, one of the earth's most fertile regions. They estimated that about 108 tonnes of eathworm castings are left on half a hectare in the Nile valley, and this is the real reason why this region has been fertile for hundreds of years!

There are so many earthworms in the soil of the United States that if all of them were weighed it would equal more than 10 times the weight of the human population!

The earthworm's body is made of two tubes, one inside another. The inner tube is the digestive system. When the worm wants to eat, it turns its throat inside out and pushes it forward to grip a piece of dirt. Then it draws the dirt back into the tube with its throat muscles. The dirt first goes into a storeroom called "the crop," and then into the gizzard. Grains of sand help the worm grind up the soil. Then it is digested, and the dirt is pushed from the body as "casting."

An earthworm has no eyes, but it has "sense-cells" on the outside of its body. This enables the worm to tell light from darkness and to feel the lightest touch. The earthworm breathes through its skin.

Earthworms live in fine, moist soil; they cannot live in sand. They come up only at night. During the winter they curl up into a ball and sleep. When you see a worm on the surface, it is because it is looking for a new home or a better feeding ground. Worms cannot live in the sunlight.

WHY DO MOTHS EAT WOOL?

There is a moth known as "the clothes moth," and most people blame it for making the moth holes in our clothes, furs, and rugs. But the moth doesn't do this damage at all!

The moth never eats. It lives only to produce its eggs and then dies. It is when the young moth is in the caterpillar stage that all the damage is done.

The eggs of the moth are laid on wool, furs, rugs, and so on. In about a week the eggs hatch into caterpillars. Caterpillar is the common name for the larvae of butterflies, moths and sawflies. What happens after hatching depends on what kind of moth it is.

The caterpillar stage is the second in the insect's life history from egg to adult. During this stage the caterpillar's main function is to eat and grow. Examples of different kinds of moth are: the case-making moth, the webbing-moth, and the tapestry moth.

The caterpillar of the case-making moth makes a little tubular case out of the wool it eats, and lines this case with silk. There it lives as a caterpillar. The caterpillar of the webbing moth always leaves a cobwebby trail of its silk and spins a silk cocoon. As the caterpillar of the tapestry moth eats into wool, it makes a series of tunnels which it lines with silk. When full-grown, it goes into one of these tunnels and stays there until it is ready to come out as a moth.

So you see that the problem of protecting clothes against moths is to make sure that no eggs are laid on the clothes. Before clothes are put away for the summer, they should be aired and brushed to make sure that there are no eggs or moths on them. It's a good idea to wrap them in heavy paper or in a tightly sealed cardboard box, for the clothes moths cannot eat through paper. Moth balls keep the moths away, but do not kill the eggs or larvae which may already be present.

WHY DO MOSQUITO BITES ITCH?

Have you ever heard the expression, "The female of the species is deadlier than the male"? Well, it certainly applies to mosquitoes. Only female mosquitoes suck blood. The bill of the female has some sharp piercing organs, arranged around a sucking tube. When the mosquito bites, it injects a poisonous liquid into the blood. This poison causes the pain and itching and produces the swelling.

Next to its bite, the hum of the mosquito is probably most annoying. This hum is very important to the mosquito, however, for it is a sort of mating call. The males make a deep, low hum by vibrating their wings rapidly, while the females have a shriller note.

Mosquitoes are found all over the world. But wherever they may live, all species begin their lives somewhere in the water. The females deposit their eggs on the surface of ponds, in pools, in rain barrels, in the oases of deserts, even in tin cans. Each female lays from 40 to 400 eggs. These may be laid singly or in compact raftlike masses.

Within a week, small footless larvae hatch out. These larvae wriggle through the water so actively that they are usually called "wrigglers." Since they cannot breathe under water, they spend most of the time on the surface. There they take in air through the breathing tubes on their tails, and weave bits of animal and plant matter into their mouths with the feathery brushes on their heads.

As the wrigglers grow, they molt, or shed their skins. The fourth time

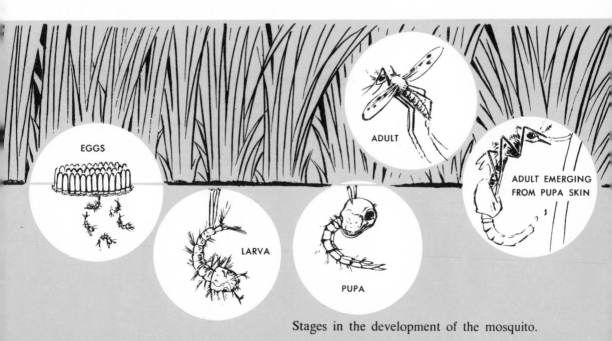

EGGS

ADULT

ADULT EMERGING
FROM PUPA SKIN

LARVA

PUPA

Stages in the development of the mosquito.

they molt, they change into pupae. The pupae spend most of the time near the surface breathing through hornlike tubes on their backs. The pupae do not eat, but after a few days their skins split and the full-grown mosquitoes crawl out.

Adult mosquitoes usually live only a few weeks. In some species, there are 12 generations of mosquitoes during one year!

WHY DO CRICKETS SING?

The cricket is an insect that has won a special place in the affection of man. In many countries there are superstitions about crickets, such as that if one lives in your house it is a sign of good luck, and that if one leaves your house this will mean bad luck. In Italy, North Africa, and Japan, crickets are kept in little cages because the people love to listen to their cheerful notes.

But actually, the cricket doesn't "sing." He is a fiddler! A cricket makes its chirping noise by rubbing the ridged underside of one forewing against the surface of the other. Only the male crickets are fiddlers. They fiddle all day long, for it is by this music that they attract the females. Imagine what it would be like if boys had to fiddle all day long to attract girls.

Crickets have keen ears, which are located on their legs instead of on their heads. Their antennae, or feelers, are very long, and their legs are especially powerful for jumping.

The house cricket, also called "the hearth cricket," is a native of Europe. It was brought to the New World long ago and is now common in many parts of the United States. It is a small insect, about 3 centimetres, greyish-yellow in color, with brown markings. It lives in human dwellings.

It loves warmth, and is often to be found near a fireplace, where it hides in the cracks between the stones or planks of the floor. The field cricket is larger and almost black in color. It makes a little hole in the ground for a home. When courting, the male sits by the entrance and fiddles. There are also tree crickets and mole crickets. The tree crickets are especially noted for loud music.

To farmers this means trouble, for the cricket babies, or larvae, eat the leaves of the bushes, vines, or trees on which they hatch.

Did you know that in China crickets are set to fight each other in cricket fights, and the people who watch them sometimes bet on the outcome?

HOW DID DINOSAURS COME TO BE?

Scientists believe that dinosaurs came into being about 180,000,000 years ago and died out about 60,000,000 years ago. Since dinosaurs were reptiles, they must have developed from reptiles that lived before them. Reptiles, by the way, are a separate class of animals with these characteristics: They are cold-blooded; they can live on land; they have a distinctive type of heart; and most of them have scales.

The first reptiles appeared long before the dinosaurs. They looked like Amphibia (able to live in water and on land), but their eggs could be hatched on land. The young ones had legs and lungs, could breathe air, and probably ate insects.

Then the reptiles became larger and stronger. Some looked like big lizards and others like turtles. They had short tails, thick legs, and big heads. They ate plants.

The first dinosaurs to develop resembled their reptile ancestors, who were like lizards, and who could walk on their hindlegs. The first dinosaurs were slender, about as large as a turkey, and could also walk on their hindlegs. Some kinds remained small, but others grew heavier and longer. In time, many of them were up to 2.5 metres long. There were even a few 6 metres long, weighing as much as an elephant. They had small heads and short, blunt teeth, which were only good for eating plants. They lived in low, swampy places.

Then came the next period in the Age of Reptiles. Some of the plant-eating dinosaurs became so large that even four legs couldn't support them on land. They had to spend most of their lives in rivers and swamps. One of these giants was Brontosaurus, 20 to 24 metres long and weighing about 34 tonnes!

At the same time, other dinosaurs were able to walk about on land. One of these, Allosaurus, was 10 metres, had sharp teeth and claws, and fed on Brontosaurus and other plant-eaters! So dinosaurs were a stage in the development of the reptiles. They may have disappeared because of changes in the climate of the earth, which robbed them of places to wade and feed.

WAS THERE EVER SUCH A BIRD AS THE DODO?

Have you ever heard anything described as being "dead as a dodo"? Or perhaps when some person acted stupidly, he was told he was being a "dodo"? There's a reason why the dodo is a symbol of something that has died away, and also why it stands for stupidity.

You see, hundreds of years ago, on the island of Mauritius and other islands in the Indian Ocean, east of Madagascar, there actually lived a bird we call "the dodo." This bird had no enemies to defend itself against, so it didn't develop any of the abilities most birds have. It couldn't fly, it couldn't run fast, it had no instinct to fight or defend itself.

As a result it developed into quite a peculiar-looking creature. It was related to the pigeon family, but it had no resemblance at all to the pigeon. It had a big body, round and fat, about twice as large as a turkey's. Its legs were so short that it could scarcely support its own weight!

The tail of the dodo was only a little tuft of curly feathers, absolutely useless to it. The wings of this bird, since it had no need for flying, had become very small and couldn't function as wings at all. The dodo's head was very large and ended in an enormous hooked bill. The only way the dodo could move about was by waddling along slowly.

In the year 1507, Portuguese explorers landed on the island of Mauritius and discovered this strange creature. Since it looked ridiculous and couldn't defend itself, they called it *duodo,* which means "simpleton." They found that they could knock over the birds with clubs. Its nest was a heap of grass on which it laid one large egg.

Later on, men brought hogs to this island, who destroyed the dodo's eggs and young, and by 1681 the bird was extinct!

WHY DO ELEPHANTS HAVE TRUNKS?

Thousands and thousands of years ago, giant monsters known as "mammoths" roamed the earth. Because they couldn't endure the hardships they had to undergo, they perished one by one. Only two descendants of those species have remained, and they are the African and Asiatic elephants.

Elephants are the largest land animals. Even though they are so huge, they are mild and intelligent, and they have a patient, gentle nature. Elephants are more easily trained than any other beast except the domestic dog!

The elephant has an enormously heavy body, which may weigh as much as 5 tonnes. That's why their legs are short and shaped like stout pillars. Those legs have quite a weight to support!

The two ivory tusks which protrude from the upper jaw of an elephant are really overgrown teeth. These tusks are used to dig up roots for food and also as weapons of defense. In the case of Indian elephants, only the males have tusks.

The elephant's trunk is an amazing organ without which it couldn't exist. It is the most remarkable part of the elephant's body and is almost as wonderful as the hands of man. It is an extension of the nose and upper lip. It serves the elephant as hand, arm, nose, and lips, all in one!

The trunk contains a great number of muscles, probably as many as 40,000. As a result, it is very strong and flexible. Because of this great strength, the elephant can use its trunk very effectively as a weapon. The tip of the trunk ends in a sort of finger which is so sensitive it can pick up a small pin!

The trunk also serves as a hand to gather food which it places in the mouth. The elephant drinks by sucking up water through tubes in its trunk. Then it curls the trunk inward and shoots the water down into its throat. It can also treat itself to a shower bath by squirting the water over its back. Elephants, by the way, are very fond of water, and will take a bath whenever they have a chance. Despite their weight, they are good swimmers. A mother elephant will often carry baby elephants on its back while swimming.

It was once believed that elephants live for hundreds of years, but in captivity, they rarely live longer than about 90 years.

WHAT IS A VAMPIRE BAT?

When you think for what a short time man has existed on this earth, it is hard to believe that bats have existed for 60,000,000 years! There are fossil remains of bats going back to that time. There are even pictures of bats that are 4,000 years old, found in an Egyptian tomb.

Today there are more than 2,000 kinds of bats, and they live everywhere in the world except near the polar regions. Bats are the only mammals that fly. They range in size from a 15-centimetre wingspread to some that have almost a 2-metre wingspread!

Most bats eat insects. Many bats of the warm tropics eat fruit or the pollen from flowers. Other bats eat fish or smaller bats. Some eat blood.

The blood-eating bats are called "vampire bats," and it is because of them that many people are so frightened of all bats. At one time, in Eastern Europe, there were many legends about vampires. A vampire was the soul of a dead person, which assumed the form of some animal at night, and roved the countryside looking for victims from which to suck blood. During the early 18th century, explorers who traveled to South and Central America found bats that fed on blood. They came back with exaggerated stories, and soon, all the old vampire legends became associated with bats. Since that time, vampires have been thought of mostly as bats.

Vampire bats are found only in Central and South America. They have a wingspread of 30 centimetres and a body length of about 10 centimetres. The vampire bat has needle-sharp front teeth with which it makes small cuts in the skin of its victim. At one time, it was thought a vampire bat sucked up the blood, but it actually laps it up with its tongue. In fact, a vampire bat can be feeding on its victim while the person remains sound asleep!

It is thought the saliva of the vampire bat contains some substance that deadens the pain of the wound, as well as something that prevents it from clotting. Vampire bats do not prefer to feed on human beings. They are just as happy to feed on horses, cows, goats, and chickens. In some places, vampire bats transmit a disease that is sometimes fatal to the victim.

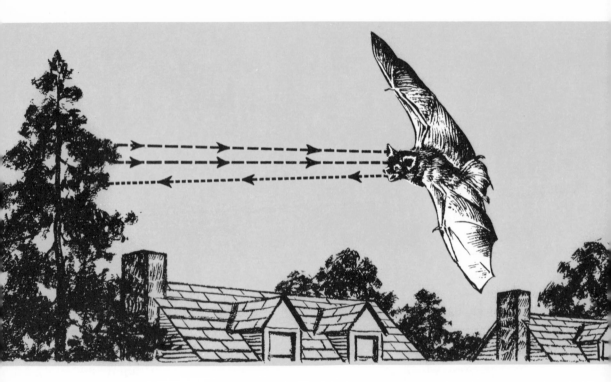

HOW DO BATS SEE?

Bats are such remarkable creatures that the unusual way they get about through the air is only one of the many interesting things about them.

Bats are not birds; they are mammals. The young are born alive and get milk from their mothers. They are the only mammals that fly!

Bats have been in existence so long that fossil remains of bats prove they lived 60,000,000 years ago! Today, there are more than 2,000 kinds of bats and they live in every part of the world except in the polar regions.

Bats vary in size from a wingspread of 2 centimetres to a wingspread of 2 metres. Most bats live on insects, but there are many bats who live on fruit, fish, other smaller bats, or blood.

For a long time, scientists couldn't explain how bats were able to fly at great speed in the darkness and through thick forests without ever touching a leaf or branch. So they made certain experiments. They hung many ropes close together from the ceiling in a room. They closed up the eyes of several bats with gum and let them loose in the room.

The bats flew about at their usual speed without bumping into a single obstacle! This proved that they didn't depend on their eyes for guidance while flying. So the scientists sealed up their ears and mouths and let them loose in the same room. This time the bats flew about helplessly, bumping into obstacles many times!

This is how it was discovered what guides a bat in its flight. As it flies, a bat utters a continuous sound, so high-pitched that the human ear can't hear it. These high-frequency sound waves strike the obstacles in the bat's path and echo back to its ears, which are very sensitive.

The bat's wings automatically react to these signals, and the bat is able to change its course and avoid flying into the obstacles! Of course, a bat uses its eyes to spot its food when it decides to go after it.

WHAT IS A LEMMING?

What makes the lemming fascinating is not what it is but what it does. A lemming is a small, mouselike rodent that lives in cold regions. It is only about five inches long. It lives in certain parts of Norway and Sweden and in Lapland.

A lemming feeds on roots, stalks, and mosses. The number of young in a lemming's nest is generally from three to five, and at least two broods are produced every year.

What has made the lemming a strange and fascinating creature is that about every three or four years certain parts of Norway, Sweden, and Lapland are over-run by an army of these creatures. This army always travels downhill toward the sea. This may mean a different direction in different parts of the country, but it is always toward the sea.

The lemmings advance slowly and steadily regardless of all obstacles. They march largely by night, usually feeding and sleeping by day. This army of creatures will cross streams and even swim lakes that are several miles wide. They move through whole towns as if drawn by some force they cannot resist.

On their line of march, they cause great damage by devouring all kinds of vegetable matter. In their turn, they are followed by crowds of beasts and birds of prey who feed on them. Many of these animals simply stamp them to the ground and kill and eat them.

Since this march to the sea may take the lemmings from one to three years, and they multiply so fast, the army actually gets bigger as it goes along despite all its enemies! And when the lemmings finally reach the sea they plunge in and commit suicide. No lemming ever returns from its march!

What is the explanation for this mysterious march? As far as we know, it is due to overcrowding conditions in their home. When there are too many lemmings to be able to live and feed at home, a migratory instinct makes them set off on a march to the sea!

WHAT IS A PLATYPUS?

The platypus, or duckbill, is such a strange creature that at first people didn't want to believe it exists. When British scientists saw a stuffed specimen in 1799, they called it a fake!

What makes it so strange? Well, it has a bill like a duck, a tail like a beaver, and heavy fur. It lays eggs and hatches them like a bird, but it feeds its young with milk like a mammal. It has webfeet and lives both on land and in the water. The word "platypus" comes from two Greek words meaning "flat foot."

The duckbill lives in eastern Australia and Tasmania. It has no external ears and the nostrils are near the end of the soft, rubbery bill. This is how the duckbill can remain under water and breathe with only the tip of the bill showing.

The forepaws of the duckbill are webbed for swimming, and when it walks on land, the webs fold under the foot and expose the claws. The female lays from one to three eggs. She holds them against her body with her tail until they are hatched.

The young duckbill laps up the mother's milk as it comes out from milk glands. The young are born with teeth, but these soon fall out and the duckbill uses tough, horny plates on the sides of the bill.

The only poisonous mammal in the world is the male duckbill. It has poison glands near the thighs. Long tubes go from these glands to grooved spurs on the hindlegs. The poison is very much like snake venom. The male probably uses it in fighting other males during the mating season.

The duckbill feeds at night on earthworms, water insects, and crayfish. During the day, it crawls into its nest which is usually deep in some mudbank.

HOW DOES A CHAMELEON CHANGE ITS COLORS?

How does the chameleon change its colors from a bright green to a grey-black or to yellow spots? Did nature give the chameleon an automatic color changer for its skin, so that it could resemble its background wherever it goes?

The strange fact about the chameleon's ability to change its colors is that it is not caused by the color of its surroundings! The chameleon pays no attention to its surroundings.

The skin of the chameleon is transparent. Underneath this skin, there are layers of cells which contain yellow, black, and red coloring matter. When these cells contract or expand, we see a change in the color of the chameleon.

But what makes those cells go to work? When the chameleon becomes angry or frightened, its nervous system sends a message to those cells. Anger cause the colors to darken; excitement and fright bring paler shades and yellow spots.

Sunlight also affects the chameleon's colors. Hot sunlight will make those cells turn dark, or almost black. High temperatures without sunlight usually produce green colors, low temperatures produce green colors. And darkness makes the chameleon fade to a cream color with yellow spots.

So we see that various things like emotion, temperature, and light cause the nervous system of the chameleon to make its color cells perform their tricks, and not the color of its surroundings.

It so happens, of course, that these changes in color help the chameleon become almost invisible to its enemies like snakes or birds. And because the chameleon is such a slow-moving animal, it needs this kind of protection to save its life.

CAN A PORPOISE TALK?

Recently, there have been some news items about experiments being conducted to test the intelligence of porpoises—and perhaps try to communicate with them!

To begin with, do you know what a porpoise is? It is not a fish—but a mammal. It belongs to the order of whales. Like other mammals, it nurses the young with its milk. And like the whale, the porpoise breathes through a "blow-hole," which is a single nostril located on top of the head. When the porpoise comes to the surface, it opens this nostril and takes in air.

Another curious thing about the porpoise is that its tail is horizontal, not perpendicular like the tails of fishes. This is to help it dive and lunge quickly. We enjoy watching porpoises swim because they move in a graceful manner. They swim in a series of long curves so that they come up to expose the blow-hole, and then as they dip downward we see the back fin.

Now as to whether porpoises can "talk." Of course, when we think of any animal or bird "talking," we mean imitating human sounds in some way. Because, as we know, most creatures have some way of communicating with each other. In some cases, it's a very simple way; in some cases (such as the bee), it's quite complicated.

The strange thing about porpoises is that they have actually been known to imitate human speech! And they will do this on their own accord. For example, there was a case at the Marine Studios in Florida where a porpoise suddenly imitated a man's voice. It did so well that the man's wife, who was nearby, began to laugh. So the porpoise imitated the sound of her laughter!

Of course, there is something about the structure of the porpoise's vocal cords that enables it to make sounds like a human. But in addition to this, it is believed that the porpoise is among the most intelligent of animals. It also cooperates with people in an amazing way.

But before we can really say that porpoises can "talk," they'll have to learn how to use words to convey meaning. And whether that will ever happen, we don't know.

DO CROCODILES ATTACK HUMAN BEINGS?

We have seen movies or travel pictures in which crocodiles are shown lurking in the water while frightened natives flee from them in terror. Are crocodiles really a menace to people who come near them?

The truth is that crocodiles probably kill more people than any other animal, with the possible exception of the cobra! Certain types of crocodile, such as the African crocodile and the salt-water crocodile, are real man-eaters. Natives who live near the regions they inhabit fear them as they do few other animals. Some of these crocodiles will not only attack anyone who comes near them in the water, but they will run up on the land in pursuit of their victim, grab them, and then carry them back into the water to drown!

Alligators and crocodiles are very closely related to certain ancient dinosaurs, huge lizardlike creatures that were about 24 metres long and roamed the earth centuries ago.

Even today, alligators and crocodiles are the largest living reptiles, and one species grows to a length of 7 metres. Alligators and crocodiles belong to the same family and are similar in habits and appearance. The chief difference is that alligators have a broad, flat head instead of a narrow, pointed one. Alligators are also usually heavier and less active than crocodiles.

Both spend much of their time in the water, lying with their nostrils, eyes, and part of the back showing. Their young are hatched from oval white eggs. The mother lays from 20 to 90 of these eggs on land in a nest of vegetable refuse and leaves them there to be hatched by the heat of the sun.

The mother waits nearby and at last helps her offspring to crawl out of the refuse. Most reptiles can't make any sounds, but alligators and crocodiles are able to emit a loud call or bellow.

Alligators live only in the warmer parts of America and China, but crocodiles can be found in Africa, Asia, Australia, and America. About a hundred years ago, it was found that alligator skin was very useful in making items such as handbags, wallets, belts, and shoes. As a result, the alligator is becoming a rarer animal.

CROCODILE

ALLIGATOR

WHY DOES A BULL CHARGE AT A RED CLOTH?

As you know, bullfighting is the greatest sport in Spain, and a very important one in many other countries. And people are quite excited about this sport. They believe certain things about it and nothing can change their minds.

One of the things most bullfight fans (and others) believe is that anything red makes a bull angry and causes him to attack. Therefore, the bullfighter has to have a bright red cape and he has to be able to use this with great skill.

Well, the sad truth is that if the same bullfighter had a white cloth, or a yellow cloth, or a green cloth, or a black cloth—he would be able to accomplish the same things with the bull! Bulls are color-blind!

Many bullfighters will privately admit they know this. In fact, some matadors conducted experiments in which they used white cloths—and they got the bulls to behave in the same way as with red cloths!

What makes the bull charge then? It is the movement of the cape, and not the color of it. Anything that you would wave in front of a bull would excite him. In fact, since the bull is color-blind, if you waved a white cape or cloth you would probably get a better reaction, since he can see it better!

DOES AN OSTRICH HIDE ITS HEAD IN THE SAND?

The ostrich is a rather strange bird, and there are many interesting and peculiar things about it, but it does not hide its head in the sand!

According to popular belief, when an ostrich is frightened it feels that it is safely hidden when it has its head in the sand. At such times, according to these stories, a person can walk up to the ostrich and capture it easily.

However, the truth is that no one has actually observed this happening! The ostrich simply does not hide its head in the sand. What may have given people the idea is that when an ostrich is frightened, it will sometimes drop to the ground, stretch out its neck parallel with it, and lie still and watch intently. But when the danger comes closer, the ostrich does just what other animals do—it takes off and runs!

The ostrich, of course, is one of the birds that cannot fly. But it makes up for this in its ability to run with considerable speed. The ostrich is the fastest-running bird in the world. It can go as fast as 50 miles an hour and is able to maintain this speed for at least a half-mile!

You sort of expect the ostrich to do everything on a large scale. The African ostrich, for example, is the largest living bird. No other bird even comes near it. This ostrich has been found to measure 2.5 metres in height and to weigh more than 130 kilograms. It would be some job carrying that weight around on a pair of wings, wouldn't it?

When it comes to eggs, the ostrich is champ again. It lays the largest eggs of any living bird. Ostrich eggs measure 15 to 18 centimetres in length and 13 to 15 centimetres in diameter. It takes more than 40 minutes to boil an ostrich egg, if you happen to be thinking of having one for breakfast!

WHAT MAKES A SKUNK SMELL?

If there is one animal in the world which you wouldn't want to be—it's probably a skunk. Yet the skunk is a friendly creature and makes a good pet. What makes him so unpopular, of course, is that famous smell of his.

What makes a skunk smell? The skunk has very powerful scent glands which contain a bad-smelling fluid. The skunk can send this fluid out with great accuracy.

The two glands are under the tail. A skunk aims at its enemy and shoots

the liquid out in a spray. The spray can travel 2.7 metres or more. The skunk may decide to send out spray from one gland or the other, or both, and each gland holds enough for five or six shots.

The spray is so strong that it has a suffocating effect, which means it makes it hard to breathe when you're near it. And if the spray gets into the eyes, it can cause temporary blindness!

But the skunk doesn't "strike" without warning. It raises its tail first or stamps its feet, so that you should have plenty of time to run away. Since skunks have been used for fur coats and are raised on fur farms, the scent glands, for obvious reasons, sometimes are removed from the young skunk.

There are actually three types of skunks, the striped, the hog-nosed, and the spotted. They live in North, Central, and South America. The striped skunk has a white line on the head from the nose to a point between the short ears, and another that starts on the neck, divides into two stripes on the back, and continues to the tail. Striped skunks live from Canada to Mexico. The largest are 76 centimetres long, with a 23-centimetre tail, and weigh as much as 13 kilograms.

The fore (front) feet of skunks are armed with long claws, which are used to dig grubs and insects out of the ground. When you see many shallow holes in the ground, it probably means a skunk has been feeding there.

Skunks are really a great help to man, since their food is mainly beetles, grasshoppers, crickets, wasps, rodents, and snakes.

DO RACCOONS WASH THEIR FOOD?

About forty years ago, if you said "raccoon" to anyone, they'd probably think of college students in raccoon coats. At that time the raccoon coat was a sign that you were "in," that you were really in style.

Today, the raccoon is still hunted for its fur and for its meat, but it must be mighty glad that it has lost its great popularity. Actually, the rac-

coon is a brave little fighter and has few enemies—except man. When raccoons are caught young, they make fine pets.

The name raccoon comes from the Algonquin Indian word *arakhumen*. Raccoons can be found from southern Canada to Panama, except in the high Rockies.

Racoons vary in size from 64 to 89 centimetres long, and they may weigh up to 11 kilograms. These mammals live in places where there are water and trees for dens. Their food, which they hunt at night, is principally crayfish, clams, fish, and frogs. But they will also eat nuts, berries, fruit, and young corn.

The year-round home, or den, where the young are born is usually in the hollow limb or trunk of a tree. Raccoons give birth to young but once a year, with four or five to a litter. By fall, the young raccoons are large enough to start their own life alone. When a raccoon family must move, the mother raccoon carries the young raccoons one by one to their new home.

Do raccoons wash their food before they eat it? The answer is that sometimes they do and sometimes they don't. Most of them seem to like to wash off their food, and there have been cases where raccoons actually refused food when they could not find any water.

They don't seem to wash their food in order to make it clean, because often the water is dirtier than the food itself! Perhaps it's just a matter of the raccoon enjoying the way the food feels in the water, rather than actually "washing" it!

WHY DO JELLYFISH STING?

The jellyfish is one of the strangest forms of life to be found in the sea. First of all, it is not even a fish! It's an animal without a skeleton. Jellyfish are members of a large division of very simple animals called "Coelenterata."

Nine-tenths of the body of a jellyfish is composed of a jellylike substance, and most of it is simply a stomach cavity. The jellyfish has no brain and no blood vessels.

Some jellyfish are very tiny, but there are others which may have a diameter of 0.5 metres. Jellyfish are a variety of shapes and colors, and there are some which seem to glow when they are disturbed.

The most interesting type of jellyfish is called "the medusa." The name comes from a mythological character called Medusa, who had writhing snakes on her head instead of hair. The medusa jellyfish has tentacles, or feelers, which hang down like snakes from the rim of its umbrella-shaped body. Around the rim are usually a number of tiny eyes, and in the center of the body underneath, is the mouth.

It's the tentacles of these jellyfish which often sting people quite painfully. The reason the jellyfish stings is that this is its method of obtaining food. The jellyfish capture other small creatures of the sea by stinging them, and this paralyzes their prey. Then the victim is brought to the mouth by the tentacles. Some jellyfish even have stinging organs in the stomach to complete the destruction of the prey. The tentacles are also used for swimming, though most jellyfish swim simply by contracting and expanding the body.

The life history of the jellyfish is interesting, too. The larva, or unhatched jellyfish, swims around by itself for a while. Then it attaches itself to a sea plant or rock and begins growing into a small polyp. Then it branches out like the stalks of a plant, and buds, each bud being a new polyp. The polyps finally take on the shape of a jellyfish, detach themselves, and swim off. Most jellyfish live on or near the surface of the water, but there are a few who live on the bottom of the sea.

CAN MARMOTS PREDICT WEATHER?

Sometimes an idea is built up, or kept up, by newspapers because it "makes a good story." This seems to be the case with the groundhog and its ability to predict the weather.

The belief that the groundhog is a weather prophet is an old one. The groundhog, or woodchuck, or marmot, is a hibernating animal. It lives in a burrow during the winter months. According to an old tradition it comes out on the second day of February, which has come to be called "Groundhog Day."

Once the groundhog gets out of its burrow, it is supposed to look over the landscape. If the day is cloudy so that it can't see its shadow, it stays out. This is supposed to be a good sign. It means the weather will be mild for the rest of the winter. But if the groundhog sees its shadow because the day is clear, it goes back into its burrow to get some more sleep. According to tradition, this means there will be six more weeks of cold weather.

The reason I say that newspapers seem to try to keep up the tradition is that it always makes a good story, and this despite the fact that most people don't really believe it. To begin with, there is absolutely no reason why the groundhog should be able to predict the weather. It has no special ability of any kind.

Another reason is that the groundhog doesn't really come out of its burrow on the second of February every year. Sometimes it comes out earlier, sometimes later. Occasionally a newspaperman will force the poor ground-hog out on the right day in order to take pictures. But obviously, if the weather is still very cold, the groundhog has no desire at all to emerge from its warm burrow.

The tradition is said to have originated in Europe concerning the hedge-hog. But the Pilgrims transferred it to the groundhog when they went to America. A rather similar legend, concerning the bear, still prevails in Hungary.

WHY DOES THE KANGAROO HAVE A POUCH?

Animals that have a pouch (and the kangaroo is only one of several animals like this) are called "marsupials."

The pouch that the kangaroo has, which is between her hindlegs, is about as snug and comfortable a little home as a new-born baby can have. It is fur-lined, keeps the baby warm, protects it, enables the baby to nurse, and provides transportation for the helpless infant.

The reason a pouch is provided by nature for kangaroos and other marsupials is that their young are born in a very helpless state. In fact, at birth the kangaroo is a tiny, pink, naked mass, not much over 3 millimetres and as thick as a lead pencil! Can you imagine what would happen if such a helpless thing didn't immediately have a place to keep it warm, snug, and protected?

The mother places the new-born baby in the pouch and for six months this is "home." In six months, the young kangaroo is as large as a puppy. But life is too good in the pouch to leave home. So "the joey," as it is called in Australia, rides around inside the pouch with its head sticking out far enough for it to pull off leaves when its mother stops to feed on tree branches,

In fact, even after the mother has taught it how to walk and run, the joey still lives in the pouch. In case of danger, the mother hops over to it, picks it up in her mouth without stopping, and drops it safely into her pouch.

There are more than 120 different kinds of kangaroos. The wallaby, which is the smallest, is only 0.6 metres high. The biggest is the great red or gray kangaroo, which is about 1.8 metres!

Kangaroos have short front legs with small paws, and very long hind-legs with one large sharp toe in the middle of the foot. With the help of its powerful hindlegs, a kangaroo takes jumps of 3 to 4 metres or more. When the kangaroo is resting, it rests on its big, long tail. Kangaroos can travel very fast, and their sense of hearing is so good they can hear an enemy at a great distance.

WHY DOES THE GIRAFFE HAVE A LONG NECK?

Giraffes have aroused the curiosity of man since earliest times. The ancient Egyptians and Greeks had a theory that giraffes were a mixture of the leopard and the camel, and they called the giraffe "a camelopard."

The giraffe is the tallest of all living animals, but scientists are unable to explain how it got its long neck. A famous French zoologist, Jean Baptiste de Lamarck, had a theory that at one time the giraffe's neck was much shorter than it now is. He thought that the neck grew to its present length because of the animal's habit of reaching for the tender leaves in the upper branches of trees. But scientists in general don't accept de Lamarck's theory.

Strangely enough, the body of a giraffe is no larger than that of the average horse. Its tremendous height, which may reach 6 metres, comes mostly from its legs and neck. The neck of a giraffe has only seven vertebrae, which is what the human neck has. But each vertebra is extremely long. Because of this, a giraffe always has a stiff neck. If it wants to take a drink from the ground, it has to spread its legs far apart in order to be able to reach down!

The strange shape and build of the giraffe is perfectly suited to enable it to obtain its food. A giraffe eats only plants, so its great height enables it to reach the leaves on trees which grow in tropical lands where there is little grass.

A giraffe's tongue is often 46 centimetres long, and it can use it so skillfully that it can pick the smallest leaves off thorny plants without being pricked. It also has a long upper lip which helps it wrench off many leaves at a time.

The giraffe is able to protect itself from danger in many ways. First of all, the coloring of its hide makes it practically invisible when it is feeding in the shadows of trees. It has well-developed ears which are sensitive to the faintest sounds, and it has keen senses of smell and sight. Finally, a giraffe can gallop at more than 30 miles an hour when pursued and can outrun the fastest horse!

When attacked, a giraffe can put up a good fight by kicking out with its hindlegs or using its head like a sledge hammer. Even a lion is careful in attacking a giraffe, always approaching it from behind!

Index

Numerals in *italics* refer to pictures.

Below is a list of words appearing in the text in American spellings:

armour	armor	honour	honor
centre	center	mould	mold
colour(ed)	color(ed)	neighbour(hood)	neighbor(hood)
colourless	colorless	nitre	niter
defence	defense	odourless	odorless
draught	draft	programme	program
favourite	favorite	saltpetre	saltpeter
fibre	fiber	syrup	sirup
flavour	flavor	traveller	traveler
glycerine	glycerin	tyre	tire
grey	gray	vapour	vapor